Biker Chicks

Other books by Arthur Veno
The Mammoth Book of Bikers
The Brotherhoods: Inside the Outlaw Motorcycle Clubs
Psychology and Social Change (Biker themed)

Other books by Edward Winterhalder
Out in Bad Standings: Inside the Bandidos Motorcycle Club
The Assimilation: Rock Machine to Bandidos
All Roads Lead to Sturgis: A Biker's Story

Biker Chicks

THE MAGNETIC ATTRACTION OF WOMEN TO BAD BOYS AND MOTORBIKES

ARTHUR VENO
& EDWARD WINTERHALDER
WITH WILL DE CLERCQ

ALLEN&UNWIN

This edition first published in 2009 by Allen & Unwin

Allen and Unwin
83 Alexander Street
Crows Nest, NSW 2065
Australia

Phone: (61 2) 8425 0100
Fax: (61 2) 9906 2218
Email: info@allenunwin.com
Web: www.allenandunwin.com

Cataloguing-in-Publication details are available
from the National Library of Australia
www.librariesaustralia.nla.gov

ISBN 978 1 74175 695 1

Set in 11/15.4 pt ITC Mendoza Roman Std by Bookhouse, Sydney
Printed and bound in Australia by Griffin Press

10 9 8 7 6 5 4 3 2

This book is dedicated to black sheep everywhere.

Contents

Acknowledgements

We acknowledge Karen Sims for contribution to chapter 2 based on data provided to her by Arthur Veno.

We fully appreciate and recognize the use of the intellectual property of those women whose stories are told in this book. It was great getting to know each and every one of you. You have all our respect and thanks for sharing your wonderful stories. Some of the women have set up their own website <www.bikerchicksbook.com> which continues their stories.

Many thanks to Wil De Clercq for facilitating our vision into another fine work of literary reality.

A special thanks to Sue Hines at Allen & Unwin for her idea to write the book on this topic and her guidance and advice in publishing our book.

Foreword

by Tanya Tucker

I never thought that I would be adding writer of an introduction to a book about biker chicks to my resume. But the whole concept of women and motorcycles has always fascinated me — ditto bad boys and outlaw motorcycle clubs. Love 'em or hate 'em, there's no denying they are an intriguing part of the fabric of our society.

Since I was a young gal, around the time 'Delta Dawn' was released, I have been independent and walked on the wild side. Riding Harley-Davidson motorcycles, which I've been doing since the early 1990s, no doubt further contributed to my 'outlaw' image in the world of country music. When I first started riding, a woman at the controls of a big bike was still considered different. If you were a woman and rode a Harley, wore shades, a leather jacket, jeans, and boots, everyone just figured you had to be a tough cookie or that you were some kind of biker mama. Unlike today, when everybody from your dentist to the CEO of a major company rides one, Harleys were still very much associated with outlaw motorcycle clubs and bad ass bikers. People tend to make associations; that's how stereotypes are born and you get pigeonholed into being this or that.

For me, tooling around on my bike is as natural as taking a stroll through the park. When I'm riding, I don't think about anything except the ride. I love to ride, because it's just me, the bike, and the elements. Even when riding with friends, I feel like I'm truly in my own space yet part of everything around me. It's a feeling you can't adequately explain to the non-rider.

Although seeing a woman cruising around on a motorcycle is a common enough sight, I think that in the minds of a lot of folks it is still unladylike behavior, because the motorcycle has been an icon of manliness from day one. Unfortunately, women who hang around with motorcycle bad boys are still thought by some to be sleazy, not very bright, and even suffering from some kind of psychological affliction. But I can't really blame people who are entrenched in those beliefs. After all, for many decades the media, writers, and movie producers have perpetuated an image of the motorcycle world that can mostly be considered negative. That's why *Biker Chicks: The Magnetic Attraction of Women to Bad Boys and Motorbikes* is such a fresh and fascinating read.

I'll be the first to admit that when I started to read *Biker Chicks*, I had my reservations, even expecting to some extent to be confronted with more of the same old, same old. I quickly discovered that this was not the case. The women's stories are a real eye-opener, at times surprising, humorous, and heart wrenching but always informative. After reading *Biker Chicks*, I not only feel even more of a kinship with my motorcycling sisters, I have more of an appreciation for the history of the motorcycle and the motorcycling community.

Tanya Tucker
Tennessee, United States
April 2009

Foreword

by Julie van den Eynde, PhD

Seated around the legal office's heavy wooden conference table was a civil libertarian lawyer, the national president of a major outlaw motorcycle club, four senior members of the club's chapter, my colleague and friend Dr Arthur Veno, and myself. I was the only woman present. This was a critical meeting, for the club had decided to take civil action against the police and they needed a strong legal team to represent them.

The outlaw motorcycle club men and Arthur introduced themselves and began to present the details of their case. The lawyer broke into the conversation and said, 'Okay, I know who you all are.' He turned to me and said, 'But I don't know who you are. Where do you fit in?' Before I could respond, the men replied almost in unison: 'She is with Arthur.' 'This is Julie.' 'She is with us.' 'Julie is helping us.' 'She's Arthur's student.' I listened to how I was being introduced and I was amused that I wasn't able to speak for myself. In those few seconds, I had not only been stripped of my voice, I had been defined inaccurately by these men.

This was the moment of decision for me. Could we really work together? Could a feminist academic and the senior men from an outlaw motorcycle club establish a rapport of mutual trust and respect? I decided to try. I cleared my voice to gain their attention and then addressed the lawyer. 'After the men have finished telling you who they *think* I am, let me introduce myself,' I said in an even voice. 'I am Dr Julie van den Eynde. I am a psychologist and a criminologist from the University of Queensland, Australia. You wanted to know where I fit in. Arthur Veno asked me to collaborate with him.'

Laughter rang around the room. The men got it. They understood my point entirely. One of the bikers spoke through his laughter and said, 'Arthur, I am going to call you Dr Julie's secretary from now on.' This caused more uproar in the room. But the introduction had been made. We were on an even playing field and we got down to the business at hand. From that meeting onwards, the men from the outlaw motorcycle club and I began to forge a respectful working relationship. Not that I would ever expect to understand every aspect of their lifestyle, nor they my choices, but mutual respect was necessary.

The connection I formed with these men gave me a unique view into a powerful outlaw motorcycle club. Rapidly, many of the urban myths surrounding the men fell by the wayside and my interest in the women who associate with them began to blossom. I had read the books. I had searched the academic literature: all gleefully reported on misogynist bikers who mistreated their 'ole ladies.' Why then were the men openly talking with pride about their women, and their women's achievements? Why did I hear all about their children and their devotion to their kids and family?

Outlaw biker Boff told me he wasn't allowed to smoke cigarettes in his home. He was laughing as he said, 'I tell me missus that I'm a senior member of an outlaw club, but I can't even smoke in my own home.' Another man continued, 'Yeah, and I have to take my colors off and hang them in the back shed. Me missus says they are filthy and smelly and she won't let me have them in the house.' Boff said seriously,

'My son has asthma. So it is fair enough, really.' Where did the stories I was hearing fit in with the widely accepted notions about brutish bikers, those men who put their club, their motorcycle, and their dog before their women?

From conversations like this, I found myself becoming intrigued by the bikers' women. Who are they? How do they manage as women, as partners, and as mothers to travel through life immersed in the outlaw motorcycle club culture? I was fascinated. But I knew I would never be able to meet any of their women until I had passed through some kind of filtering process or a test of some kind. I was very aware of being under a microscope. The men challenged me often. An ongoing challenge was to get me onto a Harley, but I always point blank refused. What could I do but be myself and not pretend to be anything else than a woman, an academic, and a feminist?

I realized I was well underway in passing the tests when two of the men sat down opposite me in a café. Ordering a latté (to my surprise!), one asked me if I was offended by their 'colorful language' and their 'substance use,' and should they 'tone it down' around me? Taken aback by their courtesy, I thanked them and assured them they needn't be concerned. From this point on, with the men's permission in place, I was invited to meet the women who associate with outlaw clubs. And once again, upon meeting and spending time with the women, the urban myths had to be pushed aside: biker women are much more than that and then some. This is where Dr Arthur Veno and Edward Winterhalder's book is so valuable.

The urban myths are addressed in Section I of the book. Here the authors run through how previous writers have reported about women who associate with outlaw bikers. They clearly reveal how the work of some of these early writers is outright lewd, some pure fantasy, some written to titillate the reader, and the remainder at best reports on women in a derogatory fashion. The usual standard sexist threads exist: for example, a woman who has sex for fun with a biker is a whore and a psychologically damaged person, whereas the biker who has sex with her is some kind of superhero. This old material is severely faulty, disrespectful towards women, and serves to detour the reader into some kind of soft-porn fantasy land. These early books were written by men who asked outlaw bikers what their women were like. The women themselves did not have a voice; they were invisible!

Up until now, readers interested in this subject have been missing out on the 'real' women of the biker world. In *Biker Chicks: The Magnetic Attraction of Women to Bad Boys and Motorbikes*, the authors relegate the stereotype to the trash heap where it belongs. They show us that the truth is far more interesting and informative than any previously generated fiction and fantasy which masqueraded as fact. Rather than asking other men what biker women are like, the authors took a unique approach. Dear reader, prepare yourself . . . they did the unthinkable. They actually talked to the women. Not only did they talk to them, they made sure the women were not misrepresented or misinterpreted in any way. Before publication, every final draft was checked and approved by each of the women they interviewed. What we have here is an accurate picture told in the women's own words. The women who associate with bikers, and the women who actually ride bikes themselves — in most cases not one and the same — have been given a voice at last.

Arthur Veno, PhD, and Edward Winterhalder have meticulously collected the stories of bikers' women and women bikers from diverse countries in various parts of the world that all have a strong biker culture and history, including the United States (the epicenter of outlaw motorcycle clubs), Australia, Canada, Scotland, Belgium, The Netherlands, and

Poland. These women will indeed take you on a ride into a world that has previously been off limits to the outsider. Some women are lone riders; others are from all-women rider groups. There are women bikers who are closely linked to outlaw motorcycle clubs . . . some aren't, as bikers' women are usually content to ride on the seat behind their man.

Before delving into the women's own stories in Sections II and III, the authors unravel the attraction of women to 'bad boy' outlaw bikers. Initially, they take us into the past to the early days of the motorcycle; look at women's roles in the developing motorcycling culture; and open the doors into the outlaw biker subculture which started to integrate itself into the motorcycle mosaic in the late 1940s. The authors also reveal for the uninitiated the magic of motorcycle riding, which is more than just getting around from one destination to the next.

Amongst the women's accounts are inspirational stories of love and devotion to their partners. Others tell of the sisterhood, and the often hidden world of women's business of supporting each other, mothering, and loving. There are joyful stories of pure sensuality; of women knowing their power and their ability to bring a man to his knees with their feminine prowess. There is the seductress, the femme fatale, and the southern belle.

I am sure some of the women's narratives will make you pause and reflect a while. At least it happened to me. For example, in older books on bikers, 'Property of' patches were used as a case in point of how men controlled and subjugated their women. Once again a quite different story emerges. Biker's woman Jane explains that 'it does take some education to those unfamiliar with the scene to understand the significance of the property patch.' Jane was absolutely correct. I needed some education.

Similarly, many women in *Biker Chicks: The Magnetic Attraction of Women to Bad Boys and Motorbikes* do not fit the traditional female mold. The insight these women provide to the reader is invaluable, and challenging. Emerging from these narratives are women who have strength of character, independence of spirit, and women making their own choices in their pathway through life. These women will challenge you with their forthrightness and frankness. Wonderful!

Finally, whilst reading the women's narratives, they evoked strong memories of Dr Clarissa Pinkola Estés's wonderful book entitled *Women Who Run with the Wolves*. Other narratives refer to the Valkyrien from Nordic mythology; some even awakened strains in me from Wagner's *Die Walküre* opera. But again, exploring these ideas would delve into the world of fantasy and mythology. There is no need. As I stated at the beginning of this foreword, women are far more interesting when we hear their 'truth.' The fiction is best left to others.

Dr Julie van den Eynde
University of Queensland
Brisbane, Australia
April 2009

A Biker's Creed

Authors' note

One interviewee sent this creed to us and we have included it because we feel it is quite representative of the way outlaw bikers and many of our interviewed women feel.

·

I ride because I enjoy it. I ride because I enjoy the freedom I feel from being exposed to the elements, and the vulnerability to the danger that is intrinsic to riding.

I do not ride because it is fashionable to do so. I ride my motorcycle, not wear it.

My motorcycle is not a symbol of status. It exists simply for me and me alone.

My motorcycle is not a toy. It is an extension of my being and I will treat it accordingly, with the same respect I have for myself.

I strive to understand the inner workings of my motorcycle, from the most basic to the most complex. I will learn everything I can about my motorcycle, so that I am reliant upon no one but myself for its well-being.

I strive to constantly better my skill of control over my motorcycle. I will learn my limits and use my skill to become one with my motorcycle so that we may keep each other alive. I am the master, it is the servant. Working together in harmony, we will become an invincible team.

I do not fear death. I will, however, do all possible to avoid death prematurely. Fear is the enemy, not death. Fear on the highway leads to death; therefore I will not let fear be my master.

My motorcycles will outlive me. Therefore they are my legacy. I will care for them for future bikers to cherish — as I have cherished them — whoever they may be.

I do not ride to gain attention, respect, or fear from those who do not ride, nor do I wish to intimidate or annoy them. For those that do not know me, all I wish from them is to ignore me. For those that desire to know me, I will share with them the truth of myself so that they might understand me and not fear others like me.

I will show respect to other bikers more experienced or knowledgeable than I am. I will learn from them all I can.

I will not show disrespect to other bikers less experienced or as knowledgeable as I am. I will teach them what I can. It will be my task to mentor new riders, who so desire, into the lifestyle of the biker so that the breed shall continue. I shall instruct them as I have been instructed by those before me. I shall preserve and honor traditions of bikers before me and I will pass them on unaltered.

I will not judge other bikers on their choice of motorcycle, their appearance, or their profession. I will judge them only on their conduct as bikers. I am proud of my accomplishments as a biker, though I will not flaunt them to others. If they ask I will share them.

I will stand ready to help any biker, when and wherever I go. I am proud to be a biker and hide my chosen lifestyle from no one. I ride because I love freedom, independence, and the movement of the ground passing beneath me. But most of all I ride to better understand myself, my motorcycle, the lands in which I ride, and to seek out and know other bikers like myself.

Anonymous

Introduction

We were patiently waiting by our telephones, continents apart, ready to do a live radio interview which was being broadcast in yet another part of the world, England. We were doing the interview as part of a publicity campaign to promote Arthur Veno's previous book, *The Mammoth Book of Bikers*. We were getting oriented for the show and we knew from prior media interviews pretty much what to expect. There would be obligatory questions about the history of modern day outlaw motorcycle clubs, followed by a question about crime and the clubs. And then there would be a question about the women associated with the outlaw motorcycle club scene.

The interview unraveled pretty well as we had anticipated. The host of the show really put the screws on Edward, asking if he would approve of his daughter being an ole lady with the Bandidos, the notorious international club Edward had at one time been a high ranking member of. He fielded the question well, indicating that he hoped his daughter would go to college and/or university and not join the club scene. After some probing by the interviewer, Edward acknowledged that he would approve of his daughter socializing with a member of the Bandidos, as long as that member was not into drugs and had a legitimate means of support.

In light of the interest and questioning we usually encountered during our promo interviews regarding women who associated with outlaw motorcycle clubs, we decided to extend the work that Dr Julie van den Eynde and Dr Veno had already done in Australia and put what we learned into a new book. To get an international feel for the subject, we would talk to bikers' women and women bikers — popularly known as 'biker chicks' — across Australia, Europe, and North America (where the secretive and powerful outlaw motorcycle counterculture originated). The response we received from the women we contacted was enthusiastic, although some didn't want to discuss their lives and simply hung up on us. Some demanded anonymity as the price for their cooperation. The stories of their lives proved both predictable and unpredictable; even for us there were a few surprises.

All of the previous works in the field, whether by academics or journalists/authors, were based on local accounts and, with a few exceptions, were done by men interviewing bikers about their women and the females who hung around the club scene. Considering the era in which many of the studies were conducted (1960s–1970s), what surfaced in print mostly reinforced stereotypes that the public had already come to perceive as truth. We realized that a serious flaw existed with these earlier attempts at defining who the biker chicks really are. We knew the only way to get to the bottom of things was to actually interview the women and let them speak for themselves.

We started out with a few contacts and used a research method called the 'snowball technique.' This meant we asked each woman to provide us with their account of life as an associate of a club or outlaw biker, and then asked them to recommend further contacts. As a comparison group, we contacted women who had no apparent links to the outlaw motorcycle scene, but who were motorcycle riders themselves; we did this because we wanted to know whether, and how, the two groups differed. We tried to restrict the biker women to Harley-Davidson riders, as this iconic American motorcycle personifies the hardcore biker. But we gathered a few accounts from riders in Europe, Australia, and New Zealand who did not own a Harley due to cultural issues and/or the prohibitive cost of a Harley-Davidson in countries other than the United States.

In the end, two hundred and twelve women were contacted, of whom seventy-one agreed to tell all. Some of the women chose to remain anonymous for obvious reasons. These reasons included fear of reprisals or harassment from the outlaw motorcycle club members who were their partners or from the clubs themselves; to protect their children and immediate family members; to safeguard their careers; or due to courts of law gag orders that prohibited them from naming names, etc. However, whether the women in question used their actual names or pseudonyms to tell their stories, it does not change the veracity of their stories in any way, shape, fashion, or form.

In the vast majority of cases, we would telephone the women and ask them a series of questions about their family histories and how they came to be in the scene. The interviews commenced in September 2007 and ended in June 2008. The process was a difficult one, as each woman stayed involved, as per our intentions, right up to the final draft so they were assured of being accurately represented. It is easy, when transcribing, paraphrasing, and editing, for information to slip out of context and thus the original meaning is lost. A few of the women, like Amy White, asked if they could write their own accounts from scratch. We agreed to this on the condition that we reserved the right to edit their words where necessary. As with the other women they received a final draft to sign off on.

During our research we found the attitude to women of outlaw motorcycle clubs was surprisingly broad and ranged from seriously misogynistic to amazingly female and family friendly. Indeed, these differences were apparent between various chapters of some national clubs, making generalizations about how women are treated almost impossible. We also discovered that the same situation applied to the international community of women bikers: there is massive diversity therein. With respect to their connections to outlaw motorcycle clubs, the women riders seem to be best described in the words of Dr Barbara Joans as a 'stepping stone connectedness.' That is to say, some women bikers abhor and avoid any contact with outlaw motorcycle clubs. Others have some contact and connectedness, while yet others are full-on women bikers who happen to be bikers' women.

Dr Joans, who is Chair of the Anthropology Department and Director of the Anthropology Museum at Merritt College, Oakland, California, saw things very differently from our perspective with respect to definitions: she defined 'biker women' as women who ride, while those who didn't ride were simply passengers. We acknowledge her formulations so well described in her fabulous book *Bike Lust*, but for our account we choose to call all of our women biker chicks.

Biker Chicks: The Magnetic Attraction of Women to Bad Boys and Motorbikes is the result of the interviews we conducted and the gathering of other pertinent information. It is a completely new look at what is widely regarded as the most under-researched aspect of the bad ass outlaw biker world: the women who are drawn to it like the proverbial moth to a flame.

Section I
The History and Evolution of Biker Chicks

1

A Brief History of Motorcycles and Women Riders

There is a certain magic to the motorcycle. It appears to be inherent in the experience of riding. Motorcycles predate the automobile by twenty-five years and the airplane by thirty-six. Basically an offshoot of the early bicycle, at the end of the nineteenth century the motorcycle was the first form of personal mechanized transport to emerge from the industrial age. The motorcycle captured the imagination of the public from day one and continues to do so to this day. To its inventors and early developers the motorcycle was intended to be nothing more than a new, modern form of transportation. But the two-wheeled motorized vehicle was destined to become much more than that. The motorcycle evolved into a cultural icon, one that changed with the times to become next to immortal. Even more than speed, grace, and agility, the motorcycle symbolizes the abstract themes of rebellion, progress, freedom, glamor, adventure, nonconformity, sex, and danger.

Simply put a motorcycle is a single-track, two-wheeled vehicle that is powered by an engine ranging from a miniscule but nonetheless potent 50cc to a powerhouse 2450cc. There are numerous styles of motorcycles, but they basically consist of three classes: road, off-road, and show (custom). In countries such as the United States, where automobiles rule the road, motorcycles are a minority, but in many parts of the world they dominate. With the rising cost of fuel, the motorcycle may soon become a vehicle of choice. For those who wish to leave a smaller carbon footprint on the earth, it is also an attractive alternative.

Whether shunned or embraced, the motorcycle is many things to many people. Aside from its utilitarian purpose the motorcycle is a technological marvel and a work of art, especially in the case of custom and personalized bikes. In the summer of 1998, the venerable Guggenheim Museum in New York held an exhibit of ninety-six motorcycles under the moniker 'The Art of the Motorcycle.' Although the exhibition stirred up a swirl of controversy, it demonstrated to a wide public the addictive fascination of motorcycles and the lure of riding them. In the exhibit's companion book, also titled *The Art of the Motorcycle*, Guggenheim director Thomas Krens refers to the motorcycle as a 'quintessential symbol of the insecurity and optimism of our time.'

While they may not deny the aesthetics of the motorcycle many people fear them, because they consider the two-wheeled powerhouses dangerous and/or intimidating. That's why to ride a motorcycle is special: it sets the operator apart from the masses and creates a kinship that is totally alien to the world of automobile drivers. Although a certain stereotype exists, bikers are anything but typical. They come in all shapes and sizes, creeds, colors, backgrounds, and occupations.

Broadly speaking, though, motorcycle riders fall into one of three very different groups with very different levels of commitment to what is called the 'biker lifestyle.' The first type consists of utilitarian riders. These people may not really care about the biker lifestyle at all and ride for a number of practical reasons, like getting from point A to point B. People in the second group, motorcycle enthusiasts, consider riding motorcycles to be important in their lives, but for these riders, the motorcycle is probably best described as a hobby with various levels of enthusiasm and commitment being demonstrated. Motorcycle enthusiasts neither live to ride nor ride to live as the third and final type of rider does. Hardcore bikers clearly form their life around their commitment to riding. It is in this third group of riders that we find those motorcyclists who are usually the ones written about by mainstream press. They are well known and often feared. They are the outlaws of the biker lifestyle.

At the extreme end of the hardcore bikers groups are the 1%ers. While they form only a small part of the motorcycle world, the vast majority of press and mainstream media constantly scrutinize them. They make colorful press! One-percenters not only live to ride, their lives are totally consumed by their passion for the motorcycle and the club. The club is front and center. They do other things — marry, work, and lead varied lives — but nothing engages them like the motorcycle. Each wishes to be a member of the dominant club in the area and will often fight to achieve or maintain that position. They define themselves with their own laws, bylaws, charters, and legal documents. To join a leading outlaw clubs takes years of association, and not everyone makes the cut. Outlaws may only represent a small part of biker culture, but their influence is huge. Arguably, they form the foundation of the biker subculture.

Not all 1%ers ride on the criminal side of the law, but many have been known to do so. Drug and gun trafficking is currently the most prevalent of their criminal activities, but they have been known to commit a vast range of crimes. Despite the lurid press and tales of murder and mayhem, not every outlaw biker breaks society's laws. What they all break are society's rules. They are part of a true counterculture, because they reject the typical norms and values of the society they live in.

One of the most significant of their rules is the 'code of silence,' which is a tenet of most organized criminal organizations like the Mafia and the Asian Triads. Another rudimentary rule is 'brotherhood.' Rules of silence are easily understood but the rules concerning brotherhood must be explained. When a club member is in trouble, all other members will back him up regardless of the validity of the situation. He will be backed up regardless of what he might have done. All club members will come to each other's aid at all times. No matter what the member has done, even if he has committed acts that the others would normally not sanction. If the member is in trouble, he will be supported and protected. Brotherhood is the most defining club value and it is constantly reaffirmed. The club, the brotherhood, and the bike, in that order, are the central aspects of their identity. Nothing comes before the club, the brotherhood, and the bike. For the 1%er the club is his family.

Why ride?
Although men still comprise the majority of motorcycle riders, according to the US Motorcycle Industry Council women now account for approximately twelve percent of motorcycle purchases depending on the brand; that's up over twenty percent in just five years! This number is expected to gradually keep rising over the next five years.

But ask any man or woman why he or she rides and in just about every case the answer given is the sense of freedom, vitality, energy, and adventure experienced while at the controls of a motorcycle. A deep passion for riding, whether hardcore throttling on the highway or just tooling around loose and carefree along winding back roads, is the common denominator of both. The thrill of flicking gears, twisting the throttle, leaning into curves and having the bike respond like a well-trained thoroughbred is inexplicable to the uninitiated. Riding a bike is communing with the environment, and as stated by Internet blogger and motorcyclist Ian Chadwick, it is 'variously exciting, relaxing, enlightening, and enabling.'

There's no denying that some people ride motorcycles for banal reasons. There are men who ride purely for the sake of macho posing and to inflate their egos; motorcycle culture has oozed machismo from the very beginning. Some women ride just to demonstrate to their biological counterparts that anything men can do, they can do just as well. Hence the riding can also be considered an ego boost or an enforcing agent for self-esteem. No doubt, for many bikers these elements subconsciously filter into the equation even though their actual motivation for riding has nothing to do with testosterone or estrogen. After all, riding a motorcycle is cool. It's about individuality. Riding a motorcycle makes a statement!

In *The Perfect Vehicle,* author Melissa Holbrook Pierson sums up her love affair with motorcycles as:

> From my mother I learned to write prompt thank-you notes for a variety of occasions. From Mrs. King's ballroom dancing school I learned a proper curtsy and, believe it or not, what to do if presented with nine eating utensils at the same place setting. From motorcycles I learned practically everything else. Riding on a motorcycle can make you feel joyous, powerful, peaceful, frightened, vulnerable, and back to happy again, perhaps in the same ten miles.

Riding a motorcycle is about being connected to your immediate surroundings — feeling the wind in your face, smelling the roses — and sometimes about doggedness — gritting your teeth and persevering no matter how miserable you feel. But on a bike, even feeling miserable can have redeeming value; it underscores the old adage 'When the going gets tough the tough get going.' Motorcycles are all about control. There is practically no margin for error. Piloting a motorcycle means your entire body is applied to the act of riding. Every motion made, even the most subtle, produces a result. The slightest of movements translate into significant reactions; major movements trigger major reactions. It is impossible to ride and not be aware of how you are positioned on your bike. Your torso, arms, wrists, hands, shoulders, legs, and feet all play a key role in maneuvering your motorcycle, whether it's a lightweight or a heavyweight superbike or cruiser.

When riding the open road or exploring off-road trails, it is easy to suspend your everyday worries. The senses are engulfed by the environment of the road and there is an all-encompassing need for constant awareness. This leaves little room to be concerned about the problems and minutiae of daily life. Robert M Pirsig, who wrote *Zen and the Art of Motorcycle Maintenance,* a testimony to the joys of motorcycling, pointed out the sense of immediacy and connection experienced by bikers compared with the isolation of car drivers who are always in a compartment, passively observing what transpires around them. Pirsig maintains that a biker is 'completely in contact with it all . . . in the scene,' because the actual process and experience of piloting a motorcycle demands that the rider be totally in the present. Many motorcycle enthusiasts like to go for a ride just to relieve stress . . . to clear the mind.

While driving a car can be an exhilarating experience it can never match that of riding a bike, even in the great outdoors where 4x4 utility vehicles are purported to offer the ultimate driving experience. In an essay entitled 'Why We Ride', Chadwick compares the automobile to a wheeled isolation chamber. He notes that when traveling in a car:

> We see the world as if it were on a television screen. Outside exists on the other side of the glass, another, slightly unreal

world that doesn't conform to our controlled environment inside. The real world is experienced through the filtering windshield, seen but not participated in, a cartoon of reality. On a motorcycle, the real world is never excluded from the experience of traveling. We ride in the world, never merely past it. We can smell the world we travel through, feel the wind buffet us, hear the sound of traffic; we are aware of environmental relationships, of the road conditions, and of our surroundings. We are acutely aware of other vehicles on the road, even if the car owners are blithely ignorant of us. We notice pets, pedestrians, and potholes. You cannot run over anything. We are vulnerable when we ride, to both the physical and emotional realities of the world.

Nobody can deny the inherent risks of riding a motorcycle, but the 'risk factor' is often part of the attraction. It's about living on the edge, a theme that in the biker world recurs again and again. Those who ride readily accept the risks, feeling safe within their control of the bike, being at one with their machine. While most people prefer the bodily protection afforded by a car, the experience offered by each vehicle is as different as night and day. Relative safety, comfort, separation from the environment, and protection from the elements are the hallmarks of driving a car. Danger, various degrees of discomfort, unity with the environment, and braving the elements are the hallmarks of riding a bike.

In his book *Hell's Angels*, Hunter S Thompson writes of the joy of pushing a motorcycle to its limits on the open road: 'With the throttle screwed on there is only the barest margin, and no room at all for mistakes . . . that's when the strange music starts, [and] fear becomes exhilaration.' Similarly, TE Lawrence, better known as Lawrence of Arabia, wrote of the 'lustfulness of moving swiftly' and the 'pleasure of speeding on the road' on a motorcycle. Milan Kundera, author of *The Unbearable Lightness of Being*, noted that: 'Speed is the form of ecstasy the technical revolution has bestowed on man. When man delegates the faculty of speed to a machine [such as a motorcycle], from then on, his own body is outside the process, and he gives over to a speed that is non-corporeal, nonmaterial, pure speed, speed itself, ecstasy speed.'

Toni Sharpless, one of the first women to make a name for herself in road and endurance racing at home in Canada as well as in Europe and Japan, said that 'High speed is a different world, really. It's a very addictive one. The best part is becoming totally comfortable with high speed by focusing and slowing everything down in your brain. You always have to have a plan at high speed, because it is going to happen faster than you are ready for it if you don't. I think the challenge of trying to manage the risks of high speed is the real thrill.'

Speed draws many people to motorcycling, as the power-to-weight ratio of even low-power motorcycles rivals that of an expensive sports or muscle car. Furthermore, the power-to-weight ratio of high-power sport bikes is well beyond any mass production automobile. And all this for a fraction of the cost of a car. Not all bikers have a need for speed, but even the most conservative and timid rider will now and again give in to the desire to ratchet the throttle just an extra notch; the adrenaline rush of sudden acceleration is not to be denied. Ask any biker and he or she will agree that high speeds on a motorcycle are more exhilarating than high speeds in a car. The sensation of speed on a motorcycle is greater, as the rider is not separated from the environment of the road like the driver of a car.

Speed demons, however, don't belong on the highways and byways of the world. Those who are serious about speed are often attracted to sanctioned racing or club racing, either off-road or on paved circuits. At least the responsible ones who are concerned about the dire consequences that can result from threading their way through traffic at high speeds look towards sanctioned or club competition as a means to satisfy their craving for life in the fast lane. It is ironic that the majority of professional motorcycle racers do not like riding on public roads. Many avoid it totally!

Birth of the motorcycle

The history of the motorcycle, like that of its predecessor the bicycle, is fuzzy at best and historians are often at odds as to whom to credit for inventing it. Instead, the concept seems to have occurred to numerous engineers and inventors around Europe more or less simultaneously. Within a decade, starting in the late 1880s, dozens of designs and machines emerged, particularly in France, Germany, and England. Although Europe was a hotbed for motorcycle development, imaginative young men who had a propensity for things mechanical were tinkering with similar ideas in places like the United States, Canada, and Australia. But the motorcycle was slated to become more than just a mode of inexpensive transportation — it would become part of a cultural phenomenon, the most dramatic of which was the birth of the outlaw biker counterculture of the 1960s.

The first commercially produced motorcycle arrived on the scene in 1894. It was called the Hildebrand & Wolfmuller Motorad and was built in Germany and France. It featured a two-cylinder four-stroke engine that propelled the bike to a then impressive speed of 29 mph (40 km/h). In addition to the water-cooled 1488cc internal combustion engine, the bike featured a hollow tube frame, both of which were innovative for the time. While the first functioning motorcycle is undoubtedly a European invention, coining the name of the new vehicle has been credited to the American inventor Edward J Pennington, who demonstrated a motorized bike of his own design in 1895. However, his 'motor cycle' was a prototype that never made it into the public realm.

The entrepreneurial spirit of the growing industrialized nations quickly saw the potential of the motorcycle and a plethora of companies sprang up all over Europe and the United States. In 1902, the British bicycle manufacturer Triumph produced its first commercially available motorcycle. By fitting their bicycles with Belgian-built engines the company entered the 'motorcycle business.' Triumph would go on to become an industry leader and one of the few survivors of more than eighty British motorcycle companies that morphed onto the scene between 1900 and 1930. Like their counterparts in Europe and the US, many British motorcycle factories ended up closing their doors as quickly as they had opened them. But some of the British pioneering firms, including Triumph, built now legendary bikes with brand names like AJS, Matchless, Ariel, and Norton.

Meanwhile, in 1898 in the United States, the Waltham Manufacturing Company, another bicycle manufacturer, got in on the motorized cycle action. They called their machine the Orient-Aster, which has been credited as the first American-built consumer motorcycle. In 1901, the Hendee Manufacturing Company designed a prototype motorcycle that went into production a year later under the brand name Indian. The company, which was reincorporated as the Indian Motorcycle Company in the early 1920s, would, until 1914, enjoy the distinction of being the world's number one motorcycle manufacturer. Following closely on Indian's heels was the Harley-Davidson Motor Company which was founded in 1903, the same year as the Ford Motor Company. It took William S Harley and his boyhood friend Arthur Davidson, and Arthur's brother Walter, until 1905 to put a dozen 405cc motorcycles on the market. Their machine's advanced loop-frame design took it out of the motorized-bicycle category and would help define the modern motorcycle in the years to come.

For nearly the first two decades of the twentieth century, motorcycles were the most inexpensive method of motorized transportation. Although they were still too costly for many people, for the average-income family it was a prudent purchase. The price ticket on the average bike was around $275 (US); for another $75 to $100 the purchaser could bolt a sidecar to his machine. Meanwhile, Ford's Model T cost about $850. What proved to be a real boon for the motorcycle industry, especially Harley-Davidson, was America's entry into World War I. Between 1916 and 1918, Harley geared up production to 25,000 units for the US military alone. Conversely, the end of the war saw the collapse of the motorcycle industry, not just because there were no more military contracts to fill, but because Ford had begun mass-producing the Model T. The car's price had been reduced dramatically, selling for $300 or less. And sell they did! By the early 1920s, the company celebrated production of its ten millionth vehicle. Meanwhile, only three motorcycle companies survived the onslaught of the automobile industry: Indian, Harley, and Excelsior. After 1931, Indian and Harley-Davidson would be the sole survivors; only one of them was destined to keep operating past the half-century mark.

World War II, as the Great War before it, boosted sales for Harley-Davidson and Indian. From 1953 onwards, however, Harley was the only motorcycle manufacturer left in the United States. It would also become the motorcycle of choice for hardcore outlaw bikers, a distinction it carries to this day. This, however, could be construed as more of a curse than a blessing, for it stigmatized the Harley from the early 1960s well into the 1990s. Whether it really affected sales is hard to say, but no doubt the negative outlaw biker image swayed a lot of 'citizens' — as outlaw bikers call the rest of the population — to buy foreign bikes or seek out other brands of vintage American bikes.

Today, Harley-Davidson is a favorite bike and status symbol not just for many well-heeled blue collar baby boomers looking to recapture their youth, but actors, rock stars, and countless professionals. For most of these 'weekend warriors,' donning leathers, a half-helmet, and straddling their brand new Harley allows them to put the drabness of their everyday life on hold for a few hours and pretend they are the bad boys they will never be. For them, a Harley-Davidson key isn't just a key to start their bikes, it's a key to the world of the biker subculture — it opens the door to dreams and fantasies. Most hardcore women riders also consider a Harley to be the only bike they want to be seen on. Few motorcycle companies can claim the fanatic brand loyalty that is part and parcel of the Harley-Davidson rider; a good example of this is the Harley tattoos found on so many of the world's Harley riders.

First ladies of motorcycling

Although from day one the motorcycle has been primarily a mode of transportation and/or recreational toy for men, women have been part of the motorcycling community since the first reliable motorized cycle was produced at the turn of the century. In the early days, however, women faced considerable social and personal obstacles in their quest to be a member of that community. Before they were grudgingly accepted by the brotherhood of motorcycle riders, these women were considered to be oddities, misfits, and interlopers. In an era that was still very much a man's world, the women who dared intrude into that world, whether political, civil, or social, were independent, resourceful, brave, bold, and tenacious. They were definitely not the kind of women who had been neutered by compliance or who were, like many of their sisters, intimidated by men. These were women who scripted their own destiny and broke down barriers just like those who pioneered the suffragist movement, who opened the doors for women into the arts and sciences, employment, and sports, and who knew that anything men could do they could do as well.

Many women had already embraced bicycles for the mobility and freedom they offered, in defiance of the prevailing conventions of femininity. Bicycles, and later motorcycles, were considered to be a means of getting around for men only. While men took freedom and mobility for granted — actually believing it to be a male birthright — women were not encouraged to ride a cycle, with or without a motor. It was actually considered 'unacceptable behaviour.' But the bicycle and motorcycle were more than transportation vehicles; they were vehicles that helped take women on the path to liberty and equality. Prominent American civil rights leader Susan B Anthony said that the bicycle did 'more for the emancipation of women than anything else in the world.' That women were destined to ride motorcycles was a given. But in the early days, and for countless decades afterward, 'ladies' weren't considered the type of women to straddle such a noisy, smoky contraption. This attitude wasn't just shared by most men either; many women as well considered female motorcyclists gender traitors.

When women first lifted a leg over a motorcycle is anybody's guess, but it's safe to say they were either convention busters and/or members of liberal-minded families whose father, brother, uncle, cousin, husband or boyfriend taught them to ride. In rural areas, especially on farms, being able to handle one of the newfangled 'iron horses' was an asset that benefited not just the women themselves, but the menfolk as well. While high-profile individuals helped to popularize and further the cause of women motorcyclists, it was grassroots women who really made it happen.

In addition to not being your typical turn-of-the-century female, pioneer women motorcyclists possessed the physical strength required not only to kick-start the engine and operate the lumbering machines over uneven terrain, rutted out, rock strewn, dusty or muddy roads, but to pick up their bikes when they dropped them. They also had a knack for things mechanical, which was a near prerequisite for riding a vehicle that required ongoing basic maintenance and which was prone to break down, anytime, anywhere.

Historical records of women motorcyclists prior to 1910 are hard to find, especially of prominent women who advanced the cause of female riders. In fact, there is next to nothing on the subject. But starting in the early 1910s a number of women began attracting the kind of media attention that would immortalize them and encourage others to get behind a set of handlebars. By this time, however, women riders were not to be outdone by their male counterparts: they did everything on a motorcycle men did, from long-distance excursions and racing to simply enjoying a carefree Sunday afternoon ride with friends. In the *New York Times* Sunday edition of January 15, 1911, journalist Frank Libbey Valiant wrote a very positive article about the growing popularity of women motorcyclists entitled 'Motor Cycling Fad Strikes Fair Sex':

> There is an old saying, but nevertheless a very true one, that a woman can turn her hand at almost anything and in this day of advancement it is never surprising to hear of a woman accomplishing any sort of difficult feat — feats that naturally are supposed to require the strength and nerve more universally possessed by the opposite sex. It is no uncommon thing to hear of women driving automobiles, or now, even aeroplanes, and with the last year American women are beginning to ride motorcycles . . .

One of the first American women to achieve some notable success in the world of motorcycles was Clara Wagner. In 1910, the then eighteen-year-old participated in a gruelling 365-mile (587 kilometer) endurance race from Chicago to Indianapolis. She braved rain, muddy roads, and odd looks from people and male competitors to win the event. Not surprisingly, the Federation of American Motorcyclists — a precursor of the American Motorcycle Association founded in 1903 — of which Wagner was a member, refused to recognize her victory. She was deemed 'unofficial.' In honor of her accomplishment, Wagner was later presented with a gold pendant purchased with money collected by some of her more fair-minded men rivals. This demonstrates that for the true-of-heart biker it's not a matter of being a man or a woman motorcyclist, but being a motorcyclist period — at least in a perfect world.

In 1915, the year the first tube of lipstick was sold, a mother–daughter team, Effie and Avis Hotchkiss, rode a Harley-Davidson from New York to San Francisco and back. They didn't take the direct route to the west coast, either. These two adventurous souls meandered about the countryside covering a daunting 5,000 miles (8,000 kilometers). Twenty-six-year-old Effie, who was employed as a bank clerk in New York City, piloted the bike while her mother rode in a sidecar rig. At this time much of the west was still considered 'frontier country.' There were few paved roads and cowboys and Indians still roamed around as did opportunists, conmen, and outlaws. For two women to travel alone through such hostile country was bold and dangerous, and unique enough to make newspaper headlines everywhere. There is even a romantic angle attributed to their journey. According to legend Effie met her future husband in San Francisco when she literally ran over him in the street as he crossed in front of her motorcycle.

One year after the mother and daughter team's milestone ride, two socialites gave the public's perception that riding motorcycles was 'unladylike' behavior a serious kick in the pants. The Van Buren sisters, Adeline and Augusta — descendants of former US President Martin Van Buren — completed a transcontinental journey of the United States, albeit via a more direct route that totalled 3,300 miles (5,300 kilometers). Sponsored by Indian Motorcycles and Firestone Tires, the Van Burens took a side trip to Pikes Peak on their way west and became the first people ever to ascend and descend the venerable 14,110-foot (6303-meter) mountain on a motorcycle. Like the Hotchkisses, they made headlines everywhere they went and had to contend with many unpaved roads, extreme temperatures, rain, mud, and prevailing social mores. In one town, the sisters were arrested and fined for publicly wearing trousers.

Another female motorcycle celebrity was Bessie Stringfield, dubbed the 'Motorcycle Queen of Miami' by the media, from which she got plenty of attention. During the 1930s and 1940s, Stringfield, who was of African American descent, meandered on her motorcycle through all of the lower forty-eight states. Her journeys took her through the Deep South, where she braved racist hostility and prejudice. 'I'd sleep on my Harley at gas stations at night. When I found black folks, I'd sleep next to their children because no one would rent me a motel room,' she recalled in a newspaper interview. 'All along the way, wherever I rode, the people were overwhelmed to see a Negro woman riding a motorcycle.' This was a time when black women were still limited to servile roles such as cook, laundress, cleaning woman, or maid. Stringfield is credited with breaking down color barriers well before Jackie Robinson broke baseball's color barrier in 1947, and well before Rosa Parks sparked the Civil Rights Movement in the 1960s. In addition to completing eight solo cross-country tours of the United States, Stringfield rode her Harley — during her lifetime she owned twenty-seven of them — in Europe, Brazil, and Haiti. During World War II, she proudly served her country as a US Army motorcycle dispatch rider.

Across the ocean, British-born Theresa Wallach became renowned as a motorcycle adventurer, military dispatch rider, engineer, author, motorcycle dealer, mechanic, racer, and riding school instructor. In 1935, Wallach and a close friend, Florence Blenkiron, who was an equally adept rider and mechanic, rode a 600cc Panther with a sidecar rig from London to Cape Town, South Africa, a distance of more than 6,000 miles (9,660 kilometers) as the crow flies. Throwing everyone's discouraging remarks to the wind they set out on their most excellent adventure and vowed to return home. The sceptics had other ideas, saying such a journey would be a daunting task even for men to complete. On their way to Cape Town, Wallach and Blenkiron crossed the unforgiving Sahara desert and equatorial Africa, becoming the first known women to achieve this remarkable feat. Even today an odyssey such as this would be considered extremely dangerous — and, no doubt, would be the subject of a reality television show.

After emigrating to the United States, Wallach worked as a motorcycle mechanic, founded a motorcycle riding school, and wrote an instructional manual entitled *Easy Motorcycle Riding*. In a 1977 interview with *Road Rider Magazine*, Wallach articulated her love affair with motorcycles, saying 'When I first saw a motorcycle, I got a message from it. It was a feeling. The kind of thing that makes a person burst into tears hearing a piece of music or standing awestruck in front of a fine work of art. Motorcycling is a tool with which you can accomplish something meaningful in your life. It is an art.'

Australia also had its share of adventurous women riders. In 1934, two members of Wollongong-based Two Wheel Tootsies Motorcycle Club entered and won the inaugural

Redex Bash for motorcycles. This run was from Sydney to Perth and back via Broken Hill, Adelaide, and Melbourne, a trek of 3,030 miles (4876 kilometers). Like their roaming sisters in America and Europe, they were not intimidated by the prevailing social mores, atrocious roads, dirt tracks through the desert, no roads at all, or the elements, which consisted of temperatures that ranged from a low of 25 degrees Fahrenheit (-4°C) to a high of 122 degrees Fahrenheit (50°C). Crossing the outback on a motorcycle was no mean feat; it was a daring adventure in a conservative time and place. Their journal tells of hostile receptions in small towns and, conversely, how they captured the imagination of people along the way.

In keeping with their conviction 'what men can do, we can do,' women like Margaret 'The Mile a Minute Gal' Gast, May Williams, Jean Perry, and Louise Scherbyn proved their mettle as motorcycle daredevils. They demonstrated their riding skills at carnivals, circuses, and fairs, performing in motordromes, which were advertised as The Wall of Death to lure spectators. In essence, motordromes were giant barrels with a platform around the top edge from which spectators could look down on the riders speeding around the inside of the vertical walls, held in place by centrifugal force. Although motordromes had been around for many years, the death-defying attraction gained increasing popularity in the United States and Europe during the 1930s and survived well into the 1950s. These motordromes were reborn as Thunder Dromes in the late 1980s and exist to this day.

As Clara Wagner had discovered fifteen years earlier, women were not exactly welcomed with open arms at motorcycle racing events. More often than not they faced outright hostility. But that didn't dissuade the legendary Dorothy 'Dot' Robinson from mixing it up with the boys and showing them a thing or two about racing bikes. If ever there was a 'first lady of motorcycling,' a title she would eventually wear with grace and dignity, Robinson fit the bill. She was born into the world of motorcycles in Australia on April 22, 1912. Her father was James Goulding, a respected sidecar designer and amateur racer. According to legend Mr Goulding loaded Mrs Goulding into one of his sidecar rigs when she started to go into labor. Together they dashed off to the hospital, he at the control of his motorcycle, Mrs Goulding hanging on for dear life in the sidecar. No sooner did they arrive at the hospital than Mrs Goulding gave birth to a baby girl, whom they christened Dorothy.

In 1918, the Goulding family emigrated to the United States, where they saw more potential to make a living from the motorcycle business. Eventually the Gouldings settled in Saginaw, Michigan, where they opened a motorcycle dealership. Not surprisingly, a precocious Dot started riding motorcycles at a very young age. In 1930, Robinson made news when she podiumed in the Flint, Michigan 100 Race. Five years later, she set a transcontinental endurance record. In 1940, the year she won the prestigious Jack Pine National Enduro, Robinson became the first woman to garner an AMA National Championship. But Robinson, who operated a Harley-Davidson dealership with her husband Earl Robinson, is best known for her selfless work with the Motor Maids, a women's motorcycle club she co-founded with Linda Allen Dugeau. This national organization, under the leadership of Robinson and Dugeau, was instrumental in raising the profile of, and attracting countless women to, the joys of motorcycling.

The silver lining of war

The exploits of women like the Hotchkisses and Van Burens did not go unnoticed by the American military. Eventually that bastion of maleness came to accept the fact that women could ride motorcycles and were capable of serving as dispatch riders. It was a long way from combat duty and equality in the military, but it was a start. In fact women motorcycle advocates like Robinson and Dugeau would soon benefit from an unexpected source in their bid to popularize the motorcycle as a means of transportation and recreation for women: one of the great scourges of humankind, war! One of the four horsemen of the apocalypse and a life-changing event for all involved, war serves as a catalyst for radical upheavals in society, some of which can be deemed constructive, albeit at a horrific price. For example, in England at the end of World War I, Parliament passed *The Representation of the People Act* (1918), which gave women over thirty who met minimum property qualifications the right to vote in the United States. Of course, the Suffragette movement had achieved this in other Western Nations much earlier. Notably, Australia and New Zealand granted electoral equality to women almost twenty years previously. This enfranchisement was in recognition of the contribution made by women to the war effort. It would take another ten years before full electoral equality was granted and women could vote at the age of twenty-one; but war got the ball rolling.

During World War II, the lives of women in all countries affected by the conflict were altered in many ways. As with most wars many women found their roles, opportunities, and responsibilities expanded. It was liberation by necessity. With their men off to war, working, or stationed in other parts of the country, women had little choice but to pick up a lot of what were considered male designated responsibilities. With fewer men in the workforce, women were called upon to perform traditionally male oriented jobs ranging from machine operators, welders, and riveters, to mechanics, etc. Women in both Allied and Axis countries heeded the call. In the United States, they applied for jobs at staggering rates: several million entered the workforce, joining those women who were already employed in conventional jobs of the time such as secretaries, receptionists, stenographers, telephone operators, waitresses, cashiers, etc.

In the military, in order to free the men for combat duty, women performed many tasks that had also been the domain of men. For women like Rosalie Myers, Theresa Wallach, Dot Robinson, and Bessie Stringfield, wartime put them at the controls of a motorcycle as couriers or dispatch riders. Another ardent woman biker from the era and member of the Motor Maids, Nelle Jo Gill, repaired airplanes, chauffeured generals (including Dwight Eisenhower), and was promoted to sergeant in the WAFS (Women's Auxiliary Ferrying Squadron). As in the private sector, however, equality of pay and power were a long way off, but progress towards equality was being made . . . it was a changing world where stereotypes and women's roles were redefined.

For women motorcyclists or those interested in becoming one, World War II would prove to be their zenith. In many cases, motorcycles fitted into the national war effort equation like a bullet into a rifle. With gasoline rationing in place, the motorcycle was the most economical mode of transportation. Riding one was deemed patriotic. And women needed transportation. For many of them, it was a simple case of learning to ride the bike, if they hadn't already, that had been parked in a shed or garage by their husband, brother, father, or boyfriend before they went off to war. Almost overnight women motorcyclists were no longer considered different or an oddity, at least by the less uptight members of the population. For many of these women, especially those who were trapped in or subscribed to the prevailing gender roles of the time, riding a motorcycle would have been the farthest thing from their mind before the war. Suddenly necessity and opportunity opened their eyes to the fact that they actually could ride their men's bikes, whereas previously they believed or were told that riding pillion or in a sidecar was as good as it got.

Jean Collingwood, a mother of two whose husband was stationed in England, recalled:

> I lived on the outskirts of town so it would have been difficult for me to take a job at the local rubber factory. I wanted to do my bit and with my mom, who lived a few houses away, volunteering to look after the kids, the only thing that stood in my way was the distance to town. My dad couldn't drive me because he worked at the opposite end of the county. But he had an old Henderson motorcycle in the basement, an item from his youth. He offered to fix it up and teach me how to ride it. I was actually scared of the thing and of riding it. But I thought about my husband flying bombing missions into Germany, and said to myself that nothing could be scarier than that. Before I knew it, I was working at the plant and getting there on the bike. My fear of riding quickly turned into exhilaration. I rode to work six days a week. Sometimes on Sunday I even went for pleasure rides with a couple of other factory ladies who rode. If it hadn't been for the war, I seriously doubt I would ever have gotten on a motorcycle. I didn't ride much after the war, but when my daughter turned eighteen she started riding. If I had never ridden myself, I would have been horrified. But how could I deny her the joys and freedom I had experienced myself as a biker girl.

During the war years and for a time beyond, the American Motorcycle Association (AMA), which, like its predecessor the Federation of American Motorcyclists (FAM), welcomed women members, devoted a section of their monthly magazine to women bikers called 'Our Girl Riders.' The section bristled with the adventures of the Motor Maids, which was considered a ladies' auxiliary of the AMA and the premier women's motorcycle club in the United States. Clubs like the Motor Maids were picking up in popularity at the time and reflected the growing number of female riders. These women wanted contact with other riders, not just in their own area but in other parts of the country. Belonging to a motorcycle club fit the bill.

Before World War II, many women who entertained the thought of riding didn't ride simply because they worried it might affect their reputation or jeopardize their jobs and career opportunities if they happened to be employed. Not surprisingly, quite a number of women who were ready to flaunt convention did it in a covert way and were closet motorcyclists. But the war changed society's perception of women bikers — they were, after all, doing their best to contribute to the war effort. Anyone who believed that some kind of motorcycling equality had been established permanently was in for a serious reality check, though. After the war, gender roles were redefined again. Women were relegated back to home and hearth and many of the negative attitudes towards women riders resurfaced. Only the boldest and most independent of women retained some of the advances they had made during the war, including riding a motorcycle.

The age of the 'nuclear family' was dawning. Soon that new invention, television, would churn out gender stereotypes and idealized sitcoms like *Father Knows Best* and *The Adventures of Ozzie and Harriet*. It wouldn't be until some four decades later that the sight of a woman mounted on a motorcycle, whether for transportation, recreation or competition, became commonplace. But before this was achieved women would face yet another hurdle, one that was much more demeaning than anything they had encountered. And it all came about with the dawning of the outlaw motorcycle clubs in the late forties.

Enter the clubs . . .

From time immemorial people have flocked together, first as family units and clans, then as tribes and eventually distinct social groups and cultures. All of these staked out territories that would lead to the formation of city states and countries demarcated by defined borders. It was all about strength in numbers, support, common interests, and control. And from time immemorial subgroups formed within the populace. In turn, these subgroups became more specialized and sophisticated as civilization evolved. From the caves of the Stone Age emerged leadership groups and hunter/warrior castes; spiritual/religious hierarchies arose; later came the intelligentsia cliques, sects and cults of various kinds, guilds/societies, fraternities/sororities, and clubs, many of which were covert and cloaked in secrecy.

Fast-forward to the late nineteenth century: clubs are being created to bring together fellow enthusiasts of the latest technological wonder, the bicycle. One such club was the Yonkers Bicycle Club, of Yonkers, New York. It was founded by George Eller, a young man who liked tooling around on his bicycle with his buddies. Membership was based on two simple rules: be a good person and treat others as you would want to be treated. In 1903, Eller and the other, more progressive-minded members of the club decided to trade their bicycles for motorcycles. Practically overnight the Yonkers Bicycle Club became the Yonkers Motorcycle Club. In the process, it earned the distinction of being the first motorcycle oriented club in the world. The Yonkers' main activities included recreational riding, staging racing events, and socializing. They were also the first club to start favoring Harley-Davidson motorcycles, setting a standard that decades later became mandatory for membership in outlaw motorcycle clubs. In the mid-twenties, Yonkers MC applied for membership in the fledgling American Motorcycle Association, becoming the sixth motorcycle club in the United States to receive a charter.

One year after Yonkers MC was founded on the east coast, the west coast saw its first motorcycle club surface in San

Francisco; it was aptly named the San Francisco Motorcycle Club. Like Yonkers it is still active today and was created with the same mandate in mind. Although some latter-day Yonkers MC and SFMC members forged ties with the outlaw motorcycling community, they have remained family oriented clubs. To this day they continue their association with the AMA, an organization that does not condone outlaw clubs. In fact, it was the AMA which coined the term in response to what were considered non-traditional clubs. Until 1946, outlaw clubs were essentially comprised of bikers who refused to comply with the AMA's rules and regulations, which ran the gamut from inspired to arbitrary. Holding races and rallies not sanctioned by the AMA (thus called 'outlaw' by the association), drinking, partying, and harmless rabblerousing were the main concerns of these clubs. These so-called outlaw clubs never even raised a blip on the nation's radar screen until one fateful weekend in 1947, when a single event would forever change the meaning of the terms 'outlaw clubs' and 'outlaw bikers.'

The cornerstone of the modern-day outlaw motorcycle club lies in California, long known to be a magnet and incubator for off-the-wall social and counterculture movements. Its genesis can be found with the hard-riding, hard-drinking, and hard-fisted members of two clubs: the BoozeFighters of Los Angeles and the Pissed Off Bastards of Fontana. Both clubs were kick-started in the wake of World War II, when thousands of inexpensive war surplus motorcycles flooded the market. Many of those who bought these motorcycles — especially ex-servicemen looking to keep their 'anything-goes' wartime lifestyle intact — gravitated towards non-traditional clubs to ride together and let off steam. It was the rowdy presence of the BoozeFighters and Pissed Off Bastards as well as a handful of similar clubs, at the AMA sanctioned 1947 Gypsy Tour Rally in the small town of Hollister, California, that gave birth to the biker image of troublemaker and antisocial deviant.

The non-affiliated AMA clubs' usual high jinks of hard partying, heavy drinking, and tearing up the streets with their motorcycles, while not exactly Boy Scouts behavior, was totally blown out of proportion and sensationalized in news reports. The pièce de résistance, a staged picture taken by an opportunistic photographer and published in *Life Magazine*, showed a drunk on a motorcycle clutching a bottle of beer. To further enhance the effect the ground around his bike was purposely littered with empty bottles. Ironically, the subject of the picture wasn't even a member of a motorcycle club. As if heeding a clarion call, newspapers and television stations around the country began to circulate equally exaggerated and damaging reports of 'riots and anarchy' at a Hollister motorcycle meet.

All this hoopla captured the imagination, if not the indignation, of the American public. Both its fear and fascination with outlaw bikers took hold and became ingrained in the consciousness of the ordinary citizen. Ever since the incident at Hollister, the media has modelled its coverage of anything related to outlaw bikers on the irresponsible precedent set by *Life Magazine* and its initial imitators. In the process, the perpetuation of the biker as an undesirable element stigmatized the motorcycle community — not to mention the motorcycle itself. Simultaneously it created a popular counterculture mythology from which the biker emerged as an iconic figure. While this was strictly an American phenomenon, it would gradually spread overseas, starting in 1954 with a movie seductively titled *The Wild One*. It was Hollywood's version of Hollister. The movie contributed to Marlon Brando's growing fame while adding to the growing infamy of motorcyclists.

The bad press following Hollister and the implication that bikers were out-of-control punks and hoodlums triggered a flood of outraged letters from motorcycle enthusiasts across America. They felt that the image of motorcycling had been tarnished by an isolated incident which hardly reflected the behavior of the majority of law-abiding motorcycle riders. The AMA, in a frantic bid to distance itself from the negative publicity, released a statement penned by its then secretary, Lin Kuchler, which read: 'The disreputable cyclists were possibly 1% of the total number of motorcyclists. Only 1% are hooligans and trouble makers.' It wouldn't be long before outlaw bikers adopted the term 'one-percenter' as a badge of honor.

The Hells Angels, founded in Fontana, California, in 1948 by dissatisfied members of the Pissed Off Bastards, were the first to wear the 1%er badge. For the next two decades, the Angels commanded the most media attention — all of it bad! Many of its members were only too happy to live up to the deeds ascribed to them and the image that was being created. Their notoriety would grow exponentially and inspire wannabe Angels across the country. With their dire winged death's-head emblem, the Hells Angels would set the standards to which all other outlaw clubs aspired. Only three, however, would rise to join them at the top of the biker world's hierarchy: the Outlaws, Pagans, and Bandidos.

Like many traditional motorcycle clubs of the era, the chapters of some outlaw clubs allowed women to join their ranks and even hold office. Among these were the Hells Angels' San Francisco and San Bernardino chapters. While some women rode pillion with their man, others rode solo on their own hulking machines. But whereas women bikers had been perceived by many as unladylike before the era of outlaw motorcycle clubs, their mere association with these clubs and its members would earn them names and reputations that could only be whispered in polite society.

During the 1950s, the basis for bad boy outlaw motorcycle clubs was thoroughly established. While some of those who sought membership in these clubs were bona fide troublemakers, the majority of the men and women were basically decent working-class individuals looking for a good time. In many cases, they came from dysfunctional families, were a little rough around the edges, dissatisfied with the status quo, misfits or disillusioned with their lives. Many of those who joined outlaw clubs, in addition to sharing some or all of the above traits, were hopeless romantics and dreamers. They were throwbacks to an era defined as the 'American Wild West', when 'freedom' still had a more tangible meaning attached to it, and riding a horse was the very expression of freedom and a carefree, mostly lawless existence.

But what nearly everyone who joined a motorcycle club had in common was a desire to belong to some kind of family in which riding together, looking for adventure, and partying were their main concerns. Weekend warrior types, wannabes, and posers looking to enhance their fragile macho image were quickly weeded out — true outlaw bikers are born, not made. After the debacle of Hollister, however, all motorcycle club members, and even independent riders, were viewed with suspicion not only by the public, but by the authorities as well. Thanks to the media depiction of the motorcyclist as barbarian, people had a difficult time differentiating between traditional motorcycle clubs and their antithesis, the outlaw motorcycle clubs. In the public's perception, motorcycle clubs were made up of criminals and dangerous individuals who were to be avoided at all cost.

This perception would only gather momentum with each passing decade to the point that 1%er clubs have been classified, or are on the verge of being classified, as criminal organizations in most countries where they have a presence. But this train of thought goes back more than two decades. According to a

1985 FBI report, 'not all OMGs (Outlaw Motorcycle Gangs) fit the definition of organized crime; many of the estimated 800 motorcycle gangs operating in the United States do.' By the mid-sixties there were hundreds of outlaw motorcycle clubs in the United States and Canada. The Hells Angels, which was the first of the big-four 1%ers to expand outside the United States, had already set foot in Auckland, New Zealand in 1961; by the end of the decade they had arrived in London, England. This was just the beginning. Starting in 1970, the world became their oyster. The Outlaws and Bandidos were not far behind.

Women and motorcycle clubs

A steady diet of singular vision Hollywood bad ass (and mostly bad) biker movies released during the sixties, and highly publicized and exaggerated biker incidents, most of which were isolated cases, only fuelled the myth that motorcycle riders were indeed the type of people who should be put aboard a rocket capsule and shot into space on a one-way trip to nowhere. As the number of outlaw motorcycle clubs increased by leaps and bounds the role of women in these clubs decreased just as quickly. Once the sixties were entrenched on the calendar, women had been banned from joining outlaw motorcycle clubs, period! The closest they got to these clubs was by association — either as wives or girlfriends. Riding alongside club members, however, was a no-no. For most of the bikers' women this wasn't a problem, as they had no desire to ride their own machines.

Women who associated with the outlaw biker element, and even those independent riders who had nothing to do with them, did not escape stigmatization. Whereas previously they had been considered unladylike or just plain different, they were now degraded to the level of sleazy lowlife white trash. In the collective societal mind, no self-respecting woman would find herself in the company of outlaw bikers, nor would she ride a motorcycle. A scooter, maybe, a small or mid-range motorcycle from Europe or Japan, possibly, but a Harley, which had become synonymous with outlaw bikers — never! It is interesting to note that in the early 1960s, Honda marketed its bikes in the United States under the slogan 'You meet the nicest people on a Honda.'

While a lot of American women (and men) shunned Japanese bikes in the early years, opting instead for British bikes and the lighter Harley-Davidson models, Indians, and other used vintage American bikes still around in abundant numbers, it was only a matter of time before they were buying the more inexpensive and easier to ride and maintain imports from a nation that had been defeated by America in World War II. Hardcore bikers, however, wouldn't be caught dead on them and condescendingly referred to them as 'rice burners' or 'jap crap.'

After the war, the number of women riding motorcycles started to decline dramatically. But this had more to do with women going back to their housewife roles and the rising popularity and affordability of the automobile. By the 1970s only one percent of motorcyclists in the United States were women, which was considerably less than during the 1940s. No doubt, the growing stigmatization of 'motorcyclism' affected many women who considered taking up riding, especially those concerned about their reputations, peer pressure, and their jobs. But because it took an unconventional type of woman to ride a bike in the first place, the not so squeaky clean image may even have contributed to the attraction of being a biker. And there were more and more clubs appearing on the scene founded and joined by women who truly loved and resonated with motorcycling. The mandate of all these clubs was to promote, encourage, and support other women to take up the sport.

When exactly the first women's motorcycle club was founded is difficult to determine as documentation, just like that of the early days of women riders, is scarce and often ambiguous. The Motor Maids, founded in 1940, have been cited as being the first such club. While, no doubt, it was the first influential and high profile national American club, it was predated by smaller, localized clubs in North America, Australia, and Europe. Most of these were comprised of like-minded friends who had no interest in expanding beyond their own circle. In many cases these clubs were disbanded when other priorities, commitments, or interests got in the way.

Today, there are hundreds of women's motorcycle clubs worldwide. Some are one-chapter city or regional clubs with very limited memberships; others are multi-chapter national clubs totalling hundreds of members; and finally there are the mega-chapter international clubs which boast thousands of members. Most clubs are open to women of all creeds, colors, and sexual orientation and are not brand biased; some are not and could be considered racist and/or homophobic. The majority of women's clubs fall into the traditional mold; a few here and there operate along the same lines and ideologies as outlaw biker clubs — this includes riding Harleys only. But they all have one thing in common: uniting women motorcyclists.

Clubs like the Motor Maids were the epitome of women's motorcycling respectability and were the darlings of the AMA for a number of decades. The Maids' display team — resplendent in smart blue uniforms and quaint white gloves — often did formation rides around a track at the start of racing events. They turned heads wherever they went on their immaculately kept machines. For many impressionable girls and young women, all it took to catch motorcycling fever was witnessing the Motor Maids in action. The Motor Maids projected poise and perfect control of their machines, proving that riding a motorcycle was not just the domain of men. Women like Dot Robinson, always immaculately groomed and coiffured, personified femininity while demonstrating that a woman could ride as well as any man.

Together with Motor Maids co-founder Linda Allen Dugeau, Robinson spearheaded the expansion of the club throughout the United States. The original requirement for membership still stands today: women who legally own and operate their own motorcycle or one belonging to a family member. This is a prerequisite for membership in the majority of women's (and men's) motorcycle clubs. In her time with the Motor Maids, Robinson reportedly logged up to 50,000 miles (80,500 kilometers) a year to help increase the visibility of the club and motorcycling in general. During her lifetime — she rode until two years before her death at the age eighty-seven — Robinson estimated she had covered over 1.5 million miles (2.4 million kilometers) on her various motorcycles.

Although Dot Robinson, who was born in Australia, is the best known of all women motorcycling pioneers, there are many other women of her era, and right up to the present, who have made substantial contributions. Louise Scherbyn, founder and first international president of the Women's International Motorcycle Association (WIMA), and Theresa Wallach of 'London to Cape Town' fame, who was involved in WIMA's formation and was its first international vice president, were equally passionate in their pursuit of forging a strong women's motorcycling community. In addition to performing in motordromes, Scherbyn enjoyed a career as an endurance racer and stunt rider. In 1940, she was one of the stars in what was billed as 'America's First All-Girl Motorcycle Show'. Like her pioneering sisters, Scherbyn traveled extensively on her motorcycle and was an ambassador for the sport. She has been credited as the first American woman to ride a bike from the United States across the 49th parallel into the Canadian north, reaching Ontario's Temagami Forest in 1937.

In 1950, Scherbyn founded WIMA in an effort to unite women riders worldwide. Scherbyn was active in many clubs including the AMA, the CMA (Canadian Motorcycle Association), the BPC (British Pathfinders Club), and the Motor Maids. During World War II she corresponded with women from other countries in order to satisfy her curiosity about sisters riding motorcycles abroad. It was this correspondence with like-minded women overseas that led her to found WIMA. 'I believed there should be a worldwide organization for all women motorcyclists,' Scherbyn said in a magazine interview in 1952. 'Why not unite as a body in exchanging ideas and opinions, problems and advice? And with this came the initial step of the founding of the Women's International Motorcycle Association.'

WIMA has grown into an organization stretching from North America to Australia and New Zealand in the southern hemisphere to Sweden and Finland in the Arctic north, and from Central Europe to Japan. One of the first international members of WIMA was Hazel Mayes of Sydney. She joined the organization in its fledgling days after receiving a personal invitation from Scherbyn to start a branch Down Under. Australia wasn't the only country to get in on the ground floor. Other branches of WIMA established during the early 1950s include France (Agnes Acker, founder), the Czech Republic, then known as Czechoslovakia (Lida Abrahamova, founder), Germany (Ellen Pfeiffer, founder), and the United Kingdom. WIMA, whose motto is 'Motorcycling is Good for Women, Women are Good for Motorcycling', has arguably done more to unite women motorcyclists from across the globe than any other organization. Although men are not allowed to join, husbands and boyfriends are welcome at many WIMA events and runs.

In more recent times, clubs including Women in the Wind, the Chrome Divas, and Women on Wheels have attracted large numbers of members and local chapters across North America. In addition to offering support, camaraderie, and riding together, these clubs are very active in charitable fundraisers and other community work. These all-female clubs are not just popular in the United States, but elsewhere in the world where women ride motorcycles.

While there are numerous women's motorcycle clubs, organizations, and mixed gender clubs worldwide, no club can match the scope of the Harley Owners Group, more affectionately known by its acronym HOG. The organization was founded by Harley-Davidson in 1983 and nurtured by the company to the point where today it is active throughout North America, Europe, and Asia. HOG's impressive website, which ties everything together in a neat package, features the slogan 'The Harley Owners Group is much more than just a motorcycle organization. It's one million people around the world united by a common passion: making the Harley-Davidson dream a way of life.'

HOG membership is comprised of men and women while an offshoot, Ladies of Harley (LOH), is for women only. Most LOH members are also HOG members. LOH's mission statement is representative of most women's motorcycle clubs, but it does have its own signature or aims. These are:

To encourage solo lady riders and lady passengers to ride and promote the feeling of freedom and the Harley experience.

To promote a comfortable environment in which solo lady riders and lady passengers can feel like they are of equal value to the chapter.

To encourage men to be supportive of women riders and passengers so they may both feel comfortable helping and encouraging lady riders.

To instil a sense of camaraderie, fellowship, learning, and fun.

It is evident from the commitment Harley has made to HOG that it doesn't consider itself a company which only sells motorcycles. Its vision is 'We Fulfill Dreams,' and fulfilling dreams has required significant investment by the company. While clearly a marketing device — the strategy provides an exemplary business model of how to create a consistent, distinctive, and motivating brand experience — HOG is much more than that because the people at Harley are as passionate about their motorcycles as their loyal customers. 'We actively engage with our customers. We encourage our people to spend time with our customers, riding with customers, being with customers whenever the opportunity arises,' said John Russell, vice president and managing director of Harley-Davidson Europe.

Founded in San Francisco in 1978, Dykes on Bikes Women's Motorcycle Contingent is an organization committed to creating a local, national, and international community of women motorcyclists and friends of women motorcyclists. The club's mission is to support philanthropic endeavors in the lesbian, gay, bisexual, transgender, and women's communities and beyond, and to reach out to empower a community of diverse women through rides, charity events, pride events, and education.

Women in the Wind, one of the more prominent international clubs with more than 1,400 members in over seventy chapters across the United States, Canada, the United Kingdom, and Australia, was founded in Toledo, Ohio, by Becky Brown and eleven other women riders. Brown, who is an industrial electrician, got the club rolling in 1979. On her personal website, *Becky's Stuff*, Brown describes herself as the average grandmother next door who happens to ride a motorcycle. 'When I am not riding my motorcycle you will find me gardening or traveling as much as I can. I am just a fluffy biker, I have all my teeth, I am not covered with tattoos, and I don't cuss like a truck driver,' she said.

The Chrome Divas, which was founded in 2002, are technically not a motorcycle club and have members who ride bikes and some who don't. Although they are incorporated and have a trademark logo, they do not wear the usual motorcycle club colors, which are sacred to most clubs, especially outlaw clubs. The organization has chapters across the United States and parts of Canada. Expansion into Europe is currently in the works. In essence, the Chrome Divas are a motorcycle organization formed by and for women to provide a means of camaraderie, community participation, and a national link to all women who ride motorcycles and strive to be known as outstanding citizens in their communities with a preference for riding, having fun, and supporting many worthwhile causes. These include fundraisers for breast cancer research and juvenile diabetes, the Children's Home Society, Angel Flight, and rape crisis centers.

Some women motorcyclists with a knack for writing have turned their literary gift into a tool with which they have made incalculable contributions to the cause. Linda Giovannoni, an influential motorcycle journalist and rider, co-founded *Harley Women Magazine* with Cristine Sommer-Simmons in 1985. It was the first national motorcycling publication devoted to women motorcycle enthusiasts. 'There really wasn't anything out there for women riders to read. Male biker magazines tended to be chauvinistic,' Giovannoni said. 'Everything was either very technical or a skin book. That left women enthusiasts in the cold for the most part.' Harley-Davidson, which was interested in developing the women's motorcycle market, issued Giovannoni and Sommer-Simmons a license to publish an initial run of three issues using the name *Harley*

Women. 'We did those first three issues and never looked back,' said Giovannoni, who stayed involved with the magazine as editor and publisher until the late 1990s.

Giovannoni's involvement with *Harley Women*, and her membership in ABATE (American Bikers Aimed Toward Education) and Women in the Wind, of which she co-founded its second chapter in 1983, led to appearances on national shows such as *Geraldo*, *The Vicki Lawrence Show*, National Public Radio and many more. During the 1990s, the number of women riders in the United States increased substantially. Giovannoni's example and *Harley Women Magazine* have been credited as having a major influence on that trend. In 1999, Giovannoni helped program and occasionally hosted 'Open Road Radio', a Sunday night motorcycle talk radio show on WCKG 105.9 FM in Chicago. She also became a contributing editor to *Motor News Media* (a syndicated news service), and *The Shepherd Express* in Milwaukee. In 2005, she accepted a position as a regular contributor to the motorcycle section of the *Daily Herald*, the third largest newspaper in Illinois.

Giovannoni's *Harley Women* founding partner, Cristine Sommer-Simmons, was active in promoting motorcycling through her roles as motorcycle journalist, author, and columnist. In 1990, Sommer-Simmons sold her shares in *Harley Women* to Giovannoni and moved to California, where she began working as a freelance motorcycle journalist, writing extensively for several magazines in the United States, including *American Iron*, *Motorcycle Collector*, *Iron Works*, *Easyriders* and *V-Twin*, as well as magazines in Japan, Spain, and Australia. Sommer-Simmons started riding a road bike at the age of fifteen, basically teaching herself the ropes by learning to ride the bike off-road. 'I had five brothers and people always assume my brothers got me into riding, but it was the exact opposite. I taught four of them how to ride.'

It has been estimated that one out of every ten bikers on the road today is a woman. Without the pioneering spirit of the women who preceded them it is doubtful the women's motorcycling community would be where it is today. The passion, commitment, and enthusiasm that women like Dot Robinson have brought to the scene, much of which has benefited men as well, has not gone unnoticed by the motorcycle community. All of them have been honored and recognized in one form or another, including the bestowing of awards and inductions into various motorcycle halls of fame.

2

A Walk on the Wild Side: Exploring the Attraction to Bad Boys

Women ride. Women have always ridden. While there has always been the woman biker, there has also always been the biker's woman. She has existed in many forms throughout history. There is a story, a women's story, about the 'real' 1% within the biker culture. Women share this story with each other, but rarely share it with men. You shall see why. Often women, heterosexual women who like male energy, appreciate male companions, and prefer and insist upon male partners, find themselves in a dilemma. Women acknowledge that men can be very difficult to live with. In fact, they can be downright impossible. Women understand that most often the culture causes these relationship difficulties.

Males are socialized to behave as they do and women wind up putting up with a lot of bad stuff. Women know that they also contribute to this situation by their own responses, but this never seems to help matters. Women frequently say that if you want to get that wonderful ten percent of desired male energy, you must put up with the remaining ninety percent of the rest of him. We are told this is standard female knowledge. Normal women, typical women, women who relate to typical men, get the ten percent of good stuff out of their men. Ah, but here's the rub. Biker women, women who insist on loving and living with bikers, do not get that normal ten percent luxury good behavior. Women living with hardcore bikers wind up getting only one percent of that good male energy. Outlaw biker loving women are the 'real' 1%.

So who exactly are these bad boys of the outlaw motorcycle clubs to inspire such devotion? What do they have that the rest of the male world doesn't have? To begin to answer these questions, we need to look at the stereotype and previous works in this area. We will revisit the accurateness of the stereotype after we have presented the evidence provided by the women we interviewed.

There certainly is a stereotype of women riders. According to the US Marshals Services Outlaw Motorcycle Gang Manual, the first priority of any club member is his feeling and respect for his colors and the club. They rate equal loyalty, and it has been said members would give their life for one another. Second priority is the biker's motorcycle. The third priority is his dog or ole lady, depending on which one he owns. If he owns both, we must keep in mind that there are a few cases known where members have bought, sold, traded, or given away dogs or their ole ladies.

Many outlaw motorcycle club bikers — as well as some men, no matter what their station in life — treat women as objects of contempt. For these men, women are often regarded as necessary nuisances who, for some in the club scene, are expendable and interchangeable. With few exceptions, previous studies and books written about outlaw motorcycle club women categorize them as belonging to one of three camps or groups: ole ladies, mamas, and party girls. Some bikers are true women haters and they tend to describe women in such derogatory terms that their mothers should wash their mouths out with soap.

Women cannot formally become members of outlaw biker clubs; they can only have relationships with either the clubs or their members and these vary in degrees of association. Since the 1970s, women have had no rights within the clubs, nor are they able to hold any positions of sanctioned power. Club women are in a sense owned by the club bikers. Some outlaw motorcycle club members' women can only wear a belt with the name of the club. Other clubs allow a vest with a 'Property of' patch to be worn, but in most cases only in the presence of the member to whom she 'belongs.' Some bikers' women can wear the patch even while riding alone, but again they need the permission of the member who is their ole man. The rules vary from club to club.

Unquestionably, some women associated with outlaw biker clubs have been involuntarily exposed to the sexual rituals of 'pulling a train,' which involves them having vaginal, oral, or anal sex with all the men present in the club; the men earn 'wings' for their performance of particularly outrageous sexual acts with the women in front of other club members.

Outlaw biker men appear to have access to sex galore and they do not have to abduct women off the street. For some reason, many women seem to fall all over outlaw bikers; according to several reports they are deemed to be worse than rock star groupies. These women are mysteriously drawn to outlaw bikers like moths to a burning flame, either wanting to become somebody's ole lady or to satisfy whatever agenda drives them. Way back in 1967 when he wrote *Hell's Angels: The Strange and Terrible Saga*, legendary American author Hunter S Thompson was told by a club member's ole lady that: 'Man, you ought to see the girls who flock around when the Angels are on a run, and just because they're Angels.'

In their 1987 book *Mafia Assassin: The Inside Story of a Canadian Biker, Hitman and Police Informer*, Cecil Kirby and Thomas Renner pointed out:

> ... bikers don't need to grab women off of the street and rape them — the women flock to them like bees to honey. That's the truth. For some reason, girls fall all over bikers, no matter how scroungy they look or how badly they smell. Most of them come asking for sex and companionship and wanting to be someone's 'ole lady.' They have no families, or they're on drugs and they need money. So what happens to them? Most people don't care. Their families don't even care enough to tell the cops they're missing.

Strangely enough, there is absolutely no shortage of women who are willing to risk 'taking a walk on the wild side' with an outlaw biker. The intrigue of association with a bad boy outlaw biker acts as a powerful magnet for women. Consequently, an unlimited number of good looking — even gorgeous — women are drawn to the bad boy, macho image the bikers embody, and to the excitement of a hedonistic lifestyle. From the outside the life appears to be as exciting as a rollercoaster ride: fast motorcycles, macho men, drugs, alcohol, parties, guns, topless bars, the thrills of flaunting social norms, and any-way-you-want-it sex according to the many who have written about the outlaw biker culture.

Obviously, biker women themselves are a goldmine of information, but in the past they have been reluctant to speak to outsiders. This is not surprising, because some who did open their mouths were tortured or executed for violating the outlaw biker code of silence. In addition, most of the writing on outlaw biker women has been penned by men, and their assessments of the women are beyond insulting. In *Hell's Angels*, Thompson states that invariably the girls who pursue the Hells Angels are 'in the grip of some carnal urgency, and some are just deranged sluts.'

Barbara Joans accurately states that previous reports and journalistic pieces on outlaw bikers' women have some deep flaws in the way the research was conducted. Primarily, most of the information was obtained by asking the outlaw motorcycle club members about their women. With the exceptions of Columbus Hopper and Johnny 'Big John' Moore, along with Randall Montgomery and Dan Wolf, other writers view outlaw bikers' women totally from the perspective of the men. However, even these male authors spoke directly with outlaw motorcycle club associated women while their men were present. They offered little information about the girls and women who socialize with the clubs and individual club members. These male researchers definitely failed to explore and understand the experiences of bikers' women. Hopper and Moore recognized this when they said that 'from the standpoint of the extant literature, biker women have simply not existed: they have not had personalities or voices.'

No studies, articles, or even fictionalized works have specifically examined the phenomenon of women who are attracted to the bad boy biker with the exception of Betsy Guisto's obscure 1997 PhD thesis (not in print) entitled 'Mi Vida Loca: An Insider's Ethnography of Outlaw Bikers in the Houston Area.' Guisto, writing from experience, said: 'I have always felt a strong attraction toward walking on the wild side, and the one-percenter lifestyle embodies the height to which wild can go.' Until now, Guisto alone presented and represented the voice of women who are attracted to the bad boy biker in North America.

Glennis Donnelly from New Zealand wrote a book in the same year as Guisto entitled *Girls in the Gang*, which is now out of print. Unfortunately Glennis included street and ethnic gangs in her account, from which one could not differentiate between the outlaw motorcycle club scene and these gangs, leaving Guisto's work the sole voice about women involved with outlaw motorcycle clubs. Finally, in 2003, Holly 'Throttle' French published her work on protocols for bikers' women. The book, entitled *The Biker Babe's Bible: How to Keep Your Ole Man Happy*, stands as the first book authored by a woman about the outlaw motorcycle club scene. Holly's book has been picked up by a few of the outlaw motorcycle clubs as required reading for their associates and prospective members, and provides some insight into this secretive world.

Everyone has heard about outlaw bikers' women and women who associate, however briefly, with these male clubs. Many people question their motivations, but no one has tried really hard to understand the deep impulses that drive these women. No one really knows anything about these women except for the women themselves. While the rest of us might think outlaw bikers are frightening or repulsive, to these women they are desirable, because they hunger for men who are bad to the bone. For the more conventional reader, they appear to be compelled to dance with the devil and sacrifice themselves accordingly.

Commencing with a concerted effort by law enforcement agencies led by the United States in the 1960s, outlaw motorcycle clubs became central targets for police and politicians, as a result of both their alleged and, in some cases, proven organized crime activities. With this focus on crime in the clubs came vivid and amazingly disrespectful portrayals of how women were used and treated by outlaw motorcycle clubs. The media mostly reported directly from police or law enforcement sources, with the exception of the occasional comment from Hells Angels who, in the early years, would freely speak to the media as a counter-voice.

A powerful ally of the police and government, the media soon came onboard the 'great ship of disrespect' of women associates. When academics cited misogyny as common practice amongst outlaw motorcycle clubs, it provided clinical credence to the arbitrary opinions circulating as fact. In essence, academics fueled the fires portraying women associates in derogatory and disrespectful ways by giving expert approval and further legitimization of the dominant stereotypical view of women associates. The academics also played a very influential role in portraying women associates of the clubs as falling into one of three categories: ole ladies, mamas, and sheep. In later years, the term 'sheep' was replaced by the term 'sweet butts' or 'party girls.'

The term 'ole ladies' is US slang used by many working-class men to refer to their wives in the era 1940–1960. A complementary term, 'ole man,' was used by working-class women to describe their husbands. However, this historical point was ignored and redefined by law enforcement and researchers who claimed outlaw motorcycle clubs used it in a derogatory fashion. 'Ole ladies' became a term which defined women who were the sole property of a particular club member. This portrayal appears to have been adopted to both marginalize and amplify the deviance of the clubs by the way they were said to treat the women in their lives. Life partners, wives, and girlfriends of outlaw motorcycle club members were said to have little or no real value to the club members other than sexual or economic. Ole ladies were said to be largely strippers and prostitutes who dutifully gave the money they earned through the provision of sex — voyeuristic or actual — over to the club members.

Ole ladies were said to have been offered for sex to visiting dignitaries from interstate and international fellow club members and the like, particularly in the North American scene. However, there is no evidence of this practice in other countries like Australia and New Zealand. So, in North America, at least, ole ladies became part of the goods owned

by the particular member. She could be punished at the club
member's discretion by being forced to provide sex for all
members in the 'train room,' which allegedly was a specific
room at the clubhouse used for women who wished to have
or were forced to have multiple sexual partners, acquiescing
to every conceivable form of sex. For example, a representative
punishment for an ole lady who had violated club protocol
was to engage in fellatio with all members of the club present
on a specific day.

Punishment meted out to those ole ladies who violated
the 'code' by which members lived was portrayed as cruel,
degrading, and dreadful. One example is a woman who was
crucified on a tree on a major highway in the southern United
States for allegedly not following club protocols. But, in reality,
how representative were these descriptions? What were the
women's stories of life in an outlaw motorcycle club? Nothing
was found to answer this except for former members and
prospects of clubs who nervously wrote about the topic,
realizing they were meddling with women biker culture.

One way to understand the involvement of women with
outlaw motorcycle clubs is to look at two key sets of
determinants: the first is known technically as *predictive factors*,
and the second is the *motivations*.

Predictive factors

The class of the woman's parental family is the first predictive
factor identified in the literature. Previous research purported
that women who associate with outlaw bikers generally came
from lower-class families in which the low status afforded to
women was not remarkably different from that in the outlaw
biker subculture.

The second predictive factor identified by previous
researchers was how well the parental family functioned. Did
something in the women's childhood drive them to the outlaw

biker scene? Hopper and Moore certainly believed that many women who associate with outlaw bikers were raised in dysfunctional families, where very little love was shared. Parents can be very destructive to their children and many of these women suffered years of physical, psychological, and/ or sexual abuse in their childhood. According to Sheila Isenberg's book, *Women Who Love Men Who Kill*, women who are abused develop a victim mentality, and the suffering some of these women endured killed part of their souls.

In their 1990 study, *Women in Outlaw Motorcycle Gangs*, published by the 'Journal of Contemporary Ethnography', Columbus Hooper and Johnny Moore quoted a biker woman named Jeanette regarding her dysfunctional family life. 'My mother spanked me frequently. My father beat me. There was no sexual abuse, but a lot of violence,' Jeanette said. 'My parents were both alcoholics. They really hated me. I never got a kind word from either of them. They told me a thousand times I was nothing but a pain in the ass.' In the same study, Pamela, another biker woman, told them: 'I got beat a lot. My daddy and mom both drank and ran around on each other. They split up for good my last year in school. I ain't seen either of them for a long time.' The women's family backgrounds and a patriarchal society reportedly trained these women for subservience to the male outlaw biker.

In 'Outlaw Motorcyclists: An Outgrowth of Lower Class Cultural Concerns', which was published in the *Journal of Cultural Ethnography* in 1976, JM Watson reported that many women attracted to the outlaw biker subculture were mothers of illegitimate children before they resorted to bikers and consequently they viewed themselves as fallen women who had little to lose in terms of respectability. Often it is difficult to show respect to someone who does not respect themselves.

The third of our predictive factors comes from Montgomery's study 'The Outlaw Motorcycle Subculture' in 1990. He attributed women's attraction to outlaw bikers as an alleged character defect or psychological deficiency from which certain women suffer. This perspective on women associates suggests they are psychologically damaged individuals who seek a continuation of their pain. Some women believe they deserve to be treated as people of little worth and they are attracted to the controlling and manipulative personalities of the outlaw biker men. The logic of this argument is that many women suffer from low self-esteem or a fear of emotional intimacy. Therefore, they do not have the ability to have a 'normal' relationship so they attach themselves to outlaw bikers in an attempt to bolster their feelings of low self-esteem and give them a sense of importance and, for some, notoriety.

Yet another explanation for the attraction of women to biker bad boys requires us to delve into the field of psychopathology — the identification and diagnosis of this 'disorder' is defined as a mental health problem. In the case of women associates of outlaw clubs, a particular form of what is called technically a character pathology is known as hybristophilia. According to sexologist John Money, violence has sexual aspects. Money, author of *Love Maps*, created a new category of 'paraphilia,' or sexual perversion, to describe women who are attracted to men who are notorious for particularly outrageous and violent acts. Hybristophilia — as Money called the condition, which is also known as the Bonnie and Clyde Syndrome — is said to describe a condition in which a female's sexual arousal and attainment of orgasm are dependent on being with such a man. A woman afflicted by this perversion is sexually turned on only by a partner who has a predatory history of outrages perpetrated on others. It seems a bit of a 'stretch' to define women associates of outlaw motorcycle clubs as suffering from this disorder because most of these men do not commit such heinous crimes, but this theory has been posited by others as well. The diagnosis is generally reserved for women who write to prisoners whose high-profile crimes attract them. Most major correctional facilities are linked to a huge database monitoring such correspondence and the database is called the Hybristophilia database.

Some women are risk takers and get a thrill from living a life on the edge. 'Good girls' associating with outlaw clubs satisfies the needs of these women for excitement and risk taking. Risky behavior fills the women with vigor and enthusiasm. Having said this, to simply label the attraction as a character disorder or to define this behavior as a mental health pathology does little to explain what inside the woman's mind makes her act the way she does. In any event, it is important to understand that part of the attraction to the motorcycle itself is an adrenaline-filled rush that riders and passengers define as riding at its best. All riders are adrenaline junkies and risk takers to one extent or another, as you will see in later chapters.

Another predictive factor claimed by some previous researchers is relatively poor education. These researchers identify school dropouts and generally low levels of education as characterizing club women.

So, it seems that so-called 'predictive factors' define women associated with outlaw clubs as a quite deviant group of women, which is consistent with the depiction of outlaw biker men as sleazy and trashy. These kinds of findings support the stereotype. Taken together, the stereotypes of these men and women paint a picture of criminality bred in the under classes of societies around the globe. Clearly, the stereotypes work well to increase police funding and budgets as well as supporting the political agendas of fear-mongering and law and order campaigns. Viewed in this manner 'predictive factors' are dependent upon the stereotypes being accurate — the women's stories in this book challenge the accuracy of these stereotypes.

Motivations

If the stereotype is wrong in relation to factors aiming to predict whether women become involved with the outlaw motorcycle scene, what does the existing literature tell us about their motivations for wishing to be club women? One key motivation suggested is rebellion. Both Hooper and Moore, and Dan Wolf, suggest that many of the women attracted to outlaw bikers were rebellious teenagers. Indeed, many women were rebelling against their parents, against the world, and some of the women were just plain rebelling to rebel. To strike back, they voluntarily attach themselves to bad boys — men that their parents would have nightmares about.

Quite apart from women in the outlaw club scene, women ride motorcycles — long regarded as the ultimate expression of rebelliousness — to express that rebellion. These women ride motorcycles to project nonconformity as their self-image. Biker magazines print many stories from women who openly state this as their primary motive for riding. Dan Wolf suggested that a woman may view her entry into the outlaw biker subculture as an act of rebellion in the name of personal freedom. In Wolf's book, *The Rebels: A Brotherhood of Outlaw Bikers*, one of the women he interviewed explained:

> . . . for me, it was like a rebellion, mainly against my father and my lifestyle, all the boring superficial people. It was a way to break away from all of the rules and more of an opportunity to be myself. I relate to this [biker] lifestyle because you don't really care what other people think about you. I don't feel like I have to do anything anymore that I don't want to. No, I have no desire to ride my own bike. That would take away from it. I'm perfectly happy on the back. My trip is to be John's woman riding on the back of his Harley.

Biker woman Barbara told Hooper and Moore:

[I] was rebellious as long as I can remember. It's not that I hated my folks. Maybe it was the times [1960s] or something. But I just never could be the way I was expected to be. I dated 'greasers,' I made bad grades and I never applied myself. I've always liked my men rough. I don't mean I like to be beat up, but a real man. Bikers are like cowboys. I classify them together. Freedom and strength, I guess, are what it takes for me.

Another motivation which has been suggested is that some women who lead dull and boring lives may take a walk on the wild side with socially unacceptable macho men who lead dangerous and exciting lives. They find the romanticized image of the outlaw biker erotic, glamorous, and extremely exciting. Bad boys are never boring — they are stimulating in many ways. By flirting with dangerous men these women give their dull lives some purpose and meaning. Men who wear suits and ties are seen as boring by these women. They consider bikers as real and, furthermore, real men ride only Harleys. The exciting lifestyle attracts women looking for any-way-you-want-it sex and party drugs. Further, the lifestyle attracts women who are looking for something more than a life in the workforce or being barefoot and pregnant in a kitchen with a nice hubby working a nine-to-five job.

In 'Women in Outlaw Motorcycle Gangs', Hooper and Moore quote Barbara, a woman who exemplifies those who are attracted to bikers because of their no-nonsense approach to life:

Compared to bikers the guys around here [her university] have no balls at all. They hem and haw, they whine and complain. They try to impress you with their intelligence and sensitivity. They are game players. Bikers come at you head on. If they want to fuck you, they just say so. They don't care what you think of them. I'm attracted to strong men who know what they want. Bikers are authentic. With them what you see is what you get.

Another motivation for some women becoming involved with bad boys is that they are seeking notoriety. They are motivated by a desire for titillation and a chance to share in the infamy of being with a feared, dangerous, and deadly outlaw biker. Other women attach themselves to charismatic outlaw bikers who, they feel, exude power. In Wolf's *The Rebels: A Brotherhood of Outlaw Bikers*, a quote from Deborah sums it up thus:

> When it comes right down to it, most of the guys are really nice. Some, like Caveman, are pretty awesome. I guess you could say scary. But then that's a big part of [the attraction]. These guys are action. I get a lot of stares [while riding on the motorcycle] from straight chicks stuck in boring cars. And I just know what their fantasy is. Just being around, being part of the [outlaw club] scene brings an excitement all of its own.

Another motivation suggested in the literature for the attention of women to the club scene is that some women worship the Harley-Davidson motorcycle. Much like the men, they are attracted to the freedom which the motorcycle symbolizes. Motorcycles are exciting and thrilling and they sexually turn some of the women on. In Hooper and Moore's 'Women in Outlaw Motorcycle Gangs', Cathy explained: 'Motorcycles have always turned me on. There is nothing like feeling the wind on your titties. Nothing is as exciting as riding a motorcycle. You feel free as the wind . . . If you don't ride a Hog, you don't ride nothing. I wouldn't be seen on a rice burner [Japanese model].' In the same book, Pamela commented: 'I can't remember when I first saw one. It seems like I dreamed about them even when I was a kid. It's hard to describe why I like bikes. But I know this for sure. The sound a motorcycle makes is really exciting. It turns me on, no joke. I mean really! I feel great when I'm on one. There is no past, no future, and no trouble. I wish I could ride and never get off.'

Another motivation cited as a reason for women's association with outlaw clubs is the appeal, attraction, and belongingness that is known as 'the sisterhood and camaraderie' offered by riding with others. These feelings transcend involvement with any formal club and are often reported in biker media as the experience of some women who simply ride as a group of friends. This motive is certainly evident in the sisterhood and identity offered by outlaw club life. All outlaw clubs have a sisterhood comprised of the women associates which is as strong as the brotherhood of the club. Some women go looking for the extended sense of family or sisterhood and achieve this by becoming someone's ole lady. This belongingness, sense of extended family, and sisterhood result in a woman completely integrated into the club scene and is often expressed as a form of identity. In *Hell's Angels*, Hunter S Thompson includes a comment from Donna, who said: 'Everybody believes in something . . . some people believe in God. I believe in the Angels.'

Holly French's *The Bikers Babe's Bible: How to Keep Your Ole Man Happy* captures this sentiment extremely well. So, this motivation for sisterhood and extended family becomes an important factor in the attraction of women to outlaw biker clubs. Obtaining acceptance within that core group appears to be difficult for many, however. The women accepted by the sisterhoods of the clubs must be willing and able to tolerate their men's and his club's brothers' behaviour under all circumstances with a subservient response — at least in public or in the presence of other people. Alone with her man, the story is different . . . the fuming, offended woman let's it all out on her man and that is the norm.

Another often cited motive for women associating with outlaw bikers is drug use and abuse. Some women attach themselves to outlaw bikers because they have plunged recklessly into a netherworld of alcohol and drugs. In the clubs, there are plenty of drugs and drug-fuelled parties.

While obtaining illegal drugs may be the motive for some women who associate with outlaw motorcycle clubs, there is another chemical which certainly drives women to associate with the bad boys — adrenaline! Riders and passengers both speak of the adrenaline rush of the ride. The ride focuses the mind. One comes alive by living on the edge. However, a woman can get adrenaline rushes any number of ways and it is unlikely that this accounts for the specific attraction to bikers or even bad boys. However, it tells us a lot about women's attraction to motorcycles.

Love is another motive for women associating with the scene. Love comes in many shapes, from the perverse to the practical. Love is little understood and in recent years researchers have actually begun to study the psychology of love. One good example is Sheila Isenberg who, quoting Ethel Spector Person, PhD, author of *Dreams of Love and Fateful Encounters: The Power of Romantic Passion*, suggests passion is the greatest moving force in people's lives and a need for love motivates people to act and seek out love. She reported that many women use love relationships as an arena for excitement and many others use love as a substitute for other types of excitement. For example, some women find excitement by falling in love with the 'wrong' man such as the outlaw biker. Could it possibly be true that any woman thinks she can only satisfy her passions and love with risk-taking macho biker men? Perhaps, but this asks us to believe that many women who fall in love with outlaw bikers need to find excitement, satisfaction, passion, self-fulfillment, and meaning in life from a bad boy . . .

Many bikers win the hearts of their women and these women become victims of love as bad boys make them feel truly alive. The women who actually marry outlaw bikers are fiercely proud to be a partner of an outlaw motorcycle club member. Consequently, they endure the hardships of being a biker's lady, because they truly love their man. So, many women who live or 'hang out' with outlaw bikers are very devoted to their man and some of these women are just as dedicated to the club as the members themselves.

At first glance, another motivation for women to associate with club men is quite odd: mothering. We found it mentioned by Hunter S Thompson in his book about the Hells Angels. He describes the Oakland Chapter's 'bondsman' as a handsome middle-aged woman with platinum blonde hair named Dorothy Conners. She has a pine-panelled office, drives a white Cadillac, and treats the Angels gently, like wayward children.

To believe this motive true we must believe that, in the woman's view, biker men need some serious mothering. Consequently, the woman derives satisfaction from mothering club members. For those women more closely associated with the men of the club scene, life revolves around taking care of her man. Furthermore, the clubs as a whole are considered to be the women's extended family and she must (at the least) act as if she derives pleasure from this mothering protocol. Public displays of 'cheekiness' or non-subservience is a sure way to be rejected by the club and give her man an ultimatum — me or the club. Depending on the club, era, and attitude of her man, some women are expected to provide sexual favors to club brothers and visiting dignitaries. However, at a more mundane level, Hunter S Thompson notes in *Hell's Angels* that 'girls cook for them, waitresses give them "credit" at greasy diners, and there are always the married men, whose wives rarely balk at feeding five or six of the brethren at any hour of the day or night.'

•

The reasons why women associate with outlaw bikers are diverse and varied, just as the women themselves are very different. However, there are some clear consistencies in the literature.

Biker chicks certainly are women who choose to live an unconventional lifestyle. There are attractions to the motorcycle, the adrenaline high obtained by riding and, for many, the sisterhood of riding motorcycles collectively.

For those women who are attracted to outlaw motorcycle clubs on an ongoing or long-term basis, there is said to be an attraction to bad boys which is motivated by rebellion from parents and/or the dominant host culture. The stereotype of these women is that they come from lower-class backgrounds and dysfunctional families. They engage in sexual practices and use drugs profusely. They tend to be women who work in the sex industry, suffer from profound low self-esteem and tend to burn-out of club life.

There has been a change in the stereotype of these women in recent years. A sisterhood of women who rider either as a 'true' biker chick or who simply passenger has been ever so faintly suggested. A woman associated with a club member as an ole lady is eligible to belong to this sisterhood and this, in turn, provides a sense of extended family to the woman. So, how accurate is this stereotype?

Section II
In Their Own Words

3

Biker Chicks of Australia

Lizzy from Brisbane

I was born in 1979 into an immigrant family from Holland. My dad held down a job in a car manufacturing plant and my mother was a fulltime homemaker. I have two older brothers. I recall my family as being strict to the point of suffocation. During the years of my father's employment in the automotive industry, he recognized an entrepreneurial opportunity which was to change my otherwise lower working-class life. Rags were used to fill the seats of cars built in Australia in those days. The factory had difficulties finding rags and resorted to buying new cloth for the fillings. My father managed to gain access to clothing industry disposals and I went along with the whole family on forays into these waste bins to collect the rags for use by the car manufacturers.

Life for me, up to my graduation, was nothing special or unusual except for the stifling family environment, which included searches of my room, listening to my telephone conversations, and the like. Graduation from high school at eighteen meant I was now able to try and escape from my dire family situation. Consequently, I found work in an old folk's home and started on a Certificate in Aged Care at a local trade school, and moved away from my parents. It was predictable that I would rebel against my family values at the first opportunity and I started to hang around the pub scene with a few like-minded girlfriends.

I also started to dabble in recreational drugs, especially methamphetamines, better known as speed. The confidence attained by the use of speed soon saw me being a regular user. On one night out, I spotted this bikie whose street name was 'Tiny' and went over to him and said, 'Here are the keys to my apartment. Would you look after them for me?' I know it's a corny classic Aussie pick-up line, but I enjoyed the thrill of doing this to him. Part of the thrill was thinking about what my family would say if they knew what I was doing. The other part was the thrill of walking on the wild side.

Tiny was in the process of divorcing his wife and he took me up on my offer. Soon, he and I moved in together. At first we lived in Tiny's house in the lower middle-class Brisbane suburbs. Around this time, a turf war broke out between Tiny's club and a rival club. As a precautionary move, Tiny went to a sheet metal manufacturer and bought us a bullet-proof bed casing, which could be sealed by a lid hinged on one side. Both Tiny and I jokingly described the metal enclosed bed as 'the safest sex possible.'

After the war, Tiny and I went to rehabilitation for our speed use, as it was out of control. Clean, we moved back into the house and started life, he as the president of a 1% club and me as his girlfriend. In spite of my oppressive family environment, or maybe because of it, I was very passive and basically did what Tiny told me to do. In essence, it seemed like I just traded in one form of oppression for another. I guess I have to admit that I feel like a rebel and my association with Tiny allowed me to express that aspect of my personality, whereas my parental family did not allow me to do this. Tiny's club did not have a 'Property of' patch yet. I certainly fit the bill with respect to the stereotypical biker's woman. Tiny frowned upon tattoos and I don't have any.

Soon, Tiny was invited to be the bouncer at an infamous Brisbane brothel. Part of the payment was a flat located above the actual brothel. The owner lived above the brothel as well, on a third floor. It wasn't long before I found work at the reception desk. My girlfriends and I took up pole dancing for recreation and exercise. However, I was deeply shamed about where I lived. My dreams were life with Tiny in a nice house with a white picket fence.

On runs where partners ride with club members, I took days planning what I would wear as the girlfriend of the chapter president. I'm a biker's woman and my fashion and apparel should leave no doubt in anyone's mind whatsoever that that is exactly who I am. When dressed for public display, I usually choose traditional bikers' women attire: skimpy black tops and vests, skin-tight leather pants with 'top shelf' shoes, and carefully chosen silver studs and jewels to complete the view of my figure. I guess you can say I proudly flaunt what I've got for all to admire.

When I enter a room, I like to make an immediate impact on all present. Dressed to kill, with my blonde hair cascading to my waist, words people have used to describe me include beautiful, glamorous, statuesque, and gorgeous. Some say my character is sweet-natured, effervescent, generous, and that I project an appealing innocence which actually belies the realities of my life. Women who are jealous of me, and there are a few of them, use different words to describe me. I've heard comments, behind my back, of course, like, 'Wait till she has a baby, her titties will hang down to her waist.' Whatever they have to say means squat to me.

I was quite happy keeping Tiny happy. I liked being on display on the back of his motorcycle and by his side during club events. I had no interest whatsoever in riding a motorcycle, rarely read, and seemed to spend my days happily doing nothing while perched in front of the television set. Like any partner of a club member, I dutifully made his brothers feel at home when they visited. I didn't feel like I fit in with the other club women. However, I had a few friends who were women partners of the club members. Most of the other club women were older and had children. The women got together when the men left on their runs and I was quite happy to be free of my duties during these times of absence, as were they.

Only a few of the club members' partners ride motorcycles. A few had girlfriends or wives who worked in the sex industry, but most were just sort of average women who seemed to be attracted to the traditional roles of women as homemakers and wives. I can't say that I was aware of any hardcore biker chicks among the club's women. I was not aware of any member who would pass their wife or girlfriend to another for sex; that just didn't happen with this club.

I think that women are attracted to club members for the protection and safety they offer, and to the secret identity of a bad girl. Tiny's cheating really upset me. I had to learn to live with it, but I didn't like it at all. That resentment seems to be pretty common amongst all the club women, although there were those women whose partners didn't cheat on them. I also think that women hope they can change the bad boy, and this is a big reason why some women are attracted to them. They fall for them, then they want to turn them into something they're not. So I guess it kind of has two edges — the women are attracted to the image as it defines them as rebellious, too. But they also want to control their men to be better boys.

My favourite saying is 'Don't do anything your heart tells you not to do.' I like a quiet life and try hard not to rock the boat and to get with the program. I am one of those women who like the traditional roles of women and I feel like I need someone around as a partner to protect me. I know it sounds strange, but I am very rebellious at heart, and at the same time feel a bit afraid or lack the self-confidence to do it . . . that is, to rebel alone. I can't say that I have any heroes except for Tiny.

Veronica from Adelaide

I work as the manager of Richo's, a strip club located directly across from Parliament House. It's not a position I just walked into but one I worked my way up to. I started at the club five years earlier as a performer, meaning I was a stripper and a pole dancer.

When one thinks of strip club owners one thinks right away of seedy characters or mobster types, but Richo, after whom the club is named, has the reputation of being the kindest and most gentle nightclub owner in the city. He tries to get the women who work for him to resolve their personal issues and strongly supports their obtaining training and education to further their career prospects prior to when they age past the point that they are employable as strippers.

I gratefully took advantage of these opportunities, and recently finished my third year of university studying psychology and business. People say I have a sharp intellect, that I'm accomplished, urbane, and confident. That may be true but I don't think of myself in those terms. As far as I'm concerned, I'm just a regular working girl.

Part of my job at Richo's is to deal with outlaw motorcycle club members when they grace the premises with their attendance. I don't consider the work I do very difficult; my prime management technique is to flatter the male ego. I do this without being patronizing and always come across as sincere. The guys may know I'm just doing my job, but they appreciate the way I do it.

The only real problems we encountered with respect to outlaw motorcycle club members were during the times of interclub wars; things could get a little tense if rival club members dropped by at the same time. Guys whacked out on 'whizz' [methamphetamines] are usually the worst to deal with. It's hard to get through to somebody who's in an artificially induced space of their own, especially one fuelled by a drug like that.

When things get out of hand, I use the outlaw motorcycle club structure to intervene, if any intervention is necessary. I have the personal telephone numbers of all office bearers of the outlaw motorcycle clubs in the area and I simply call the president or other high ranking guys if one of their members behaves badly. We want everybody to have a good time but not at the expense of other patrons. Calling on the club's officers is always a last resort, because I like to handle problems myself, diplomatically and with tact.

Honestly, when it comes right down to it, I find the majority of outlaw motorcycle club members quite easy to manage, a lot easier than some of the men who come in wearing two thousand dollar suits. A lot of the outlaw motorcycle club guys may have bad ass reputations when it comes to push and shove, but at Richo's they know they need to keep things in check. I don't feel intimidated by them and I've never really been threatened by any of them.

Linda from Margaret River

I was born in 1970 on a farm in the isolated southern wheat plains of Western Australia. My family can be traced back to the early pioneers in the area, who raced across the desert in search of gold. When I was born, my parents were wheat farmers. Unfortunately, with an annual rainfall of fewer than ten inches [25 centimeters], my family's farm went broke.

My parents and two uncles pooled resources and bought the general store, which served local farming families. My childhood was ideal. I was left to my own devices to make my own world in this small rural community. I am an only child with devoted parents and two attentive and involved uncles. I believe these early years of my life formed both my independent spirit, and the model of the type of man I would later accept as my life partner.

Riding was not a part of my early life, nor that of the other children [in the area]. My life revolved around my parents and my uncles, my dogs, the local wildlife, the kangaroos, lizards and emus, as well as reading anything I could find that came through my parents' store. It was my uncle, who was remodeling an old Harley in the shed, who sparked my interest in bikes when I was about fourteen.

I was content with my life, but my mother realised I would need to experience more than what was offered in this remote southern part of Western Australia to make a decent life for myself. My parents decided that I would train as a nurse at the nearest city hospital located [150 miles] 240 kilometers away. I did not fit in with the other training nurses. I became an outsider who observed and watched from a distance. I kept my own interests and life to myself. I did get my nursing degree, and still continue to work as a midwife specialist.

During my training years, it was my desire to return to my rural community that sparked my other passion — bikes. My uncle had offered me a motorcycle as the means of transport to get me home on weekends from the city training hospital. Before I began my nurse training, my uncle taught me to ride, and taught me how to maintain and repair my bike. For me, my bike became my central passion, the means to express my independence and to flee the strictures of nursing school. In short, my bike was my freedom!

During these years, I had a few short relationships with men around my age, but these young men did not match the qualities I was accustomed to in my relationships with my dad and uncles. Neither did they share my passion for riding and freedom of the road. The man who did keep my attention was an older man who rode a Harley-Davidson Softail. I soon struck up a friendship with him. I had no idea he was a senior member of an infamous outlaw motorcycle club, as I met him when he was working for a small construction company as an executive.

My nursing career was established and I had purchased a small property in the foothills surrounding the city, where I operate a wildlife shelter for injured, sick, and orphaned Australian native animals. The Harley riding man revealed his association with the outlaw motorcycle club, and gradually exposed me to the culture and lifestyle. I found myself at ease with the bikies; the club events I attended were fun, the rides with the club were outright exhilarating. The hierarchy in the club and respect between members was a system I could understand. He and I decided to start our lives as a couple, and we decided to live on my property. We kept our finances separate; he bought into my property as an equal partner. Part of our attraction to each other was that we were not dependent on the other: we both had independent lives and interests and earned good salaries.

The biggest adjustment I had to make was the invasion of our home, which became the center of the club's informal business. In the beginning of our relationship, I found this invasion of my privacy very difficult, and this caused tension and arguments between us. Over time I accepted this inevitability, and with my deeper immersion into the sisterhood of the club, I have found my fabulous extended club family. I now understand and enjoy the friendship of most of the men of the club.

Over the years, I learned to fully grasp the rules of the club, and I recognized that my position as ole lady to the president of the club gave me a special status within the club as a role model for other wives and partners. My position involves more than being a role model, as I am expected, along with a few other outstanding members' ole ladies, to actively teach the new women how to be staunch club women. My instructions on how to abide by the outlaw motorcycle club protocols include:

- To earn respect women should dress decently, maintain good manners, and treat other bikers' women courteously and respectfully.
- To maintain respect women should not use drugs or alcohol, and should not try to 'party' with the club.
- Women need to know the rules of the club, and they should support their men in upholding these regulations.
- Always be a gracious host when members arrive at your home, no matter what the time. Provide meals, snacks, and drinks to all the men. Provide a private place for members to discuss business. Ensure there is always a clean and comfortable bed available for your guests.
- Whenever club business is being discussed outside of the designated room for this activity, women must leave.
- When a club member brings a guest to your home, the guest must be afforded the same respect and courtesy as the full club member.
- It is wise to treat noms [prospective club member] with the same respect as a club member; this is a future investment, as they may be full members one day.

For me, understanding the outlaw motorcycle club protocols, and supporting my man in his role as a senior club member, has been a pleasurable task over the years. As well, my man's involvement in the club has allowed me to maintain my space and my own life. In reality, I cannot have, and do not want total involvement in the club. My own life continues as a dedicated midwifery specialist in the city general hospital, and with my private passion of tending to injured animals in my wildlife shelter. I sold my own bike years ago to finance my animal shelter. It was not just the purchase of the shelter which made me come to that decision; I was pregnant at the time. Things change when you have young children, as you feel a safety issue that wasn't there before: you have more than yourself to consider before throwing your leg over the motorcycle.

There definitely are factions in the sisterhood. Some are employed in a variety of occupations, others stay at home. The women form into smaller friendship groups based on where they live, interests, and personalities. A few of the women are abused by their partners; I would estimate that only a small segment of the sisterhood has to deal with this issue. The women who have very low levels of self-esteem are a problem for the sisterhood. They tend to get into the drugs and their tolerance for abuse disgusts the hardcore, long-term sisters. These women also tend to grapple with dependency and addiction issues and as a rule can't be trusted. They usually are not around very long and it is quite tedious acting like they are sisters when we know they are only passing by.

I have observed other women who just hang around the clubhouse and all club activities the public is allowed to attend. For some of these women, their motives are clear — drugs. However, there are a very few who seem to be just at loose ends and looking for a way to belong to something or someone. The sisterhood doesn't want anything to do with these women. As far as we are concerned, they are simply club whores. I can't say I know many club whores, but the one I do know of was a close friend of one of the sisterhood. The woman in question was seen with several members of the club on different occasions. It was an ugly scene when the sister learned of her friend being a club whore.

Most of the women are not riders in their own right and prefer to ride behind their men, if at all. I traveled to Melbourne four years ago to see the Ned Kelly Museum. This was my favourite ride, as it was just three couples from the club who traveled, taking it easy and loving life. I can't say why, but it was just magic! The friendship, camaraderie, and the journey itself just seemed to all come together making for a fabulous time.

In my opinion, women are attracted to the bad boy biker image for many reasons. First, they are so damned good looking. Second, the women can sense that the man is a bad boy, because he has issues which she believes she can help him with. The women see a fellow rebel and believe they can help out the bloke, and she will have a strong man to keep her own strong will in check. I look back on my other relationships and see that I have intimidated the other younger boyfriends/men in my life, except for my uncle. I'm not proud of it, but that is the way it is. My bad boy leaves no question as to who the ultimate authority is in our family. But that comes with a mutual love and respect for each other's separate life and passion. I do indeed love my bad boy because he is who I need to keep me in line.

My heroes are my uncle and my husband. Both are real men who live life to its fullest. After them, I think Ned Kelly. He was a similar kind of man who had the guts to stand up to authorities and say 'get fucked.' I lead the life I love and love the life I live . . . I guess that would be my favourite saying.

Nyleta from Rockhampton

At the age of twenty-seven, I found myself a single mother of four children. I had two important relationships up to this point. The first had been a physically and mentally abusive one. The second had been a knee-jerk reaction, where I had married a man who was the exact opposite of the first. He was kind, polite, educated, and didn't have a bad bone in his body. After separating from my second husband, I found myself lost with no real idea of who I was or who I wanted to be. I was wandering though life, just going through the everyday motions of being a mother, daughter, and employee. Then I was involved in a traffic accident; a truck slammed into my car and I ended up with soft tissue damage [whiplash].

The work I was doing at the time was very physically demanding so I had to give up my job. And I could no longer do the everyday 'mom' things like the washing, ironing, cleaning, going to sports games, or even bending down to tuck my kids in at night. I ended up depressed, as the things in my life that made me who I was were no longer there. My mother moved in to help me because when I was in pain, which was nearly every day, I had to take painkillers which made me sleep or too tired to do anything at all.

As I slowly got better, I had a lot of time to think about where I wanted to be and what I wanted to do with my life. I came to realize that I wanted to start to live. I wanted to push the boundaries I had put up and do things I had previously been too scared to do. My first decision was to attend a course at university called 'Steps,' which would give me the skills to pursue a university degree. I had not completed grade ten at secondary school so taking this first step was scary. I started to engage in social groups and by halfway through the three-month Steps course, I had more confidence and found myself wanting to go out and do things I had never done before.

One night, two other ladies and I got together for a night out on the town and one of them mentioned that we had all been invited to the local clubhouse of the Rebels Motorcycle Club by a member whose name she said was Johnno. I had actually met Johnno once before at a social group 'coffee night.' The lady running the coffee night had to pick him up at the train station on the way to the social and Johnno found himself tagging along with her. She had told us that Johnno was into motorbikes. But the 'real' Johnno, whom I would discover later, was hidden behind a façade that included jeans and a long-sleeved shirt, which hid his tattoos. He also wore his hair tied back.

His new appearance surprised me. He had long graying hair, a potbelly, tattoos and piercings all over him. On his wrist he sported a tattoo that said 'Rebels RFFR' [Rebels Forever, Forever Rebels]. I was very shy to start with, as I had never spoken to a real bikie before and was intrigued by his appearance and the image he projected as a real man: a dead-set, fair dinkum bikie. Despite my concerns and trepidation, I found myself outside with him having a smoke while my friends attended to other matters. Johnno was quietly spoken and we chatted about tattoos and he even recommended a good place for me to get the work done if I ever decided I wanted one.

Before my friends and I went to a local pub to plan our night out, we dropped Johnno off at the Rebels clubhouse. After having a few drinks at a nearby bar, we decided we would go over to the clubhouse for a little while just to check out the scene. I think I agreed to go because I was sick of living on the outside of life and felt that in going to the clubhouse, it would be a walk on the wild side and a story to tell the grandkids someday.

When we arrived, we knocked on a huge solid door which had a security camera mounted on the wall just above it. We pushed a button and waited for the red light to go green and turned the handle. I was apprehensive about going in, as I had images in my head of what I thought the place would be like, with bar fights, drugs, strippers, and the men having control over the women. As we stepped inside, I was taken aback by how much it looked like any other sports bar, with memorabilia, a pool table, jukebox, and wide screen TV on the wall. We had to sign in and then ordered our first drinks, which were very inexpensive compared to other bars.

Karen, the lady who had brought Johnno to the social night and who told us of the invite to the clubhouse, had been there before. It turned out that she had worked for the Rebels in a different chapter and was confident that we would have a good time. She took us out the back of the clubhouse through another set of heavy solid doors to the courtyard. The door opened up and the first thing I saw was a row of Harleys and an airbrushed image that took up most of the back wall depicting a skeleton, clutching a joint and a can of beer, riding a Harley.

We went back inside the clubhouse and I immediately saw Johnno. He was sitting with two other men at a picnic-style table. Because he was the only one there we knew, we sat down opposite him. Once again I found myself being very shy, only saying 'hello' for the first hour or so. People came and went from the table and the members greeted each other with a handshake that ended with them hugging and patting each other's back. After a few drinks and realizing that the clubhouse was nothing like I had pictured it was going to be, I calmed down and started chatting with Johnno.

There were more people present than I expected. A lot were not members of the club or even invited, but were just there for a good night out. I was surprised by the amount of young people in attendance. One young man in particular, who was a blow-in, kept coming up to Jane, one of the ladies I was with. He was obviously interested in her.

Jane and I played a few games of pool and then I left her playing with someone. By this stage, my two friends and I were quite drunk and I felt like dancing, a common side-effect of too much alcohol for me. Jane was happy playing pool and Karen didn't feel like leaving so I just started dancing near the end of the table. Karen made a joke that I should get on the table to dance. There was no way I was going to do that, as I felt it would be disrespectful to the club. Even though I was intoxicated, I still had in the back of my mind a keen eye on my actions so as not to offend anyone. However, after some encouragement from the members that were at the table, I did in fact get up on the table and dance. It was a strange feeling getting up there to dance. There were about six people sitting around the table talking, but no one seemed to bat an eyelid. My experiences in regular bars or nightclubs had shown me that when you dance anywhere other than the dance floor, you end up with unwanted attention from men. But this didn't happen because I was seen as invited by a specific member.

I remember the blow-in coming up and saying to me that if I wanted to keep dancing up on the table I would have to take my top off. I got down so quick it wasn't funny. Johnno asked me why I had stopped dancing. When I told him, he said I didn't have to take anything off and that he was enjoying watching me. He left for a few moments and came back and asked if I would get back up on the table. I didn't find out until a few weeks later that while he had been gone he had told the people in charge to get rid of the blow-in, because he was harassing some of the women present.

I got back up on the table for a little while, but by now it was close to 2 am and I was starting to wind down from too much alcohol and the late hour. I sat on the end of the table to get off and found myself with my legs pushed up in the air and Johnno playfully bit me on the inner thigh. I was laughing so hard I could hardly get up. A few jokes were made about eating at the table and having table manners. After that, my friends and I said our goodbyes and we went home.

The next morning we got together to have a chat about the night before, with all of us coming to the same conclusion of how much we had enjoyed ourselves. Jane and I, who had never been to a clubhouse before, were amazed by the whole night. We both had bikie stereotypes built up in our heads, which had proved to be nothing of the sort. I can't speak for other motorcycle clubs, but our experience at this particular Rebels function was memorable in a very good way.

I had exchanged phone numbers with Johnno early in the night, and found by lunchtime he had sent me a poem he had written for me. Things progressed and within a few weeks we were going out on dates. Whenever we were together, I had a feeling of being completely safe, that no matter what happened I would be protected. When he went away I still felt protected, because I knew that if I called one of his brothers with a problem, they would come and help me, no questions asked.

Johnno took me on a few bike rides and it was so different from the back of any other bike I had been on. When we rode with a pack of his brothers, all on rumbling Harleys, nearly everyone on the street stopped and turned their head. Whether it was from fear or envy is hard to say, but look back and stare they did. The feeling of being on the back of a Harley with an outlaw bikie is one of such freedom, openness, and trust, it is totally exhilarating! I'm not surprised so many women are attracted to the scene.

My mother, who has had small motorbikes all her life, was still very cynical about the whole bikie scene. She would hardly talk to Johnno and ignored him completely when she could get away with it. She grudgingly came along to the clubhouse one night as it was Johnno's birthday; we nearly had to drag her through the doors. For the first hour or so she just sat near the corner trying not to make eye contact with anyone. Then one of the members' wives came over to talk to us both and Mum started to open up a little. Soon enough Mum was laughing and joking and actually enjoying herself. I think she started to realize that her opinions about bikers and the clubhouse had been unfairly formed.

Mum ended up having a great time and by the end of the night had chatted with most of the people there. Many of the members were only a few years younger than she, and had been around in her heyday — it was almost like she had run into a bunch of old kindred spirits. By the time 1 am came along, we just about had to drag her out of the door. She saw a different side to Johnno and bikies in general and it differed quite a bit from what is commonly portrayed in the media. Mum had expected fights, rowdiness, cussing and swearing, and drugs — much as I had the first time around — but she saw nothing of the sort.

The next morning she told me about the tattoo she was going to get and where she was going to get it — the place Johnno had suggested, of course. My fifty-nine-year-old mother had finally moved into the twenty-first century. For her sixtieth birthday, I paid for her first tattoo. She now has a large eagle near her right ankle. Mum has told me many times since that night she would prefer to go to the Rebels clubhouse rather than any other pub or club she has been to. She couldn't get over the fact she had been treated with more respect at the clubhouse than at many of the public drinking establishments in town.

Unfortunately, Johnno and I didn't work out as a couple, as we had a large age gap between us. I have a young family and his children were all grown up. We are still good friends, however. Yes, another myth went down the tubes: I had thought that in breaking up with him I would be in trouble with the club. This was not the case. I have seen many of the members since then and they still treat me with respect and dignity. My experience with the outlaw biker scene, that is to say with the Rebels, opened my eyes to the fact that they are mostly regular type guys. The only difference is they live the way they want, not dictated to by society's norms. And who in his heart of hearts wouldn't want to live like that?

Roxy from Melbourne

I was born in 1973 to a middle-class family in Melbourne. To provide me with a quality education was their priority; they insisted on creating a little lady. Unfortunately for them, that was not meant to be, as I was a tomboy. I loved being outdoors. When I was about five years old, I learned how to ride a Yamaha 50cc motorbike. I loved the freedom I felt when I rode bikes, knowing I was the only one in control. I continued to ride motorbikes with my neighbours, much to my parents' dismay.

I graduated from senior school really uncertain of what career I wanted to pursue, so my parents made that choice for me. Much to their dismay, I ended up a university dropout. That is when my life changed. Mum told me to get out of the house so I moved in with a friend and her children. Around that time I met P at a local bar; he was a biker but not a member of a club. I guess I was attracted to him because of his non-conforming lifestyle. That was how I wanted to live my life. I felt like I was the black sheep of my family, and when I was kicked out of my family's home I did exactly what I wanted to do. Of course, what would upset my parents the most is what I pursued — hanging out with the bad ass bikers.

I ended up moving in with P and his friend and learned how to party. They were great guys and we had a lot of fun. I got my motorcycle license and saved for a 250cc Yamaha, but that didn't have enough power for my liking so I used to ride around on P's 1100cc Kawasaki. I recall one old friend at the pub saying to me that I could ride his Harley anytime, after he watched me ride the Kawasaki. He was amazed at the way I could handle the bike, considering I couldn't even touch the ground with my feet when I was on it.

Eventually, I ended up moving out of P's place after his mad mate moved in; there was something about this guy that made me feel uneasy. Later P and the boys moved back to South Australia and P and his mad mate ended up becoming members of an outlaw motorcycle club. While I was with P he introduced me to his ex-girlfriend. My first impression was complete intimidation. This woman was covered in tattoos, rode a massive Harley and projected a 'no one's gonna fuck with me' attitude. But somehow I was drawn to the lifestyle even more, because if this woman could ride that big bike so could I. I didn't want to be a pillion passenger, I wanted to get out there and ride around myself. At that stage, I also knew that by having my own bike I wouldn't owe anyone any favours.

I was keen to pursue adventure and enjoy my life to its potential so I kept hanging out with her. She introduced me to her tattooist, and eventually I ended up with a beautiful work of art covering my back. I have won numerous tattoo competitions at club parties. Since then I have had half my upper arm tattooed, artwork designed to connect to the one on my back, giving the impression of one big tattoo. I have the highest admiration for the artwork and respect my tattoos as a form of art and beauty.

I started cruising with P's ex and her hubby, and a group of male and female riding enthusiasts. We used to get together on the weekends to go for rides; sometimes there would be up to twenty of us roaming the countryside. In time, I met this guy through my friends and he rode a Panhead; and yes, I convinced him to let me take it for a ride alone. Wow, what a buzz! However, this relationship was not meant to be. He was hanging out with an outlaw club and he showed his true colors eventually at a club function we attended. That's when his disrespect for women and drug abuse surfaced. I didn't have time for shit like that and I quickly ended the relationship.

I partied hard and rode hard, but always watched my back. I was really wary of outlaw motorcycle club members or any men within this subculture. All I wanted was just to ride my own bike. It was obvious that no guy ever showed any interest in my intellect, just my long blonde hair, my youth, and my feminine attributes. I did receive a proposal from an outlaw club prospect one year. However, I politely declined, as my female intuition advised me to stay away from this guy. I was right on the ball, as a couple of years later he shot one of our friends in the knee. There were no reprisals from our friend or the police, just fear and the well-known code of silence.

It took a while, but eventually I purchased a brand new Harley Dyna Super Glide. This was my pride and joy — I would ride everywhere. I did a lot of solo riding and basically just drifted around the state. I got the evil stares from patch members; on the other hand I got some hilarious reactions from members of the public. When I had to stop for fuel in the countryside, I found people's reactions highly entertaining. But I was polite, answered curious questions, and then rode off to my next destination. I just loved riding. One day some friends and I got caught at the top of mountain; it had been snowing and it had turned to slush. I could feel my rear tire just sliding and I was shitting myself. This was turning out to be the most exciting lifestyle; pure adrenaline rushes over and over again. I finally felt free!

My 'aha' experience came in 1996 on a road trip with some of my friends. I was struggling to keep up with them, as they were on the throttle. My speedometer was at 110 miles per hour (180 kilometers per hour) and climbing. I was holding on for dear life riding my 1340cc Harley. I weighed only 138 pounds (63 kilograms) and this proved to be a challenge. But what an adrenaline rush! Then a lovely gentleman, aka TOG [Traffic Operations Group] Police, decided to chase me down for breaking the speed limit. I was to find out I was doing more than double the legal limit. I eventually pulled over and the police officer could not believe I was a female riding this big bike, or the fact that I actually owned my own Harley. In the end, that nice police officer sent me away with a warning.

My freedom of riding didn't last much longer. Unfortunately, I was involved in a serious accident and my body and my bike were broken. I was riding in the city one spring afternoon and a young driver accidentally hit me at just 9 miles per hour (15 kilometers per hour). I was seriously injured and totally devastated, but lucky to be alive. I had permanent injuries and spent a lengthy time in hospital, then in a rehabilitation center learning how to use the left side of my body again. After some time and lots of physiotherapy, I managed to get reasonable use of my leg and arm. I decided to ride again, but I had a lot more difficulty handling the heavy bike now. And bearing in mind all the medication I had to take, it wasn't safe for me to get around on what had been my pride and joy. I did the responsible thing and on our day or weekend trips, I traveled as a passenger in the car, listened to music, and drank Jim Beam. I still had fun, but it wasn't the same as riding my own bike and feeling the wind in my face.

A couple of my friends were invited to an outlaw motorcycle club party and they wanted me to come along. I agreed to go and this is where I met J. I was just sitting around with my friends, having a quiet drink and watching the crowd watch the strippers, and I noticed this man was just staring straight at me. At first I felt a bit uneasy, like 'what the fuck does this guy want?' He then approached me and we ended up chatting all night. I learned that he was not a member of the club, but that his brother had friends who were. He also told me that his brother was soon to become a prospective member. One of my friends warned me about J and his family, said they were bad asses, violent, and drug users.

I never listened, of course, and I soon found myself entering a chapter of my life that would really open my eyes. I would end up hiding a pistol for one of J's family members. I sat and chopped marijuana plants for weekends at a time. I watched them weigh up speed and count the cash they made from their illegal activities. I sat with them listening to the police scanner, living a life of paranoia. Later, I heard police interview tapes when one of the brothers got busted for drugs — it's amazing how frustrated cops get with the code of silence during questioning.

J and I started our relationship a couple of weeks after that initial meeting. He never owned a bike, in fact didn't even own a car. It turned out his entire adult life was spent bludging from one female to the next. He hardly ever paid his debts and just drifted around the countryside. Basically he was a shithouse catch, but I guess in his eyes I was a free ride for him getting a bike. I owned a Harley I couldn't ride. I owned my car and I had savings and a job. At this stage, I was vulnerable, had low confidence and low self-esteem because of my accident. I was naïve to the fact I was about to be taken on the biggest ride of my life. J eventually got his license and I let him ride my bike, then things changed. The relationship became possessive, and physically, emotionally, sexually, and financially abusive.

I saw no way out so I lowered myself to his lifestyle and developed a daily marijuana habit to numb my pain and fear. I was very unhappy and depressed . . . simply put, I had lost my freedom. Surprisingly, J would take me out to accompany him to the club parties, but I dared not speak to or even look at any other man. Four years into our relationship, I decided it was time to take the sober path. This upset J, as he no longer had control over me. After being subjected to another violent physical and sexual attack, I finally mustered up the courage to leave. However, it didn't last long for I discovered I was pregnant. For the baby's sake I reluctantly gave J another chance. It only lasted a year and by that time I was pregnant with our second child. In spite of this, I threw him out after he broke my toes.

I decided to make something of my life. After our second child was born, I enrolled in university. I wanted to support other victims of domestic violence, and drug and alcohol abuse. I believed that if I could just help one person from my life experiences it was all worth it. Although I was still young, I had been through experiences that some women twice my age had not been exposed to, especially the many evils human beings are capable of. I didn't realize at the time I would be assisting a member of my own family.

One of my cousins, who is close to me like a sister, was abused in many ways by her now ex-husband. We worked together to help her find her inner strength and the courage for a better quality of life for herself and the children. Today, she is a completely different person — very happy and fulfilled with where her life has taken her.

In the meantime, J began associating more with a local outlaw motorcycle club; he had an instant girlfriend and didn't bother much with our children. The funniest thing was that J bitched and whined to members of the club about how he lost his bike — my bike, actually. However, my friend and tattooist, who is very protective of me and has known me for many years, managed to clear things up for me when a full-patch club member happened to mention how unfortunate J's life was because of me. After that, J didn't have a great deal to do with that particular club anymore. Things changed when J saw I was moving along with my life;

he decided to take me to court. At the time it was very traumatic, but a good learning tool.

Nowadays, the children go and visit with their father every second weekend. After one of their visits, when the children told me they accompanied J to a factory with pool tables and a bar, I knew exactly what kind of place this was. When I confronted J about what the children had mentioned, he informed me that he was the president of an outlaw motorcycle club and they had been building a new clubhouse. We talked about his new situation and we both agreed it was no place for our children and they have not been there since.

Meanwhile, my lifestyle has gone from free spirit, party hard, ride hard, drugs, bourbon, cold pizza, and McDonald's to quite the nerd. I have taken it upon myself to become healthy in every aspect of my life. I no longer ride motorcycles. However, I really do miss the wind blowing through my hair and on my face. I have replaced riding with bushwalking in my local national park, and I often feed the kangaroos and wallabies. I am raising three beautiful children, two lovable dogs, and a cuddly cat. I exercise daily and feed my body nutritious food now. I love reading and learning, I continue to work away for my bachelor degree at university, and I also study alternative therapies. I am currently working in a rehabilitation center for females with drug, alcohol, and domestic violence issues.

My life experiences have assisted me with a greater self-awareness, self-regulation, self-motivation, empathy, and awesome social skills. I have no regrets. I am proud of who I am and everything I have achieved in my life so far. I truly believe I had to experience this roller coaster within my life to get me to where I am today. I have now realized that the journey of adventure, freedom, and happiness I was pursuing was within me all this time.

I'd love to say I have heroes who have inspired me, but I believe we are all equal and heroes to ourselves for living our lives how we choose to live. A quote that is very important to me during hard times is: 'The key to happiness is realizing that it's not what happens to you that matters, it's how you choose to respond.'

Nabila from Brisbane

I was born into an extremely privileged family in the Middle East in 1960. My grandfather owned and operated a vast network of enterprises and companies. In turn, he passed the responsibility for running these concerns on to my father and his other male family members.

My early life was that of a spoiled rich girl. Chauffeurs, nannies, and the like . . . anything I wanted that could be bought I could have. But when I turned seventeen I was in for a dramatic change. I had become of a marriageable age and my father used all the right networks to find me the best husband possible. The suitor who my father chose was, on paper, an excellent candidate. He had a PhD from a prestigious university and was living and working in one of the Gulf countries. With the confidence that he was doing the right thing for me, my father agreed to have me marry the suitor. I was a seventeen-year-old bride — my husband was twice my age.

I know there are many in my culture who are in favour of arranged marriages, but I am not one them. I never grew to love the man who was now my husband. He certainly was a guardian and protector, but it was a loveless marriage. We had our first child when I was nineteen years old. Our son was beautiful and I took to caring for him. However, my husband was very controlling and abusive towards me. We stayed in the Middle East until I was twenty-two; then we moved around the globe to Australia, where my husband had been offered a new job. When I arrived Down Under, I had no knowledge of English, as I spoke only Arabic and French.

Once we were settled in our new home, I was keen to further my education in order to overcome the feelings of isolation. However, each time I would bring the topic of my education up for discussion with my husband, he would start in about having another child. Not having a choice in the matter, I gave birth to our second child at the age twenty-four. It was another beautiful son, however, and I loved him as much as our firstborn.

When I was twenty-nine, my husband was sacked from his job. This gave me some leverage in our relationship and when we moved for him to take up another job, I decided it was now or never and enrolled to obtain my university degree in science and technology. My husband continued his abusive ways and tried to sabotage my life and that of our sons through physical and psychological abuse. Somehow this only made us stronger and we grew in our mutual dislike for him. I realized that I had to be the cornerstone for my sons, which made me resolve to be even more focused on forging a new life. Meanwhile, my family back home was unaware of my situation, as my husband withheld all mail from them. Likewise, he destroyed all the letters I wrote, which I believed he mailed to them for me.

But another major change in my life was on the horizon. When I turned thirty-nine, it would be an eventful year for me. I had come to the conclusion that I needed to live my own life, be happy, and be free. I filed for divorce, and with my children writing depositions to support my case, the court ruled in my favour. My soon to be ex-husband was given two days to leave our house. The divorce was like a wall being removed from out of my path — a burden of repression suddenly had been lifted. I became a free woman. I realize now that my life had been like being in prison until the courts opened the gate.

My sons and I had formed a strong relationship based upon love and achievement in education and I felt I could take a brief leave to visit my family in the Middle East. It was during this visit that I learned no mail got through to them and they realized no mail got through to me. After my return to Australia, I continued to study and work in the IT area and eventually became a senior manager of IT services at the university.

At age forty-two, I met a man who had that 'edge' of thrills and excitement for me. For the first time I came to know true love between a man and woman. Around the time I met him, he bought a Moto Guzzi 1100 motorcycle and, of course, he wanted me to go riding with him. I soon learned to love that motorcycle. There is something about the sexy image of a sleek bike and dressing in leathers. We soon started to ride on weekends and holidays with a small group of friends, an experience I thoroughly enjoyed. The motorcycle provides me with a clearing of the mind — all other things are put aside while riding. I get an adrenaline rush every time out and each ride is special. I now have plans to get my license so I can ride my own motorcycle.

I especially admire women riders. I understand and relate to the feeling of freedom, the wind in your face, and the ability to control the beast between your legs. I adapt to situations quickly and I am a great believer that a person must take things to the limit, right to the edge, in order to live life to its fullest. It is there, on the edge, where one is truly alive. I have no problems understanding the attraction felt by women for bad boy bikers. After all, good girls are attracted to bad boys, so the saying goes. To me there is a certain look of the untamed about them. I find that it excites me and I love to ride behind my man feeling like I am with a bad boy. I'll take a biker over a man in a suit any day.

My favourite saying is 'Happiness is comprised of three elements: something to do; someone to love; and a goal to work towards.' My heroes are my sons. They have inspired me to become the woman I am today.

Jo from Sydney

I was born in Devon, England a long, long time ago! I started riding bikes at the age of sixteen, which was the legal age to start operating a motorcycle. I learned in a field full of cows and, when that got slippery, a tennis court. When I got fed up with the weather and lack of space, I departed the United Kingdom and moved to Australia. The Land of Oz was a welcome sight — it meant the end of being seasick.

From that day on, bikes became a passion, not just riding but learning everything and anything related to them. Around 1993 I rode in my first Sydney Mardi Gras; since then I have seen the number of women riding increase from a dozen to two hundred and fifty. After that experience, I joined Dykes on Bikes and have been on the committee as secretary, president, vice president, and ride leader many times. The club has continually strived to give back to the community by combining our passions of bikes and women.

I am passionate about bikes — all bikes! There is a touch of rebelliousness to them. They give you a sense of freedom, and there is nothing that fulfills the mental and physical accomplishment achieved when you combine body, mind, motorcycle and a road to make it one.

My best ride was the latest one with some of the Dykes on Bikes girls. We left Sydney early Saturday morning via Bucketts Way, Thunderbolts Way, and the Oxley Highway to the Long Flat Pub. It was an awesome ride with a great bunch of women. And one of the friendliest, best value accommodation places I have yet come across. The ride back was wet and long and memorable, because only two of us braved it! My favourite annual ride is a children's cancer fundraiser in the Snowy Mountains. Approximately 2,500 other bikers took part in the most recent ride, which makes for a weekend of camaraderie and beautiful scenery even better because it's for a great cause.

Motorbikes became a life's addiction for me leading to my current choice, which is a Triumph Scrambler. I commute around town on one, travel long distances on one; in short the bike is my hobby, sport, and my lifestyle. Dykes on Bikes enable me to combine all this with other women who have the same interests. This is my thirtieth year in the club and to celebrate I am hoping to get my 1988 Matchless G80 on the road. It was designed and built in Devon, my home county. For me that will be a dream come true — riding a bike from the county where I was born.

I don't have any connections with outlaw motorcycle clubs, but I don't have a problem with them as long as there is no violence or abuse to humans or animals. I'm a believer in 'to each their own.' I don't have any heroes, but I admire and respect anyone who puts time and effort into making positive change, especially volunteers. However, I must thank my beautiful partner, Jodie, who supports my addiction!

My pet peeves are drivers and riders who can't use a roundabout or an indicator. My favourite saying is 'I will not be broken.'

4

Biker Chicks of the United States

Victory Lynn from Florida

I was born in New York City as the eldest daughter in a family of three children. My dad was a lawyer and my mom was a fulltime homemaker. I have one brother and one sister. I remember my family as a good place and have fond memories until I turned about fourteen. I was a rebellious teenager and this caused a lot of friction between me and my parents. I stayed in New York until I was sixteen.

I was in my junior year of high school when a boyfriend asked me to meet him in Miami, Florida, where he was going during the school holidays. I hitchhiked my way down to Florida to meet him. When I got there, I waited for him at the place we agreed to meet, but he never showed up. For a few weeks I survived by panhandling and sleeping on the beach. I considered hitching my way back home, but I had decided I couldn't possibly live with my mom. I started fruit picking as an itinerant farm laborer for a safe place to stay and to make a few bucks to live on.

Being so young and apart from the city and family, I felt as though I couldn't take care of myself and was desperate to find a boyfriend to look after me and take care of me. I met a man who looked like a bad boy, one my mother would surely disapprove of. He was obviously a biker. He had that edge of dangerousness about him. Although he proved himself to be a controlling type of individual, and I felt repressed being in our relationship, I stayed with him.

About two years into my relationship with him, my family came for a visit. I couldn't wait to see the expression on my mom's face when she saw this hardcore biker. When he met my family, I couldn't believe my mom's reaction — she loved him! She liked him a lot. My grandmother, however, did all the things I had expected my mother to do. She rolled her eyes, groaned, and gave a look of strong disapproval.

I guess I had just not understood that my mother was a lot like me when she was growing up in the 1950s. Later, she told me she preferred men's company to women and she, like me, hung out with the boys. I was growing up in an America which was at the high point of alternative cultures and anti-establishment attitudes, and my man was quite acceptable to her. I didn't tell my family or friends, but my man had a drug problem. One day three years into our relationship, he died of an overdose. I was nineteen years old at the time; I didn't want to be on my own. Why did he leave me? I was angry — I still am to this day.

It was at this time that I started dancing as a career. I did exotic dancing, stripping, and many other kinds of dancing. I made a lot of money, as I was very pretty and I liked the physical work as well as the attention. I met my husband to be while working at a strip club. He was a senior national office bearer for the Outlaws Motorcycle Club. He was seventeen years older than me. This didn't bother me at the time, but later I felt like I was hanging around with a man who was too old for me; it was like being married to my father.

Like my first biker husband or partner, he was very controlling. Due to his position as a national officer, he kept me away from the other women in the club and the other members. Fortunately for me, he was not part of the 'he-man woman haters' of the club who would pass their partners around for sex and other 'duties.' He made sure that I was treated with respect, unlike the club members who so disrespected their wives and partners.

The women partners of the club were almost all workers in the sex industry except for a few stay-at-home mothers and a very few who had straight jobs. In my opinion, these women with straight jobs were not involved in the sex industry simply due to the fact they weren't good looking enough to be hired. As I said, the club members who passed around their wives and partners were basically women haters. Their women just had no respect for themselves and the men had no respect for them.

Six years into my marriage with this member of the Outlaws, he was arrested by federal authorities for violating the *Racketeer Influenced and Corrupt Organizations Act* (RICO). I was astounded to discover during the trial that over one hundred pictures of me were presented in evidence relating to the RICO charges. I probably was the best 'protected' girl in Florida, judging by the incredible amount of surveillance photos produced by the prosecution at the trial. I wasn't charged, but I was certainly watched and considered to be a 'person of interest' by law enforcement.

The jury came in with a guilty verdict for my husband and other members of the club; he was sentenced to twenty years in prison. Following the sentencing, each member of the club was sent to different prisons throughout the United States. My husband was to do his time at the Federal Penitentiary in Memphis, Tennessee, so I did the good wifely thing and relocated there and went on with life. I was still dancing and making plenty of money so I easily found a job in strip joints and clubs around Memphis. I hated Memphis; it was a dirty place and sleazy. I saw the town as a complete ghetto.

There was a local chapter of the Outlaws in town. For me, it was a nightmare meeting the members of this chapter. They were even worse women haters than the Florida-based chapter. They were much more redneck and had even less respect for women. The local chapter tried very hard to get me to come to the clubhouse to be a pass-around. I told my husband about the situation and the pressure from the local club weakened. However, two club members were overheard in a bar discussing how to scoop me up and get me to the clubhouse. The discussion overheard indicated that I was pre-trained — that they wouldn't need to train me.

I stayed on in town, but I was desperately lonely. I was allowed to visit my husband once a week for a brief period. After about fifteen months, I met someone new. He was a bouncer at one of the clubs where I was working. He was a former member of the Hangmen Motorcycle Club, but he had dropped out of the outlaw scene. We soon commenced an affair. I told my husband that I was having the affair and, of course, he was violently opposed to it. It seems like the situation just kept getting worse with each visit I made to the jail. Three months after I first told him of the affair, I fronted up to the jail for my weekly visit and simply told him that I wanted a divorce.

He was beside himself with anger, but I was adamant. He said, 'I love you, I need you.' I had never heard these words from him before. Previously he had told me that he loved me in his own way. To me this translated as 'I love you, like I love my dog.' It just was too little, too late. I had had a gutful.

The new man in my life was separated from his alcoholic wife and two children. He went to New Orleans and gathered his children up and came back to our place in Memphis.

One night, when I was coming home from dancing, he had arrived back and I looked in the children's room. There I saw a vision which filled me totally with love: two beautiful boys, one almost two years old and the other almost five years old. My dreams had come true. I could be 'mommy' to these wonderful little children.

We stayed another two years in Memphis while divorces were settled and we made plans for the future and our little family. We then moved back to Florida. It was now 1987 and the club scene had changed dramatically. My new husband attended and graduated from the American Motorcycle Institute and worked his way up the ladder from being a motorcycle mechanic to a master mechanic. I was still dancing and earning enough to make it worthwhile.

I have a wonderful family tattoo: it's a bracelet of flowers with my sons' and husband's initials. My eldest son has a tattoo which is the same as my husband's tattoo, but a smaller version. My younger son has a tattoo of konji symbols, with our family's initials surrounded by the wonderful symbols which are associated with family, warmth, happiness, and the like. In 1997, our eldest boy graduated from high school and became a body piercing artist. Both my husband and I have lots of tattoos so I guess he just wanted to continue on with the chosen lifestyle of his parents. Our youngest boy graduated from high school in 2000; he joined the US Navy as a submariner.

I finally quit dancing in 2001. Yes, I was making less money, but the real reason is that you will find in every strip joint the woman who is sitting by herself just hoping to be asked to dance. Well, I didn't want to become that woman. I have never had the slightest desire to ride a motorcycle. However, I have ridden many hundreds of thousands of miles as a passenger.

Although I have never operated a motorcycle, I have had an 'aha' ride as a passenger. My partner and I were traveling from Memphis to Nashville. Torrential rain hit and hit hard. We rode a few miles and the rain was so heavy water was coming in through the bandannas we wore so we couldn't breathe properly. We had to stop and we pulled over at one of the many little country stores that dot the roadways of rural Tennessee. Coughing and spluttering we went inside the store to take shelter from the storm. A guy in the store watched us and then came over to us and said, 'I'm headed to Arkansas. What do you say we load up your bike and take it to my friend's house to wait out the storm?' We both gladly accepted the offer.

When we arrived at the house, there were a few bikers there . . . a welcoming fire was burning in the fireplace. We were provided with a meal and I curled up near the fire and went to sleep. When they woke me up, the rain was still going strong. The trucker and my husband had agreed that he would take us to Nashville, which was totally out of his way. He drove us all the way to our front door in Nashville and departed. We never found out his name or any other personal details about him. I learned from that ride about the camaraderie between bikers — this is what fellow bikers do for each other.

When it comes to heroes, I would put my mom first. No matter what I have done, she still loves me with no strings whatsoever attached. She gives me unconditional love. That is my mom. I have the best mom in the world. Wolf is another personal hero of mine. He was convicted of murdering a rival club member way back in the 1970s. Wolf originally was sentenced to death and spent many years on death row. His sentence was eventually commuted to life. I still write to him on a weekly basis. He is my hero because even through the darkest of times he maintains his optimism and love of life.

Even today, at every parole hearing, he is positive he will be released. He is the most optimistic person I have ever met. Wolf has the best state of mind. He has the best reason to just give up, but never does. Third is my husband. He has had severe accidents that have left him slightly disabled. Even though he constantly lives in pain, he works hard to better himself and his whole family respects, and loves him; he is a quiet achiever.

My favorite quote may sound corny, but it's the old saying 'Be true to yourself.' This is the quote that got me through the tough times, when I followed my heart to leave my second husband to be with my current husband. What attracts me to bad boy bikers? Well, they are just so damned good looking. To me they are real men. They have charisma and power. The power is to be strong and reject the pansy filled straight society. Their whole look says 'I think for myself. I love my lifestyle and will kick ass for it.' They are men in chaps, not men in black. They are the American dream of individualism and reject the host society while still living the American dream.

Kirsten from Florida

I have two siblings, both boys. My mother worked in the insurance industry. My father was an entrepreneur of sorts. At one point he owned a marina and several property holdings which he also managed. Sadly, my father died unexpectedly of a heart attack when I was in grade eleven.

Throughout my elementary and junior high school years I was the ultimate tomboy. I liked doing the things boys did and hanging around with my older brother. He was interested in motorcycles so not surprisingly I was, too. We both developed this interest from the enjoyment of seeking thrills and taking risks. For us, world famous motorcycle stunt performer Evel Knievel was the definitive thrill-seeking icon. In a bid to emulate Evel, and other daredevils, we built ramps to test our ability to see how far we could jump. We used bicycles rather than motorcycles, however. At age eleven, I enjoyed my first ride on a Harley. It was awesome! The engine noise and wild feel of the ride made me think that I was going to get one when I was older.

I would describe myself as the athletic type while in high school. At the age of eighteen, I decided to move into one of my dad's properties, in order to keep up a visible presence. I attended night school to become an accredited court stenographer. During the day, I worked at a psychologist's office whose services included diagnosis and therapy. When a much better paying job presented itself, that of lingerie model, I jumped at the opportunity. This job allowed me to go to school fulltime and I completed my studies when I was twenty-two years old. Around this time, my brother bought a Honda Ninja and subsequently several other bikes. Eventually he gave me an early Honda off-road bike, which I rode frequently.

In 1997, when I was twenty-four, I met my first husband. The only thing that was important to me was the fact that he owned a boat and a pair of water skis. It sounds pretty lame now, but my adventurous desires were fanned by these thrill-seeking aspects to the man. He worked in the transport industry and I kept my job as a court stenographer. We had a daughter two years after our marriage.

Early on in our marriage my husband bought a Harley Sportster, which, of course, I had no problem with. The two of us had some great runs and we developed a network of eight couples, located around our neighborhood, and rode together whenever we could. It was a call to the lifestyle I wanted — living on the edge. I ended up attending the state-sponsored motorcycle safety course and subsequently purchased a Honda Virago. After I bought my bike the other couples followed suit and our rider group now numbered sixteen motorcycles instead of eight. We were like a club but without the patch and organizational structure. I thought the sound of eight bikes traveling together was something to behold, but sixteen bikes rumbling down the highway was really music to my ears.

In 2002, a few friends and I from the original group of sixteen decided to attend Biketoberfest in Daytona, where we wanted to have a patch and our own t-shirts on display. We knocked around the idea of a name and decided it had to include divas — Chrome Divas is what we eventually chose. An appropriate patch was developed and we were received extremely well at the event, which is one of the coolest biker gatherings in the States.

Spurred on by the interest shown at Biketoberfest, we decided to manufacture Chrome Diva paraphernalia for a pending local rally called the Rally in Tally — for the uninitiated, Tally is short for Tallahassee. Prior to the rally, we incorporated and became an official organization. The founding members of the Chrome Divas had a vision for a club comprised of women riders and their associates. The idea was to establish a club for professional women. Our message was clear: if we can do it, so can you! We also set clear motorcycle safety goals and adopted a deep commitment that would see the club serving as fundraiser for various charities.

The Rally in Tally, and the website we created, worked well and saw the growth in membership swell interstate and eventually nationally. Soon Harley-Davidson outlets and shops had set up special sections where Chrome Diva paraphernalia could be purchased.

Unfortunately, despite our common passion for the motorcycle lifestyle, my husband and I were growing apart and our marriage was heading to ruin. Constant goading about my imperfections such as gaining weight didn't help. Physical looks seemed to be the only thing that was truly important to him. We decided to call it quits and divorced in 2004.

A few years later, in 2006, I married a man who had been a long-time friend; he was also the man who happened to assess my riding ability for the state-run motorcycle course. I now live in a blended family environment, where motorcycling is a key element of the marriage. What more could a gal ask for?

Throughout the hard times membership in the Chrome Divas helped pull me through; the club provides a great support system. And to this day my co-founding members and I continue to manage the international growth of the club, but we're not involved in an official capacity with the local chapter. I have been very fortunate in life and have learned that reality and dreams can be the same.

My 'aha' ride came during a discovery trip of the southwestern United States that I took with my new husband. The experience of seeing the rich variety of our country and the closeness of the motorcycle combined with the open roads produced an understanding of life on the road. The 'aha' part was discovering that the motorcycle was something spiritual. I also realized that the motorcycle was a way of being completely free.

My favourite quote has to be 'There are some people who live in a dream world. There are some who face reality. And then there are those that make dreams their reality.' My hero is Mahatma Gandhi.

Wildfire from Washington

I was born in 1974 in an urban setting in the state of Washington to a stay-at-home mom and a dad who worked as a salesman; he is now retired. I am the only child they had together. I have been around the off-road, enduro, and dirt track motorcycle world since the age of three. My half-brother, in particular, was a keen off-road rider.

There was nothing remarkable about my childhood and teenage years. After graduating from high school, I enrolled in university immediately upon graduation, majoring in criminal administration. I did this as I wished to become a lawyer one day. I have a particular interest in child protection and welfare and becoming a lawyer would allow me to help children through the prosecution of perpetrators of child abuse.

I met and subsequently married a man with whom I have three children. I dropped out of university to have children, but I intend to return and achieve my goal of being a lawyer. My husband is a motorcycle rider and, after spending a lot of time as his passenger, I recently purchased a bike of my own. This decision was partly influenced by the fact that our kids are getting older and they like to accompany us on road trips. We ride as a lifestyle option which is family oriented. We attend many public rides, like poker runs, where prominent motorcycle clubs are present. The camaraderie and freedom of the motorcycle is what I love about the machine and the lifestyle.

I am a probationary member of Bikers Against Child Abuse (BACA), and the club offers me a chance to engage my interests in child welfare. My heroes are the little victims of child abuse who sit in court and face the perpetrators of the crimes done to them. The BACA motto, 'Willing to ride to hell for one child,' is one of my two most inspiring quotes. The other is also a BACA saying: 'It's not about you, it's not about me, it's about the kids.'

From what I see, the outlaw motorcycle clubs are rapidly changing for the better. When my little girl gets off my bike at events where members are in attendance, she will run up to the biggest and meanest looking of the bunch and give him a hug. You can see this scary looking guy melt when she does this. In my mind, outlaw bikers are definitely not as bad as sources make them out to be. I feel I am very lucky to be able to have my kids around the biker family at large, whether they're independent riders, regular motorcycle club members or outlaw bikers. I know, and the kids know, that they are well protected.

Linda from Arkansas

I was an only child. I was born in 1949 into a family whose greatest passion was traveling. Mom and Dad told me of being brought home by airplane from the hospital, where I was born. In those years, birthing meant that a woman and her baby were kept in the hospital for ten days. Dad owned the airplane and he was an accomplished pilot. He owned and worked a small acreage farm and was also involved in the construction game. Mom was the homemaker as per the role of women during that era.

My parents settled into the closely knit community and remained there throughout my childhood and adolescence. Rural life instilled in me a deep value for environmental conservation. It was the era of Rachel Louise Carson's groundbreaking work in environmental degradation. Her book, *Silent Spring*, ushered in a new look at the consequences of pesticides and other long-term farming and industrial practices. Along with many others across the United States, my family took a hard look at their farming practices and I've held those values throughout my life.

I would describe my family life as unusual in that my parents strongly encouraged me to be adventurous and well-rounded. An example of that is fourteen years of classical piano training on one end of the scale and attaining a thorough understanding of mechanical objects on the other. They inspired in me a belief that there was no such thing as 'can't do.' I was encouraged to help maintain machinery around the farm so I learned a lot about motors, gears, hydraulics, and things like that.

I attended the same rural school from kindergarten to the end of high school. My friends at school were like my extended family. My high school graduating class had fifty-six students in it. Growing up in a close-knit rural community, combined with extensive travel with my parents, developed a sense of stability and competence in me as well as a burning desire for adventure and hitting the road.

I chose to go to a college located on the other side of Michigan. The year was 1967, with its so-called Summer of Love, hippies, and a time of great social transformation in the United States. The images of the traditional nuclear families represented by television shows like *Leave it to Beaver* and *The Donna Reed Show* were what I and members of my generation rebelled against. For me, the motorcycle is an icon of rebellion and freedom from those traditional stifling values.

I eloped with my high school sweetheart in 1968. The man I married, who would be the father of my first child, was a veteran of the Vietnam War. Unfortunately, he suffered from a severe case of post-traumatic stress disorder and didn't receive treatment for his condition. He tried to find the answer to his problems in a bottle and became an alcoholic through and through. Unable to deal with his escalating troubles I left him in 1970, taking our son with me.

In late 1971, I met and fell in love with another man whom I married a year later. He was a Harley-Davidson rider and worked in the construction industry. The marriage, which dissolved in 1976, produced a second child for me. In the meantime, I had attended university, graduated with a BA in business management, and found employment with an upscale business furniture manufacturer. This job required a fair bit of travel and I discovered a taste for the good life early in my career. I recognized, however, that my promotion prospects were limited with a BA. In the early 1980s, I worked fulltime at obtaining a masters degree in business administration.

From there, I worked my way up the American corporate ladder and eventually became a marketing research director. This job required me to travel even more extensively, not just throughout the United States, but Europe as well. I loved the job, but the travel and intensity of the position took its toll on me. One day, I awoke and did not know what city I was in, the hour of the day, the day of the week, or why I was there. I decided it was time to give up my job and get my life in order; the year was 1990.

I had made the decision to never marry again, but I met a man who had a PhD in accounting, with whom I maintained a close personal relationship. On one remarkable vacation we visited Milwaukee, Wisconsin, home of Harley-Davidson Motorcycles. After touring the factory, we were allowed to sit on the machines. It was fantastic! I knew I had to have one of these beautiful machines and bought one soon after. I had to have the Heritage Springer Softail lowered to effectively ride the unit; I had a blast with the bike and put a lot of miles on it. I took the state-sponsored motorcycle rider course, which I highly recommend to anyone new to biking. If you don't have a state-sponsored course, there are other riding schools which offer newbies a chance to learn how to ride the right way. I credit the taking of the course for saving my life when I was run over by an eighteen-wheeler truck. I used what I was taught in that course to avoid serious injury and certain death.

I put 40,000 miles (64,000 kilometers) on the Softail before trading it in on a brand new Harley Road King, with which I logged 46,000 miles (74,000 kilometers). On one of my many tours and road trips, I went to the Sturgis Motorcycle Rally in South Dakota. At first, I was daunted by the 'No

Colors To Be Worn Here' signs, thinking I might have placed myself in danger. My concerns were soon put aside when I met some really great people — like the biker who was camped near my tent. He was a big hairy guy wearing only a leather riding vest as a top which exposed his many tattoos. He was a very intelligent man and later I discovered he had a PhD in physics.

My all-time favorite ride was over the Rocky Mountains from Moscow, Idaho, to Spokane, Washington. I had stopped on the east side of the Rockies for a break. As I dismounted from my bike, I took off my helmet and gazed back towards the east. As far as the eye could see over the rolling hills there were fields of grain. The grain was about to be harvested and was still a bit green, but the air already smelt strongly of freshly cut grain. I thought about the song 'America the Beautiful', which contains the line 'and amber waves of grain.' That was my 'aha' experience. The person who wrote that song must have seen that view. The beauty of the wind creating waves in the grain fields was breathtaking!

Some non-riding women friends of mine asked me once what the magic of the motorcycle was to me and I told them, tongue-in-cheek, that it was a chance to have something big and throbbing between my legs. They sure weren't expecting an answer like that. For me, riding is a social thing and belonging to the Chrome Divas and HOG fulfills that part of it nicely. The ride forces you to put all politics and petty issues in your life away, because riding the motorcycle requires your full attention; it keeps you sharp, it keeps you focused, and it keeps you alive. I am happy each time I arrive home safely after a ride and I thank God for keeping me alive.

In truth, the magic of the motorcycle for me is that it allows me to face fear head-on and just go for it. My favourite quote comes from Katharine Hepburn, a woman who was ahead of her time and who called her own shots, both in the movie roles she played and in real life: 'Life is to be lived. If you have to support yourself, you had bloody well better find some way that is going to be interesting. And you don't do that by sitting around wondering about yourself.' I live my life in a way that interests me and I found my path to the expression of freedom and rebellion, and that is through the motorcycle and its attendant culture.

Sherry from Texas

I was born in 1947 to a family comprised of me and a brother who was three years younger. My father was a roughneck or rigger, working in the oil industry, and my mother was a homemaker, which was characteristic of the times. My dad's work meant that I traveled to a few of the more exotic places in the world as a youngster. I believe my dad was always in control of the family and some of that rubbed off on me.

I went to high school in Tripoli, Libya, at a United States Armed Forces base located nearby. When I was eighteen, I married a US Air Force serviceman. The marriage produced one girl and one boy. As a spouse of a GI, I was uprooted from time to time and also had extended periods of time when I was a single parent. Fourteen years of marriage ended when my family and I were in Ramstein, Germany. At the time I had a clerical job on the base and had also accepted the offer of a woman friend to work as a barmaid in a German pub.

Here I met my second husband. He was also a US serviceman and I continued to move around quite extensively. I had a daughter from this marriage. As we moved, my husband bought a Kawasaki, apparently on impulse as he never rode the bike. Yet it came with us in each change of location. The marriage lasted eleven years and in the wash-up of the divorce, I ended up with custody of the never ridden or started Kawasaki. I sold it for parts when I moved back to be near my brother, mother and father who had settled in Oklahoma.

I had never considered riding a motorcycle, as I believed it was a guy thing to do. At forty-four years of age, I found myself in circumstances where I had always been somebody's child, wife, or mother. It was time to find myself, now! I was reunited with my parental family, but I felt something was missing, something which was unfulfilled. So I started to look around and try to get involved with new things in my life.

One of these new things came from my brother, who I really respected. He had purchased a Harley-Davidson and I asked him to teach me how to ride. My brother took me to the back yard, brought out the bike and gave me fifteen minutes of training on how to start it, showed me where the brakes were located, the clutch, etc. Then, after another fifteen minutes of coaching me around the back yard, he climbed onto the back of the bike and said let's ride on the streets. I was incredibly impressed with my brother's actions. He had that much faith in me; he was willing to ride along with me.

As the roles I had played previously began to disappear into the past, I found within myself core values which included a deep-seated patriotism and a desire for camaraderie. I also felt the need to be identified as someone special — a part of a group. For me, independence was something akin to defiance from the 'normal.' It was linked to belonging to a club or scene which set me apart from others of my age.

For Christmas 1993, I purchased a new Harley-Davidson Softail Custom. After this, I found my identity and transportation. I rode extensively with my brother and friends. To complement the scoot, I traveled to Missouri to get my first tattoo, as tattoo shops were illegal in Oklahoma at that time. And because I had to travel so far, I decided to get three! I currently have eleven. 1993 was a big year for me. This was the year when I met my significant other. However, the Harley and the tattoos had already made me highly distinctive in the world of the 'straights.' I was a biker chick now. This, in turn, led to my self-acceptance.

I made a circle of friends with my significant other's contacts in the biker world scene. My man wanted to start an Oklahoma chapter of a motorcycle club called the American Veterans. He was driven to this end and I happily supported him in his dream. Dreams eventually became reality, as my man was allowed by other relevant clubs to wear the patch of the American Veterans. My man was a founding member of the club and became its first president, which he wanted to run as an outlaw motorcycle club. I happily got my 'Property of the American Veterans' patch which I liked. It, like the bike and tattoos, defined me as someone very special to the world. I wore the patch everywhere I could.

My man wasn't happy with the status of the club as a simple outlaw motorcycle club. He searched the biker scene attempting to find a club which clearly was closer to a 1% club. This occurred when the OK Riders Motorcycle Club accepted him into their ranks. The OK Riders was a support club of the Bandidos Motorcycle Club. I was allowed to wear the 'Property of' patch, at my option, during the American Veterans years, but all the other women associated with the club in Oklahoma chose not to. The OK Riders members placed some conditions as to where I could wear my 'Property of' patch, but their rules were not that different from the American Veterans. However, when my man joined the Bandidos, severe restrictions were placed on the wearing of my 'Property of' patch. Now I was only able to wear the patch in the presence of my man. This was a severe blow, so I rarely wore the patch after my man became a Bandidos member.

Throughout this period, as a founding Oklahoma American Veterans member, my man was not required to go through the prospecting process for the Bandidos; he did, however, have to probate for one year. He had done his 'hard yards' founding the American Veterans.

The women partners of the clubs are both different and similar for each club in some ways. The American Veterans women were almost without exception women who had jobs and lived their lives without fully identifying with the biker culture. A few were mothers who lived a normal family existence, like stay-at-home women, but they got along well as members' wives and partners. There were a few friendship-based factions in the club as with all clubs.

There were few women riders in the ranks of the American Veterans and only a few 'Property of' patches were worn by the women of the Oklahoma chapter during my time of association with the club. The OK Riders women culture was not much different. Although I found them to be comprised of more subservient women than the women culture of the American Veterans, there were also more full-on biker chicks. By the term 'biker chicks', I am referring to women who were integrated into the broader biker scene, characterized by their traditional apparel, tattoos, commitment to riding as an alternative lifestyle, and outlook on life.

The Bandidos were a different story. I characterize women of the brothers as being professionally employed, as well as hardcore biker chicks, and stay-at-home mothers. The women were kept at the edges of the scene and were definitely, on the whole, much more subservient. Women were relegated to belonging to their men's club and formed different groups or cliques which were based on mutual interests. The divisions in the women culture of the Bandidos basically reflected the divisions of the members of the club. So many of them disliked each other that it's hard to believe one member would dive in front of a fellow member to take a bullet for him. Maybe it's like combat, where you have men with different interests who function as a cohesive unit, but from where I stood the brotherhood was not evident in the club for that to happen.

With respect to other women who associated with club members, there are a clearly identifiable group of women whom I describe as hardcore biker groupies and who used to be called 'mamas'. I was well aware of the women who came to the clubhouses attracted to the bad boy image and for any-way-you-want-it sex and party drugs. These women posed no problem for me; let's face it, if your husband or partner is going to cheat on you, he will do that whether he's in a club or otherwise . . . it's a matter of trusting him or not.

I believe that hanging around the club scene has made me the rider I am today — fast! I do not like twisty roads, though, and prefer straight long open rides the most. However, amongst my many favorite rides, one included nothing but switchbacks. I rode with some friends who were traveling to Sturgis one year for the annual party. I objected and bitched at each stop along the way, as managing the monster between my legs was a real effort on these sorts of roads. Besides, high-speed riding was my thing. But the scenery was fabulous. I remember the feeling of a deep understanding as Mount Rushmore suddenly came into view. I stood in awe at the effort and the initiative it took to do the carving, seeing it as a patriotic action of unbelievable proportions. This greatly moved me.

One of my favorite sayings is by Robert F Bennett. He said that 'A desire to be in charge of our own lives, a need for control, is born in each of us. It is essential to our mental health and our success, that we take control.' I think that says it all — we need to take control or we go nowhere.

Jewels from Georgia

I was born into a farming family in 1952. My grandparents were share croppers in Colquitt, Georgia. I was the first child of my dad's second marriage. There were three children from his first marriage. His first wife died and he married my mom. I have three full-blood siblings, which makes for a total of seven children in my family. We were dirt poor and that meant we all worked on the farm. This instilled a work ethic in me that has lasted throughout my life.

I attended primary and high schools that were located near the family farm. My parents were aware that my hardworking childhood and exposure to only small rural schools left me unprepared for life in a city environment, where manners and customs were different from what I had experienced. Upon completion of high school, my family sold a five-acre parcel from their farm in order to send me to finishing school in Atlanta.

I decided at the age of eighteen to enlist in the United States Air Force. My training in the Air Force took me to Texas, North Dakota, and England. England proved to be a remarkable period for me. I met a fellow Air Force employee who was an avid motorcycle rider. I loved the rider lifestyle I was introduced to. Because my family situation was such that we couldn't afford anything other than tractors when I was growing up, I had never had access to motorcycles. The closest thing to a trail bike we had was a tractor we rode to a local swimming hole, Smith's Ford Landing on Spring Creek.

One day in 1973, I was riding as a passenger with a girlfriend. She came into a corner too quickly and I was thrown off the bike as the rider lost control. I somersaulted into the air and landed on my rear; fortunately I escaped serious injury. My friend wasn't as lucky. She had a clutch hand lever stuck deep into her leg. The lever had to be cut from its cable and she was transported by ambulance to the Oxford hospital for surgery to have it removed.

Although I wasn't injured physically, the accident triggered a phobic response which was left untreated. I guess, in light of my subsequent reaction, I was suffering from post-traumatic stress disorder. At first, I was afraid of motorcycles and didn't ride again for many years. Then the fear surfaced in other ways. For example, I became frightened of heights. I found that the fear response invaded my lifestyle as it generalized further to a fear of taking risks. It was debilitating, but I learned to live with the condition.

While I was stationed in England, I fell in love with my biker man and we got married in 1974. After our tour of duty ended in England, my husband and I returned to the United States and settled in Alexandria, Virginia, a suburb of Washington DC. Our first action was a big, old-fashioned church wedding in my grandparents' hometown in Georgia.

While stationed in England, I had taken courses via the University of Maryland's Distance Education Program and I continued these back in the States, eventually obtaining a degree in sociology. As this degree did not assist me in obtaining the type of employment I had an interest in, and would not enable me to obtain a higher earning capacity over time, I used my communication skills and interest in real estate to work in that field. Along with our regular day jobs, my husband and I purchased properties and renovated them for resale.

Unfortunately, in 1984 we went through an ugly divorce. Compounding an already bad year was the death of my older brother — someone I looked up to and respected. He was a motorcycle cop in Albany, Georgia, for over seventeen years and rode a Harley. The effect of these two major life events drove me more deeply into work, and life was tough for the next seven years, a time I call my 'dirty thirties.' My fear levels were still very high at this point in my life.

Either an epiphany or midlife crisis made me decide to face my fear problems head-on. The solution was action, tackling one fear at a time starting with my fear of heights. To this end, I worked up the courage to go bungee jumping in 1991. After bungee jumping, I went parasailing . . . next was my fear of bridges. A year later, with the help of friends, I crossed the Woodrow Wilson Bridge, which spans the Potomac River connecting Virginia to Maryland, on a motorcycle. It was the first time in a long time I had been on a bike. From then on, I started to live my life again without fear controlling some portions of it.

I shifted employment with my newly found zest for life and greatly reduced fear of taking risks. The job I landed was in mainstream corporate America, working for Acacia Life Insurance, a large insurance company. Now I had paid health benefits and a five-day-week working schedule, which looked great after six long years of working as a realtor seven days a week, many times ten to fourteen hours a day. After Acacia Life Insurance merged with another leading insurance/financial company, Ameritus, the office I worked out of was shut down and I was out of a job.

In 2001, I had the great fortune of being hired by Edelman Financial Services as an insurance specialist. Ric Edelman, founder and chairman of Edelman Financial Services LLC of Fairfax, Virginia, has been named the No 2 independent financial advisor in the United States by *Barron's Magazine*, the world's leading business publication.

My journey to a happier and fearless life had one more hurdle to cross in order for me to fully recover: I needed to get back on a motorcycle and ride to freedom from fear. I needed to clean out my closet in order to get rid of my emotional baggage and get back on a motorcycle. In 1992, at the age of forty, I bought a Harley-Davidson Sportster, an 883 Hugger. To earn extra money to pay for the bike, I worked evenings in a bar/restaurant as a waitress.

Having conquered my fears, life became both full and sweet. I regularly rode my bike to work and did weekend runs with friends. Each time I got on my bike the fear would resurface, but the more I rode the more I became comfortable and at one with my motorcycle. Soon, I had jumped through the last of my hoops in order to obtain true freedom from fear controlling me.

Despite the heavy demands of a career with Edelman Financial Services LLC, and two sons to raise on my own, I took on part-time waitressing, so I could earn enough extra money for the purchase of a new motorcycle. In 1994, just two years after purchasing my Sportster, I joined the Harley Owners Group, my first formal motorcycle club. With the club I learned formation riding, which is a different sort of riding where there are rules, standards, and formal roles. To ride in formation, you must be an excellent rider who has earned the respect of colleagues for riding skills and abilities. One must be able to trust in both the abilities and skills of the person riding eight hundred pounds of steel and chrome just inches away from you at high speeds. However, I still take my risks very cautiously in relation to some other riders.

After thirty-one years of working in corporate America and running the 'rat race,' I felt a deep call from within to move back to be near my family. I sold some of my properties in Virginia and had a house built in Wakulla County, in a small township called Medart, and relocated in August of 2005. Perhaps it was simply coincidence, but both Hurricane Katrina and I arrived in Florida on the same day! After several very bad jobs, and taking time off to do some soul searching and work on my personal real estate investments, I accepted a job offer with the American Automobile Association (AAA) in July of 2007.

A few months after I had settled into my new home, I joined the Tallahassee chapter of the Chrome Divas. I had heard of the club, mostly due to their excellent community service and charity work. I had never been big on women's motorcycle riding groups, but I soon learned to love this aspect of the Chrome Divas. Returning to small town life was both fulfilling and distressing. I found the levels of the rigid stereotyping of women's roles in America's Deep South hard to accept and conform to.

It is my goal to set an example for the women in my area to become more in touch with the times and I see the Chrome Divas playing a central role in this quest. Membership in the Chrome Divas provides me with the opportunity to break stereotypes. There is something in the club for all women. The club provides women the ability to self-govern and become a positive force for earning respect and making changes to reflect a more valued view of all women. For me the motorcycle is a visible presence and symbol of empowered women who have high self-esteem.

Many people, actions, and words of wisdom have inspired me. Dave Barr, who is a double amputee from injuries sustained while a missionary in Angola, is my biggest inspiration. If I ever had a hero, Dave would be it. He rode his motorcycle around the perimeter of the world from September 1990 to May 1994. He wrote a book about his travels called *Riding the Edge*. In 1997, I went to Memphis to meet him. Due to some technicality he was denied a place in history as having done the longest ride by a double amputee. So he did the same ride again, this time making it into the *Guinness Book of World Records*. Harley-Davidson gave him a new Sportster for this second trip around the world.

I believe that the complaints I hear from fellow riders are quite trivial in the context of Dave's epic journey. He has inspired me and many other riders to 'get real, dude,' when minor issues arise. Partly because of my attitude, and partly for being an assertive and independent woman, I am widely known by the Chrome Divas as 'The Bitch of the Bunch.' I earned my first road name, 'Jewels,' due to the fact that I wore jewellery and presented myself as a squeaky-clean uptown girl. My new name is rapidly taking over my current road name, but the name, as in all clubs, is used by my colleagues as an honor reflecting my high status and deep commitment to both the club and to social change.

I guess you could say my story is one of realizing the great American dream. Hard work, positive thinking, and a bit of luck took me from an early life of poverty to one of relative comfort and financial security. I'm not a rich woman monetarily, but I'm rich in the fact that I'm an independent woman, that I have wonderful friends, and that I'm able to appreciate the simple things in life — like riding my motorcycle. I intend to continue to devote my life to the passionate cause which the motorcycle represents to me, and empowering women of the Deep South to change the dominant culture's gender relations and roles for women. I have, indeed, come home and I'm ready to rumble. I'm very involved in volunteer work with military veteran causes and have spent the past five years working with our current generation of military personnel who end up at Walter Reed Medical Center in Washington DC. My favourite quote is by Julie-Gayle Hintz: 'I've always been on my journey back home.'

I would like to end my story by sharing one of my favourite poems, 'Barter,' which was written by the American poet Sara Teasdale (1884–1933).

> Life has loveliness to sell,
> All beautiful and splendid things;
> Blue waves whitened on a cliff,
> Soaring fire that sways and sings,
> And children's faces looking up,
> Holding wonder like a cup.

> Life has loveliness to sell;
> Music like a curve of gold,

Scent of pine trees in the rain,
Eyes that love you, arms that hold,
And, for the Spirit's still delight,
Holy thoughts that star the night.

Give all you have for loveliness;
Buy it, and never count the cost!
For one white, singing hour of peace
Count many a year of strife well lost;
And for a breath of ecstasy,
Give all you have been, or could be.

Val from North Dakota

I was born in 1962 in North Dakota. I am the youngest of my parents' three children and their only daughter. My parents have always been very good people and I was raised in a great family environment, filled with travel, due to my dad's affiliation with the American Legion. My earliest memories are of fun and adventure, both while traveling places for the American Legion and on our family property. My dad bought the children a small SL70 when I was ten years old. How I loved to ride that bike!

There was nothing unusual or exceptional about my early years. I was definitely not a tomboy. However, commencing with my freshman year in high school, I adopted a style of dress that I wear to this day. The style is jeans and t-shirts with boots or comfortable shoes. My life was really great and I was happy enough living in my folks' home and working locally. I had a steady boyfriend from age nineteen and again nothing unusual or remarkable occurred during the years we were together. I was quite content in my environment. A friend and I decided to go to travel school in Minneapolis to become travel agents. When we finished school, we found employment in Dallas, Texas and I moved there at the age of twenty-four, not knowing anyone in the city.

I soon became friends with a man who was into the Harley rider scene. For the next year or so, I hung out with him and his friends. This group had no desire to patch up or bother to become a club. They introduced me to other riders including a man from Switzerland who spent the cold months of Europe living and riding in Dallas with local outlaw motorcycle club members.

My relationship with men since my freshman year in high school has always been 'one of the boys.' You must understand that men do like me, as I am a free spirit and a person who does not make demands. These qualities allow me an almost unique ability to hang out with the guys and have a great time without all the sexual bullshit baggage that women seem to lay upon their men.

I slowly started to etch myself into a biker chick appearance by hanging out with bikers and my street name soon became 'Harley.' I purchased a Honda Shadow 750 motorcycle in 1996, because that is all I could afford at the time, to go riding with my fiancé. Sadly, he died in an accident the following year. Needless to say, I was really depressed. After his death, I decided to move to Austin. I sold most of my belongings and moved in 1998; it was the best move I ever made. I started to hang out with people I worked with and along the way I met more friends who were part of a family oriented club. These were the individuals that introduced me to the outlaw motorcycle club members with whom I soon became good friends.

I was one of the few women who were accepted at the clubhouse on my own. I loved the party scene at the clubhouse and if 'fun' was involved at a party, it certainly occurred with my consent. It was at a party hosted by the local 1% club that I met the man who would soon become my new fiancé. I looked around the crowd at the party and saw only one other blond besides me; I was introduced to him later in the evening.

I was on a date with a member of a family oriented club and when I saw my soon-to-be fiancé, my date warned me about him, saying he was trouble and to watch out for him. I didn't see the 1%er for a while until I ran into him at a drag race one day. Of course, I ignored the warning and began dating my blond 1% club member. That is when we started our relationship.

My closeness to the club continued to grow and I soon found myself doing odd things like buying a new motorcycle in my name for a club brother who needed help to purchase it. He was always there for me when I needed help, and to this day I still have a lot of respect for him. He is truly a good man. I was treated with respect by club members and was welcome to drop in both at the clubhouse and at the homes of my sisters from the club scene. There certainly were women who you call sweet butts, mamas, or party girls, who hung around the club scene. Many of these women seemed to me to hang around in order to be somebody or to be part of something. Other women falling into this category were women with very low levels of self-esteem and drug dependency: these women were treated with no respect.

The sisterhood of the club was a bit of a mixed bunch. There were the 'ladies,' women riders who had been with their husbands or ole men for many years; these are the guys you could call 'old school.' These women were loyal to their men and to the club. They were shown respect by the men and were responsible for teaching the newer arrivals the protocols of club life. For example, no matter how pissed off you were at your ole man, you need to act like he was the best man in the world. When you got home, you could give him hell, but public displays of subservience and devotion or loyalty had to be the public face you presented at all times in the presence of a club member. Most of the ole ladies had jobs and kids and their home life seemed very conventional. The ones who didn't fit into the sisterhood remained isolated and generally didn't last long in the club scene. There were always plenty of other temporary ole ladies, but we knew immediately if they would fit in or not.

Women did not wear the 'Property of' in the chapter my ole man and I belonged to. We could only wear a property belt with the club colors on it. In some cases at some of the functions or runs, it would have been nice to have the patch because you'd get the 'looks' from other brothers that you were not supposed to be there, or that you were a party girl and not someone's ole lady.

Unfortunately, a dispute between factions in the club subsequently occurred and to this day I am still fuming at what happened to my ole man, many others like him in the club, and me and my sisters. Many good staunch members and sisters left the club scene altogether; some members were killed and others were deemed to be 'out in bad standings.' This is nothing short of being totally ostracized from the 1%er world; you don't belong to it anymore and those who do are not allowed to associate with you in any way — even members of rival clubs respect this rule. You just don't exist anymore in their eyes.

My ole man was singled out as a problem for the local chapter for reasons that seemed to be due to his popularity with club members from other chapters. There was an incident which involved a woman riding in front of 'the pack' on an official run. Before my ole man could have action taken against the officer of his local chapter, the national officer sided with the opposing faction. In 2003, my ole man was given the choice: surrender your colors or face the consequences. He chose not to at the time. When I got home from work that day I had a house full of brothers, but not the ones who committed the rule infraction, these were the brothers that were on his side. When he eventually surrendered his colors, I lost my sisters. I am still upset about this, as I truly enjoyed and loved the biker scene. We maintained contact with many of our good friends, and sisters and brothers would visit us on the sly. We were still welcomed in a lot of brothers' houses, where the brothers who committed the infraction were not allowed.

We both had really good friends and club brothers and sisters in Austin and San Antonio at the time. However, the factional fighting seemed to permeate the club at all levels. For example, during a brawl occurring at a funeral — which in the 'old school' ways would have never happened, because funerals are supposed to be neutral territory — my ole man was blindsided by members of his old chapter, the ones who had been responsible for the infighting. It proved to me that none of these guys could stand on their own with him, one-on-one, toe-to-toe. He did not even have a chance to defend himself. One of the so-called brothers pulled out a knife, and I said, 'You stab him and I'm going to fucking kill you.' Another 1%er turned around and got in my face and without flinching I told him the same thing. After a few seconds of consideration, which seemed an eternity to me at the time, the instigator turned and left the party.

After this incident, we decided to move to North Dakota, to be near my parents. My daughter was two and I wanted her to grow up in a normal family life, and not have all the problems that I experienced during my outlaw motorcycle club years. About two years after recovering in North Dakota, my ole man spoke with me saying he didn't realize how everything that happened in the last few years had consumed his life. I believe he and I took those two years to recover from our experience of being deemed 'out in bad standings.' I am a

Angie on her Cowley Davidson with udder attached

Annick Coussement with HOG friends touring the French Alps

Annick at Harley shop in
Germany (top) and riding free
in nature (bottom)

Jeannie cruising with some Chrome Divas in Tallahassee

Angie Jourdan cruising in the old days with her husband

Group photo of Tallahassee Chrome Divas 2007

Ironheart—leader of the pack

Jane Smith's 'Property Of' patch

Sam from Covina

Ironheart (top) and
The Spirit of Annick
(bottom)

Annick posing for Ladies of Harley Run

The Wicked Bitch—Amy White from Arkansas

Amy's World—her Road King and stilettos

stronger person due to the experience and while I wanted to kill the bastards who caused the problems for us in the club, I believe in karma — what goes around comes around — and to those brothers their time will come.

We now enjoy our family life immensely. My daughter and her dad are devoted to each other. My daughter wants me to buy a motorcycle to ride around, but I'm a mom now and I think I will get a Jeep as a compromise in the name of safety. The Jeep also affords me the luxury to cover up from the rain and snow. But when the weather is fine, I can be free in the wind by removing the canopy.

I have two heroes: [actors] Charles Bronson and Sean Connery. They both had the bad ass attitude. They didn't take shit from anyone and I feel they both played the honesty role, which is something I truly believe in. I won't lie for anybody, not even my best friends. The truth may hurt right now, but lying to someone, then later when the truth comes out, it just hurts worse and makes the person angry and vengeful.

I think the bad boy biker image can easily be compared to other bad boy types, like gangsters, guys who buck the system, sports stars with a bad attitude, or what have you. If a woman is attracted to a bad boy, he doesn't have to be a biker, but there is something special about the bad boy biker image that attracts certain women. I am a black sheep in my family. In some ways I think this is part of the answer, black sheep flock together. Some misguided women want to change the bad boys into good boys, and that is a guaranteed disaster for the building blocks or foundation for a relationship. It will not last the tests over time, to which all relationships are exposed.

Most bad boys have issues which eat at them, and it is probably these issues that have made them bad boys. Some women see a bad boy and believe that they can be the person the bad boy needs to deal with his issues. These women are like me. I provide my man with the backbone and strength to deal with his issues; I am there to help him face his demons, so he can become more comfortable with his issues. To me, the combination of black sheep and this belief that I stand by him through thick and thin, to help him in the spirit of the Valkyrie, that is the attraction for me. The term 'Valkyrie' comes from Nordic legend. The shining of their shields is said to create the aurora borealis (northern lights), visible around the northern polar regions of earth. The Valkyries were mystical women who gathered the bravest warriors' souls to Valhalla, the Nordic version of heaven. These women's roles were to serve and protect the souls they personally gathered and guarded.

Red from California

I was born into a middle-class family which proved to be a highly abusive family. I no longer associate with any of them. Initially, I commenced work in a biker bar as a waitress. The bar was a regular hangout of the local chapter of a major 1% outlaw motorcycle club; in town it was well-known as a 'biker friendly' bar. The biker world was no stranger to me, for my brother had provided me with an understanding of biker culture when I was about sixteen. I have spent many years riding on what is called variously a 'pee pad,' 'bitches box,' or 'bitch's seat.'

I believe my experiences support the fact of women being attracted to bad boy bikers. One time, while working at the biker bar, I was asked by a member of the local outlaw motorcycle club to stand outside and watch the clubhouse building. I thought this was rather a curious request and didn't know what to expect, but off we went to the clubhouse, where I stationed myself and did as I was asked. All I saw was an occasional good-looking woman going into the building. I was sure that there must have been a mistake in what I was supposed to be doing so I asked the guy who had taken me to the clubhouse if I was doing the right thing. 'Just watch the clubhouse,' is all he said.

Soon, I saw the first woman exit the clubhouse. She looked like she had ridden twelve horses. She was bow-legged and her clothes were dishevelled. It was obvious she had just had sex with all members present. Woman after woman would go into the clubhouse and exit in the same state. Enough said . . . there is no shortage of women who will associate with bikers and do their bidding. My experience of club life lets me make the following comments about women associates of the clubs. One percent outlaw club members put the club before family in terms of importance and priority. The women walk in the shadow of their men; they are women who simply do what they are told to do.

There are three camps of bikers' women: the 'ladies,' the 'hardcore biker chicks,' and the 'strippers.' There aren't many, if any, 'Property of' patches worn these days. As for the women who do wear patches, they're the ones who have their clubs which are spin-offs of the men's clubs. Recent years have seen the birth of bike clubs comprised only of women who are the wives and partners of affiliate clubs like the Hells Angels. Let me make it perfectly clear. They do not like, nor will they wear, the outlaw motorcycle men's club's patches. The women's clubs, like any other establishing club, must have the approval of the 1% outlaw motorcycle club whose territory they want to base their club in. They can't just establish a club and start wearing their own patches without the approval first. These outlaw motorcycle club women want to be identified as rebels too, so they love it!

There are clearly defined groups of women who hang around a specific club. These women are called 'club whores' if they are around and available to any member for any time more than a few weeks. In fact, I know one woman like that. She's a very pretty woman. She could make it in the model industry instead of being a cheap whore. To me, anyone who's a whore is cheap. There are those women who just come by for a night of debauchery. They are college girls and middle-class women who come down to try and live the scene, with no knowledge about the scene. There was this one girl who came to our bar dressed in the 'Gothic style,' trying to be a biker chick; to me, this is a typical biker wannabe.

I have never been drawn to the full-blown outlaw motorcycle club scene, due to my strong-minded, no-bullshit nature. Nevertheless, I came across a biker who won my heart.

After about eleven years of working at the bar, we moved to a different state, where we continued to live a biker lifestyle. This new place was Hells Angels turf. Here is where my partner and I founded a club open to both men and women bikers who choose to live by the bikers' creed. We made many new biker friends who happened to include members of the Hells Angels, and their affiliated clubs.

While I have been around the bike scene for many years I didn't own a bike until 2005, when I purchased a 2005 Harley Sportster. My best ride so far was a long road trip back to the south with my biker partner; we arrived the same night as a major hurricane. I feel like I am too new at riding to have had an 'aha' experience, as the motorcycle and the road require my full attention and focus. A very memorable ride for me was with a group of bikers who rode to the site of the Twin Towers in New York, just after the attack. The ride was good, although you could see the sadness in everyone's faces; some were in tears.

My heroes are my partner, James Dean, and Elvis Presley (after he appeared on a Harley). They were all rebels and that's what being a biker chick is all about. Living a biker chick lifestyle says to the rest of society that you reject mainstream values, and choose to live life free.

Jeanne from Tallahassee

Like Jeanne d'Arc (Joan of Arc), 'I am not afraid,' although I have had challenges in my life that could weaken the resolve of lesser women. It is easy to take the straight road and behave as others expect. But when you understand what you want from life, it is easier to live it. I was born into a family of riders in the early summer of 1960 in Tallahassee, Florida. My earliest memories of my riding life are riding pillion with my dad both off and on road. I was given my first motorcycle at the age of fifteen by my family and was a keen rider throughout my high school years.

When I went to college, I met the man who was to become my first husband. He convinced me to give up riding; he was not a biker and frowned on my riding activities. It was either the man or the bike; this time the man won. In my second year of college, where I majored in computer science and information technology, my husband convinced me to quit college in order to get married and have children.

By 1987, we had two children, Caleb and Chase. I was employed fulltime in a clerical position. I divorced him on our eighth wedding anniversary. In rebuilding my life after the divorce, I took on the role of the sole supporting parent of my two children. At nights, I returned to college part-time. I had a great childhood and was committed to passing this legacy on to my two children. My divorce was the impetus for my first tattoo — fittingly, it was a broken heart.

In the early 1990s, I began to socialize with a man from a 1% outlaw motorcycle club who I still regard as a dear friend. I refer to him to this day as my 1%er. I entered into the 1% outlaw motorcycle club party scene under the protection of my friend, who evidently had told his brothers 'she's mine.' As he was then the president of the chapter, there was little question of my safety and, in fact, I wasn't at all worried or afraid while I was partying or socializing with the club. I happily became an associate and I didn't feel like I was a sex object. I guess sometimes during the wilder and fun parties I was entertainment. But, for me, it was definitely mutual fun. My association with the man continues to this day.

At the same time, I forged ahead in my career, and worked my way to being an IT engineer for the Florida State Legislature. I am very proud of my deep belief and commitment to my children and their friends. Many of my children's friends called me 'Mom,' as they came from broken homes. I even posted bail for a few of them and helped some get their general education diplomas (GED) after they dropped out of school.

In 2000, I was diagnosed with malignant melanoma and advised I had to accept the fact that I was likely to die within five years. Naturally, this devastating news plunged me into a depressed state of mind, as my children were still too young for me to leave this earth. I was advised to live life cautiously and slowly to extend my life as long as possible. However, I still managed to socialize and get along with life, believing I was likely to soon die.

After I passed the predicted five-year 'death sentence,' it was as if a weight had been lifted from my shoulders. My life suddenly returned. In fact, it was more than that; I had a new outlook on life and there seemed to be an incredible energy pouring into my being. I felt each day should be lived to its fullest, for every day was a bonus. I set out on my new life by doing exactly what I wanted to do, getting the maximum enjoyment and experience from my extension of life. I chose to do this in my own colorful way.

After about twenty years without owning a bike, I purchased a 1999 Harley-Davidson Sportster in late 2004. After four months of riding the Sportster, I traded it in for a 2001 Harley-Davidson Dyna Wide Glide. The Wide Glide made the Sportster look like a toy and I named my massive new bike 'The Beast.' Jeanne the woman biker was back!

After my recovery from cancer and my purchase of a bike in 2004, my sister and brother-in-law would visit, and all three of us would go for family rides. The 1% outlaw motorcycle club also encouraged me to go on rides with them as a solo rider. One day I heard of a club for women, whose main goal was to share the thrills of riding together and do fundraisers for various charities. In 2004, I joined the Chrome Divas of Tallahassee to satisfy my desire to ride with a group of like-minded women. After only a year of riding with the Chrome Divas, I was asked to be the director of the Tallahassee chapter. The Chrome Divas, like all formal clubs, are constituted and have office positions; the director is the equivalent of the position of president.

Currently, there is no equivalent position to sergeant-at-arms in the Chrome Divas. One key role of the sergeant-at-arms is to maintain discipline during meetings. Leading a room full of women is like herding cats, so I am in the process of having the constitution of the club changed to include a new position which will be the equivalent of a sergeant-at-arms. I have made other changes during my directorship which benefit the club, such as broadening the membership base to include women who had been previously refused admission on the grounds of sexual preference. One goal I have set for my term as director is to make the Chrome Divas more outlaw motorcycle club friendly.

I have a rational side and a wild side. I have been able to keep the biker or wild side of my life quite separate from my work side. However, the cat was out of the bag after my return to work from a recent trip to Daytona for Biketoberfest. When I told a colleague about where I had been, he looked the event up on the Internet and found a picture of me with my many tattoos, smiling astride 'The Beast.' 'Hey, Jeanne, is that you?' my colleague asked. I had always kept my tattoos under cover at work. I currently have eighteen of them, including a family tattoo which my sons and I sport: it is a depiction of Jesus climbing a cross of thorns. I also have a 'Route 66' tattoo (which I changed to read 'Route 69'), a 'heart' with my children's names, and a full back piece of a 'dream catcher.' My next artwork will include an eagle down the side of my forearm with a map of all of the places I have ridden the bike to on the inside — these should complete my first full-arm tattoo.

At the time of writing this, I have 830 days left to obtain my thirty-year retirement package and then I want to devote my life fully to the biker scene. To this end, I joined the Tallahassee chapter of HOG a few years ago. At the time, I was only the second woman member who was a rider in her own right; the rest of the women ride pillion or passenger. Last year, I was awarded the prestigious position of 'road captain,' again a first for a woman in HOG. There are two lead road captains and this year I earned the right to be one of them.

I have never had any problems with the police. In fact, once I was able to get out of a speeding fine, along with two other Chrome Divas, when I was acting as a sweeper for a breast cancer charity poker run. Sweepers are riders whose designated task is to locate riders left behind to make sure they are safe and to help make repairs, etc. This time, we were well behind the pack and my friend and I 'twisted the throttle' to get our Harleys roaring well above the speed limit. A policeman working traffic duty saw the two bikes fly by him. Throwing his donut away, he gave chase and stopped us after he eventually caught up with us. After hearing our reason for the run and why we were in such a hurry, he let us go without issuing a traffic ticket. It seems that the policeman's wife had recently been diagnosed with breast cancer. Like all riders, my biggest concern is car drivers, as I have buried three friends in the last year, all killed by cagers.

I embrace the challenges of being a black sheep in a white sheep dominated culture. I do this by living on the edge between my wild side and my more rational side. I feel I was born to do this. I hope I can help by example, words, and behavior, so that other women who are afraid to face up to their fears can experience true freedom in life.

By the way, my favorite quote is by Joan of Arc: 'I am not afraid. I was born to do this.'

Rockie from Colorado

My husband has ridden bikes since 1982. At first he owned a Honda, but when the opportunity presented itself he traded it in for an old, raked '59 Sportster which belonged to a friend of his father. Actually, he still owed money on the Honda but he couldn't resist an even exchange for the Sportster. One of his friends at work had a full-blown Harley and my husband wanted one, too. I guess my husband had learned that to be a real American biker you rode a real American bike.

Unfortunately, shortly after he got the Sportster, my husband was hit head-on by a car whose driver was going down the wrong lane. My husband survived what could have been a fatal accident and despite what had happened to him and the long healing process he underwent, he didn't lose his love for motorcycles. As soon as he was up and around he started buying different bike parts; he was going to build his own bike. That was an experience itself!

One day, at a motorcycle shop, one of the salesmen asked if he would be interested in coming to a party at the club the salesman belonged to. My husband asked if I was welcome at the party, which I was, and that's how the club scene started for us. My husband told the guy he thought that maybe he wanted to be a road captain in a club. The salesman told him he had to go to Oklahoma and get a phone book from a certain truck stop and a menu to prove he had been there, and bring it back to the party. So we bundled up, because there was snow and ice on the ground, and away we went all the way to Muskogee, Oklahoma. We got a phone book and a menu from the truck stop and still made it back in time for the party that night. I don't know what it all proved, but my husband scored big points with the guys for doing it.

About a month later, I was given the nickname Rockie; this came about because I poked the national president's ex-girlfriend in the mouth for talking down to my husband. I didn't know who she was until later, and I couldn't care less. She had it coming and my husband couldn't very well slug her himself. I liked my new nickname, however. It's a great honor in the biker community to be called by a nickname.

As far as the women in the club go you had the wives of the members and the ones that wanted to be ole ladies to the members. A lot of them would come with this idea that the less clothing they wore the quicker they would get somewhere. But you do not come into a club disrespecting the wives/ole ladies with all of your stuff hanging out. All that does is give you the rep of a pass-around and you get no respect from anybody. It was our job as wives to educate the wannabes.

We didn't do a whole lot with the first club; a few short months later it split into two factions. We went with the guys who were referred to as the bad ones. Not that I saw anything all that bad in them, they were just more open to things. We obviously made the right decision as we had a blast. With these guys, family always came first. I guess that is what attracted me to the life; it was like having two families. In order to fit in with the biker life you have to know when to keep your mouth shut and always treat the members with respect. I had no problem with that.

When we would go to biker gatherings, I didn't worry about being messed with, because we all looked out for each other. There is a sisterhood among biker women — it is very unique and strong. If you are fortunate enough you will be accepted in that circle; I was one of the lucky ones. The sisterhood would tolerate the women who didn't really fit in, but only out of respect for the members whom they associated with. These women would be kept at a distance without being totally shut out. We would give them the chance to conform and be a part of the group. You could usually tell right away if they would make it. Some survived, most didn't.

The rides I always loved were just plain getting on the highway and feeling the wind in my face; the destination didn't matter. I always enjoyed the charity rides; not only were you having fun, but while you were having fun you were raising money for a good cause. That's a real win–win situation.

I don't really have a hero, but I did admire Famous Harry; he was the president of the new club we belonged to. I didn't ever wear a 'Property of' patch because to me that makes you a target and I am nobody's property.

Skyspirit from Ohio

I was born in 1965 in Akron, Ohio. I was the youngest of four children in a middle-class family. My father has been an automobile mechanic since before I was born. He's what you might call a motor head; he likes to build cars, bikes, and anything else that comes to mind that has an engine. When I was two years old, he would ride me on his bike everywhere he went. I would sit on the gas tank facing him, with my legs wrapped around his stomach and my arms around his neck. I resembled a monkey from what I've been told. It is, of course, illegal now to ride your children like that on your motorcycle, but back in the 1960s it was widely acceptable.

My love for riding started very early. Growing up with two older brothers and an older sister, we always had dirt-bikes, mini-bikes, and always some homemade motorbikes or go-carts to play with. I loved to ride them and got quite good at pulling wheelies and hill climbing. My passion for bikes continued into adulthood. I've always loved to ride. I currently own two Harley-Davidsons. I have a fully dressed 1995 Electra Glide and a 1997 Sportster. Besides riding my passions are music and caring for children and elders. One of my guiding sayings is 'Take care of the little ones, take care of the older ones. Those in between can take care of themselves.'

I am a college graduate, having earned my degree in computer information systems and programming, with minors in both English and business. At present, however, I am a stay-at-home mother with six children and a grandson. My oldest girls have since moved out on their own, leaving the younger three at home. I have custody of two boys who belong to my cousin by marriage. She had all four of her children removed from her home, because of her abuse and neglect. I have had the two boys for the past six years and they are doing very well. My youngest daughter will be four years old in April. I also mind my three-year-old grandson every day while my oldest daughter works. It gets challenging sometimes with all the different personalities in the mix, but somehow it flows well for us.

The best ride I've ever taken would have to be Sturgis, South Dakota. Each year, for more than ten years straight, I went to the Black Hills rally. To me, there is no place on earth better to ride. We would put 1,500 miles (2,400 kilometres) on the bike in a week and a half. It is an unbelievable ride! I would describe it as 'surreal.' The first three years I went to Sturgis, I cried a lot due to the fact that it is breathtakingly beautiful everywhere you look. The high plains stretch for miles and miles, and many of those fields are covered with sunflowers. The big sky is as vast and as blue as any ocean I have ever seen. The majority of South Dakota is straight and flat, until you get to the Black Hills, where there is so much to see.

We would usually plan out our vacation to leave enough time to meet up with friends old and new. Often we'd ride in a group, only knowing in which direction we were traveling and ready for the adventure of finding out our destination. The many beautiful, breathtaking places to ride while in the area include the Badlands, Custer Park, Needles Highway, Spearfish Canyon, Crazy Horse Monument, Mount Rushmore, Devil's Tower, and Deadwood. I recall one night camping out and handcuffing myself to my bike so that there was no chance of it being stolen. Paranoia aside, it was still a fabulous ride which I cherish as a fond memory.

I do have many sayings which I use on occasion to help me get through the rough spots in my life. A few favorites are 'Never ride faster than your angel can fly;' 'Life is quick, make the most of it;' and 'Always count your blessings.' I have a sign in my kitchen that reads 'Normal around here is just a setting on the clothes dryer.' It helps to keep things all in the proper perspective. 'Normal' is what you make it.

When you're on the road, there is an unspoken code of ethics with most bikers, be they male or female. For instance, you never pass a brother or a sister and not give them 'the wave.' The wave is either the high sign or the low sign. You would never leave another biker broken down on the side of the road without stopping to offer assistance. These laws are not written down anywhere and you will probably not find them in any book. They are just 'rules of the road' for bikers.

These little things are the common courtesies that help hold the brotherhood and sisterhood together. It is the glue of the camaraderie of the biker lifestyle. This camaraderie seems to flow into a tolerance by the riding community in general towards those who would be physically or socially unacceptable to society at large.

I chose the lifestyle I live because it suits me. My passion for riding, traveling many places, and the freedom that being on a bike offers me, is precious to me. I love the smells of the different environments that I ride through and the feeling of freedom that the wind gives to you on your motorcycle. It's a completely different world out there when you're viewing it from two wheels. And the adventure in riding makes the destination seem so shallow. It's not about the destination for me — it's about the journey you make to get there.

I have seldom met another lady biker who I didn't like. Most are extremely friendly, down-to-earth, and very easy to get to know. I have many friends who are women bikers as well, which gives us all a common bond. I do find, however, that many women who belong to the outlaw motorcycle club scene are a bit rougher in their manner than those of us who do not hang around with those types of clubs. My main problem with the outlaw club scene is the drugs. I don't like what drugs do to families. I guess the adoption of my foster children drove this point home to me, as they were removed from their home because their parents were addicted to meth. They had two years to fix their addiction and in the end chose drugs over their kids.

There are many non-outlaw motorcycle clubs with which I am friends. I have had many opportunities over the years to join clubs, but I honestly can say they are not for me. I choose to stay friendly with many groups but not join them. I am far too independent and really have no need to enjoy the biker lifestyle in that way; but I see nothing wrong with being in a club for other people, it's just not for me.

I do belong to the Harley Owners Group (HOG) and also to Ladies of Harley (LOH). I am a life member of both, as I have been involved with them for more than fifteen years. I like the many events sponsored by these two groups; the brotherhood and sisterhood are alive and well. Many of the events are geared towards family, which is something that appeals to me. While I do enjoy the occasional wild party and a night with friends, I would much prefer to have the opportunity to include my children in the events planned.

I have so many personal heroes that it is difficult to identify only one. Most certainly, my grandmother is a personal hero, as she was my best friend when I was growing up. I have an uncle who tutored me when I couldn't attend school for a year. When I returned to school, I was far ahead of my classmates and he is definitely on my hero list. My mother is also a personal hero. She taught me the open-door policy for children, which characterizes my lifestyle to this day. Finally, Bikers Against Child Abuse (BACA) is a heroic club to me; the work they do with abused children is something I greatly admire.

Raine from Texas

I was born in Dallas, Texas, on Friday the thirteenth into an eccentric world: a fifteen-year-old mother from a wealthy family, and nineteen-year-old father who was a biker from the wrong side of the tracks. I joke that I got my Lalique Crystal gene from my mother and my Harley gene from my dad. In a strange way it all balances out. Being the only child of two only children was definitely an experience; however, in spite of their young ages, I think they did a remarkably good job of raising me.

I don't recall my mom riding much with my dad, as she had her own interests. In typical kid fashion, I was shy about my dad pulling up to the elementary school on one of his obnoxiously loud choppers — you could literally hear those bikes from anywhere in the school. I do recall one day as I left the school my dad had this really sheepish look on his face. I walked up to the bike and he handed me my red metal-flake helmet that was totally scuffed up. In a split second, I went from a shy 'why does my father never pick me up in a car?' mindset to going ballistic on him because my helmet was all scratched up. Seems it had fallen off the bike on the way to school. I confess that I've always had issues with people messing up anything that belongs to me — I refer to this as 'only child syndrome' — and that does extend to my father.

Dad seemed to always have three bikes being rebuilt at any given time, so the best sound system on our property was located in the garage. I learned early on that you never picked up any parts that were on the garage floor for a bike he was rebuilding or the earth would go spinning off its axis. Being the only child, one would think that this mechanically minded father might have shown me a thing or two but, alas, he did not. To this day, I am ridiculous at such basics as checking air pressure in tires.

Much like my father, I had three rides at almost any given time when I was growing up, but mine weren't bikes — they were horses. I was fortunate in that I won at shows more often than not, and I attribute all the hours of my life in an English saddle to my ability to ride a motorcycle so well today. I often do things on my bike that I don't think it was designed for, and that is why I don't trust myself with a sport bike like a GXR, because I would be silly and reckless on it.

Along the way, my father sold his bikes and never bought any more. After that, my parents moved to Florida and I muddled my way through life. I attended school for design, but ended up working in the recording industry. Then one day, my boyfriend, who is from the broadcast world, and I were brainstorming on business matters and I had an epiphany. I came up with an idea for streaming demo tapes online for both artists and professionals working in the broadcast and recording worlds. Somehow, I had found myself being a glorified paper pusher for an Internet development company I co-owned. We were doing high-profile projects for the likes of the National Football League, the State of Texas, and the Public Broadcasting Service. I felt like I had really missed my calling in life.

At some point during this spell, I started saying that I was going to get myself a big, purple Las Vegas type tacky Harley-Davidson. I guess I said it so much that it waved over onto my boyfriend and since he loves to shop, and I don't, he decided to buy his Harley first. He was trying to decide between a dark green or purple Road King. My opinion was asked so naturally I said purple. That bike, after a vicious custom fabrication and paint job, and a mere seven years on the road, has more than 120,000 miles (193,200 kilometers) on it.

It would be another month before I got my bike, which turned out to be a black Dyna Low Rider. I dubbed it 'Superstition,' as I sometimes play up that 'born on Friday the thirteenth' angle. Initially, I was going to buy a Sportster to get a feel for things for about a year before upgrading to a bigger ride. But — and this goes back to the horses — because I have a heightened sense of balance, I never got further than putting the kickstand up, due to the Sportster feeling so top heavy. I found my way to the Low Rider and I have ridden that bike throughout Texas and to the east and west coasts of the United States.

After buying my bike, I began feeling even more thoroughly disenchanted with the 'dot com' world, and I began broadening my network amongst bikers. I began receiving requests to handle media relations and sponsors for motorcycle events; because that is what I did in my capacity with the record label it was a nice fit. From there, I was asked to be the editor of one of the largest motorcycle magazines in Texas. The position offered lousy pay and my boyfriend asked me why I was doing it. I told him I wanted to see where it would lead. What the editor role ended up doing was giving me a toehold into the motorcycle media world and dramatically increasing my contacts.

During this time, it became more evident to me that a major portion of the motorcycle riding market was not being properly addressed. Yes, the custom-built shows on television were usually interesting to watch, but the reality is that few people were going to invest in a custom-built bike and at the other end, people had to be getting tired of only going to HOG dinner rides. There are more than one million new motorcycles being sold in the United States every year, yet what is out there for this market that is informative and entertaining? This is when my mind began planning a motorcycle travel series with the intention to webcast, not broadcast, so that it could hit a global market 24/7 instantly.

My pet project is *2 Wheel Passport* and it's been four years in the making. We have a handful of episodes shot now and I am anxious to finish the others in the series so that we can begin our international destinations. There is nothing like riding a route like Tail of the Dragon (US 129), which is three hundred and eighteen curves in eleven miles in the mountains along the border of North Carolina and Tennessee. I hope people will experience through the show the amazing joy it is to encounter a route like that and coming to the end of it and going, 'Wow! What a rush!'

To ride your bike across the Golden Gate Bridge in San Francisco, on the other side of the country, and then follow the coastline along the Pacific Ocean, cruising these amazing mountain routes where you don't see cars . . . it's just you and nature with the sights and sounds and aromas as God intended; you can never truly embrace that feeling in a car.

In addition to *2 Wheel Passport*, we are currently working on a documentary project related to the Patriot Guard Riders. I have a feeling it's going to be one of those projects that strikes a chord with many people. When I can make a request to interview the Governor of Texas regarding a law he signed into effect on an issue related to this project and have a positive reply within forty-eight hours, that tells me we are on to something.

Even though my personal ride is a Harley, I rarely hang out with a Harley crowd and it's not likely you'll find me on a HOG dinner ride. I'm not big on imitating the John Wayne 'slow strut' that most Harley weekend warriors do when they ditch their suits. To be perfectly candid, I prefer independent riders or groups like the 59 Club, which is comprised of Triumph, BMW, Ducati, and Norton riders, etc. The mentality is completely different and I find these riders to be more open and enjoy the fact that they are on cool toys and not concerned about pretences or riding from meal to meal.

For me, I simply enjoy the bikes. There's nothing better than testing your abilities with your ride on some amazing route or stopping in some one-horse town, because the bike is an instant ice breaker. I particularly like it when an elderly couple comes up with a smile to talk about when they rode in the 1940s and 1950s . . . those were the true rebels, because the roads and bikes were a lot different then. I also enjoy hearing stories of my boyfriend's step-grandmother, who was in the Motor Maids for years. I've only had the pleasure of meeting her once, but she lit right up when she saw us pull up on our bikes to visit her.

It's nice to see that more women are getting into biking. From my observations, it seems that women riders are of the mindset that there's more to life out there and they want to experience it. It's a sensation of freedom, independence and, for many, rebellion from the stereotypical molds women are supposed to embrace. As for bikers' women, it seems like they have a need to be part of a group and experience the camaraderie that belonging to such a group offers.

What is it about the bad boy biker image that attracts women? Well, this is one topic I could write a book on. It's not just the bad boy biker image, it's the bad boy image all around and it happens in any creative field. So many females crave that bad boy and yet when they snag him it's a bait and switch. They want to change him and switch from approval of the bad boy image to changing him to fit into the stereotypical soul destroying middle-class man whom they were not attracted to in the first instance, because then they want him to conform, dress conservatively, etc.

I've always felt this was the height of bait and switch when dealing with a guy. Why on earth would a woman want to change the very elements that attracted her to her man? Is it a challenge to see if he will change for her? Speaking for myself, I'll take a true biker over a banker any day — and a true biker is not a weekend warrior who only rolls the bike out on dry days when the temperature is 75 degrees Fahrenheit (24°C). Banker types rattle me, because there is always something hidden beneath the surface whereas a biker, or most any man in a creative industry, has his true look presented for all to see. More often than not he is a true gentleman at heart. Additionally, I have met more people with integrity and strong faith/beliefs in the biking world than I have in any other industry to which I've been exposed.

When it comes to personal heroes, this actually takes a great deal of thought. There are many people I admire greatly for their achievements in areas of life, whether it is spiritual or financial. However, for a hero, I'm going to have to go with Eleanor of Aquitaine. She was a beautiful royal rebel who was one of the wealthiest and most powerful women in the Middle Ages. Not only was she Queen of both France and England, but she also went along during The Crusades. I could so easily see her with her own motorcycle, because she had the mentality, sense of adventure, and *joie de vivre* that a girl needs to be a woman biker.

Sam from California

I was born in California in 1955. My given name is Dara, but I prefer to be called Sam. I began my life's journey in suburban Covina, a racially diverse and densely populated region of Greater Los Angeles. My story is one of traversing the country, first north to Washington and Oregon then east to New England, and later yet another move, this time southwest to Tallahassee, Florida.

My father deserted the family when I was quite young. When I was seven years old, my mother married again; this is the man I call 'Dad.' He really was my dad, as I only have a few memories of my biological father. I have a brother from my mom's first marriage and a half-sister from her second. My dad owned a gas station, which he eventually sold; but he remained in the automotive business. My mom worked in the insurance business. I always had a burning desire to learn how mechanical objects function, even before my stepfather appeared on the scene. I loved hanging around with him while he worked on his cars. Later, his skills as a car mechanic would provide me with the opportunity to gain more and more experience and understanding of mechanics.

With a change in my father's employment, my parents decided to move south to the township of Vista just north of San Diego, which was sparsely populated at the time and was comprised primarily of people of Anglo–Saxon descent. I was thirteen at the time. Dad's primary employment as salesman for an automotive parts company required him to service half of Southern California.

I attended Vista High School, but I didn't like high school at all. I was always keen on being out and about experiencing new thrills. I found school to be boring and a real drag. I was an independent and rebellious teenager who had an insatiable desire to know how everything worked, and to experience life at its fullest. My parents were pretty straitlaced and I soon learned the art of living a 'hidden life' while appearing to be a good girl. I also wanted to do what boys could do and didn't hide my frustration with the dominant values of the day. I was pretty opinionated.

In most cases, I pretty well did what I wanted to do whether it was considered boys' stuff or not. I'm an adrenaline junkie and I went hang-gliding and bike riding, and any other thrill-seeker activity that would give me the rush I was looking for. This was without my parents' consent or knowledge, of course. At fifteen, I asked my parents to buy me a dirt bike. Their reply was a firm 'no!' But three years later, I had saved up enough money to buy my own dirt bike. My boyfriend shared my passion, and it helped that he owned a campervan, which meant we could carry the bikes out to the desert and ride. I especially remember the beautiful and wild rides through the Anza Borrego desert, located to the east of San Diego.

My first introduction to American biker culture occurred when I was fifteen. My family traveled to Northern California for their annual hunting/camping trip. A group of Hells Angels camped next to us. One afternoon, I returned from a trip to the supermarket with my mom to discover my dad having a beer, laughing, and socializing with these guys. My dad said, 'Those guys are regular people, just like us. They just ride choppers and wear leather jackets.' But I was not permitted to speak or interact with them. I guess that was just the protective instinct of any father who knows from his own youth that boys will be boys. I was totally fascinated by their motorcycles, most of which were custom jobs, and I never lost my desire to ride a bike like that. I still hope to own a custom chopper some day.

Shortly after graduation from Vista High School in 1973, I moved out on my own. The next year, I moved in with my boyfriend and commenced my post-secondary education at the age of nineteen. I attended college in San Diego and supported my studies by working at a variety of jobs in the area. My boyfriend and I built a street-legal racing car and took it to the local drag strip on amateur nights; on weekends, we headed for the desert. I maintained my drive and passionate desire to experience life at its fullest, taking every opportunity to achieve the all-important adrenaline rush. It was more than the rush, though. It was my style and in my character to face frightening situations square on and go for it!

Shortly before graduation from college, my boyfriend died in an industrial accident. A year later, I married a man who was the exact opposite of him. This man was quiet, reserved, and certainly did not like taking risks. Somehow we managed to live together; it was a marriage of a wildcat and a poodle. In 1981, we moved from Vista, California — which proudly boasts on its town sign that it has the 'Best Weather in the World' — to the relatively dreary weather of Spokane, Washington. In Spokane, I got a job working for Hewlett-Packard as a radio frequency communications technician.

Five years into the marriage, I was informed that I was not able to have children. I accepted that fact and went on with living married life, but I was beginning to feel like I was losing myself. It was a vague uneasiness. After being informed I couldn't have kids, I immediately enrolled in classes again, indulging my insatiable need for knowledge in the field of electrical engineering. I could figure out how anything mechanical worked, but I needed the formal education to understand electrical technology. Then the impossible happened: I became pregnant with my first daughter just weeks before starting classes.

I didn't alter my lifestyle all that much in light of the pregnancy, but, needless to say, I didn't engage in my previous risky behaviour. I kept my job, my classes, and maintained the small farm where I lived with my husband. A few months later, I was taken to the hospital for the birth of my baby. Early in my last year of school, I learned I was going to have another child, due one month after finishing my final exams. The child was another girl. I took to parenting as I do to everything in life: full-on and the best I could. My husband was still very quiet, but he did not appear to care that I was so busy and active. But he absolutely refused to allow me to buy a road motorcycle. Still, I rode dirt bikes and other people's road bikes with friends throughout my marriage. My husband did not participate in that activity either, but he tolerated my active life in order to make the marriage work.

Something, however, was still eating at me on the inside. I attribute this to taking on too much and feeling like I was mentally and physically crashing. I tried to pull back on the activities I was engaged in, but couldn't resist the call again for more knowledge. In 1992, we moved to Corvallis, Oregon, which gave me the opportunity to go to trade school and apprentice as an electrician at Hewlett-Packard.

Meanwhile, my husband, a veterinary technician, was unable to obtain employment in his field after the move to Oregon. Money was scarce and I worked fulltime, often sixty to seventy hours a week, and did most of the work around the farm. The financial problems and my heavy workload were truly taking their toll and after nineteen years of marriage, a very ugly divorce ensued. I realized I had intimidated him all my life and I hadn't seen it. I don't think he ever liked me, or himself, very much. The bottom line is that I walked away penniless from that marriage, because I had put my own money into my husband's failing business.

I started over from scratch and moved to New England in April of 1999, for health reasons, and because of the ease of finding work there. By May I was employed; by August I rejoined Hewlett-Packard, working at a plant the company had in the area. Shortly after, I bought a 1997 Honda Shadow Ace — it was my first road bike since 1977. I was thrilled. But I had a minor spill learning about cagers in Massachusetts, a state which has the reputation of having the worst car drivers in the United States. I quickly learned to plan rides into the less populated areas so I could enjoy the freedom of riding without the stress of cagers.

In 2001, I traded my Honda Shadow Ace for a new Honda Sabre 1100cc, but I wasn't happy with it. I rode with friends who constantly copped snide remarks about my 'rice burner' from those who rode Harleys. At the same time, I had a close friend who was a Harley rider. In 2002, he took me to a Harley dealer and asked me to 'just sit on one.' He pointed me to a Dyna Wide Glide and I parked my butt on it. I actually didn't feel like I sat on it, I felt like I sat in it. That's all it took. I sold the Honda immediately and bought the Harley with my twenty-year bonus from Hewlett-Packard.

Two weeks after purchasing the Harley, I had another accident. Thankfully it was totally unrelated to motorcycling. I fell in my own back yard and broke my ankle. This didn't stop me from enjoying life on the road, however. After surgery to repair the ankle and during rehabilitation, I rode pillion with various friends. I also added custom accessories to my new Harley, waiting for the day that I could ride again.

From this point on, life seemed to focus for me. Since early 2001, I worked in the capacity of electromagnetic compatibility engineer (EMC). The job included radio frequency interference investigations in healthcare environments, which took me many places throughout North America, Europe, and elsewhere.

Early in 2007, I decided to move to Tallahassee, Florida. I now manage other EMC engineers, which lessens the amount of travel required of me. In this position, I'm able to work from home and still fly to wherever I'm needed. I also speak on a regular basis at national medical conferences in my line of work as an EMC engineer. And I'm active in the pursuit of motorcyclists' rights, and I became a member of the Patriot Guard Riders.

When I was moving into my new house, a neighbor saw my Harley and he told me about the Chrome Divas. I was impressed that women had formed such a group, as I had generally ridden with men. I decided to join right then and there. I thought the Chrome Divas would be like myself, experienced riders. I was a bit disappointed that many were actually novices, but they are all great women. They are all looking for the same things I am. My life has always been about doing all the things everyone says women can't do. Riding motorcycles is just one of the big ones. I see my fellow group of women as defying those preconceived ideas that society has forced upon us. My two daughters, now college age, have not shown any desire to ride motorcycles — yet! But if they're anything like their mom, it's only a matter of time before we will be cruising as a threesome down the highway.

My favorite quote is by Charlotte Whitton: 'Women must do everything twice as well as men to be thought half as good. Luckily, this is not difficult.'

5

Biker Chicks of Europe and the United Kingdom

Annick from Belgium

I was born in Antwerp, Belgium, in 1979 into an average middle-class family. I was first exposed to motorcycles when a friend of my father brought around his Triumph. I rode a few kilometers as a passenger behind him. It was then I decided that I would someday be the proud owner of my own bike.

My mother certainly didn't approve of her daughter riding a motorcycle. She viewed motorcycles as 'killing machines,' so I waited until I was living independently. Shortly after moving out from my parents' home, I met a boyfriend who had recently bought a Harley-Davidson. I thought that this was the perfect time to buy my first motorcycle. It was a Kawasaki 500 and was good to learn on. My boyfriend and I became members of the Antwerp Diamond Port chapter of the Harley Owners Group (HOG). After going to a few HOG events, I also became a Harley fan. In 2005, I decided I had practiced enough on my Kawasaki and purchased my own Harley Dyna Superglide Sport.

To me, motorcycles are epitomized by Harleys and the Harley Owners Group. HOG offers you an immediate group of like-minded people who share a passion for the roads and rides. They offer friendship, a brotherhood/sisterhood with its feelings of camaraderie, parties, and the riding image is kind of tough looking. No other brand of motorcycles offers you this. I love riding for the experience of being outside, in the open air and close to nature. Harley riding for thrills is best experienced on small twisty roads, as Harleys are not built for speed.

I now live with my fiancé, Geert, whom I met through my HOG chapter in 2006. We share the same passion for Harley-Davidsons and our home is full of Harley paraphernalia. In 2007, Geert gave me a wonderful gift, a brand new Fat Boy, which I love! As I work in the chemical industry as an engineer, I very much appreciate the fresh air ride after work and on weekends. I am at heart an open-air girl.

Our planned honeymoon was at an official HOG event. After we married, we got on our bikes to ride to the HOG European Rally at Lake Gard, Italy, which was scheduled for September, 2008. But before that Geert and I, along with a group of friends we met through HOG and Harley riding, organized the 1st European Posse Ride for HOG, scheduled in July, 2008.

Of my many rides, the most memorable one was a particular HOG run to Fakersee, Austria, which took me and Geert over a mountain range, where we suddenly came upon a huge snow-capped peak, the Grossglockner. That was it for me — it defined the magic of riding. The beauty and closeness to nature, with great companions, overwhelmed me with an emotion of happiness, wonder, and well-being. I felt like I was living life fully at that moment.

My heroes are my fiancé, who brought me to the world of the Harley-Davidson and helped me to find my identity as a Harley rider, and Del Hofer. Del owns a Harley-Davidson shop in Fargo, North Dakota. He is in his seventies and spoke at a HOG rally, where I met him. I felt that he was such an inspirational person that he immediately became my hero. He told of how he came to buy back his original Harley-Davidson, which he had sold many years before. To me he spoke to my heart and my passion.

My most inspirational saying is the same as Harley-Davidson's motto: 'Living the Legend.' Riding my Harley has become a way of life for me.

Angie from Germany

I am a rolling stone. I was born into a French family. My father's employment took us to various locations throughout the world, including Kinshasa in Zaire and many other exotic, adventurous spots. Recreation for me and my family was travel and adventure activities. Eventually, my family and I settled in Hamburg, Germany. Those years of traveling and adventure for recreation stayed with me through life; I hold these values to this day.

My motorcycle is not an integral part of my identity. I have been an office bearer in HOG and I am a Harley-Davidson owner and rider in my own right. I first learned to ride when I was sixteen on motorized bicycles (mopeds) and small scooters. I wasn't moved to purchase my own motorcycle until my brother got into some financial problems when I was thirty-eight. I agreed to bail him out by purchasing his Harley-Davidson Softail. And because I now had a motorcycle, I decided to ride it and thoroughly enjoyed the experience — I still enjoy riding it. I like adventure. For me, riding without risk is no fun. I have ridden many kilometers, choosing twisty, winding roads to test the limits of my riding abilities. I ride wherever I can for the thrill and adventure. I also ride off-road. I love the closeness to nature that riding provides. The television series *Long Way Down* and *Long Way Around* characterize my style of adventurous riding.

I am inclined to live life on the edge. On warm days, I will ride with no protective clothing, adorned only in a tank top and street clothes for pants and shoes. One of my most memorable experiences was picking up my boyfriend on my Harley in Berlin and traveling to Hamburg. At the end of the ride, he was completely addicted to Harley-Davidson motorcycles! He has owned a Road King since the Berlin trip. I became involved with HOG around this time while we were first living together. I am now happily married to him.

My hero is my dad; unfortunately he passed away in a car accident some twenty-nine years ago. He was my hero due to the way he lived his life and especially the way he raised his children. He never told the children, 'No, you cannot do this or that.' His style was to say, 'Well, if it were me, I wouldn't do that,' and then provide the reason why. Who else raises a family like this?

My favourite saying is 'The trouble with most of us is that we would rather be ruined by praise than saved by criticism.'

Jenny from The Netherlands

I was born in Holland, near Rotterdam, forty-nine years ago into an average middle-class family. My earliest memories include riding on a moped behind my dad, who did not own a car. As a child, I loved his moped and would sit on it or any other I could find and imagine I was riding it, making the engine noises myself. From that moment on, I wanted to have my own moped and I did when I was sixteen. After that I kept getting bigger and bigger motorcycles.

I am not your conventional 'girly' girl or woman. I was gifted with mechanical and technical abilities. My profession is that of carpenter. I was the first woman with a carpenter's certificate in my area of Holland. When the newspapers printed a story about me obtaining my certificate, the headline was 'Jenny has Golden Hands.' I have the luck that what my eyes see my hands can do, and I learn very quickly. I never thought of being a mechanic, but after years of car racing I learned car mechanics just by looking at what the mechanics did. I wanted to do all car mechanical work and soon I did. I don't know where it ends, but I love to be working and doing things with my hands.

Around the age of nineteen, I purchased my first real motorcycle. It was an off-road bike, a Honda XL500S. I had several male friends who had the same or similar off-road bikes and I fondly recall those years. Together we visited a lot of motorcycle Grands Prix, like Silverstone in the United Kingdom; Hockenheim, Germany; Spa-Francorchamps, Belgium; and Assen in my home country. During those times Freddy Spencer, Barry Sheene, and Kenny Roberts were our heroes. We went on many adventures and we had a lot of fun.

When I was in my early twenties, I felt free because of motorcycle riding with my friends. We were not an official club or group. We all just felt the spirit of being young and free motorcycle riders going to the places I wanted to go together with my friends. I really had that feeling of being free and lived in my own world. Sometimes we talked about and thought about the people around us who did not understand how or why we lived this way. It was a great time and we also had our parties with loads of beer around the campfires. But we never did things for which we could have landed in jail . . . except for speeding!

In 1982, at the Belgium motorcycle Grand Prix in Spa-Francorchamps, I met the man who two years later would become my husband. He was from Luxembourg and was attending this Grand Prix with his friends. From that day on we did a lot of riding together. Towards the end of 1982, I moved to Luxembourg to live closer to him. We upgraded our bikes a couple of times over the years to more powerful road bikes, like Honda's CB750 Bold D, CB900 Super Bold, and CB1100F. These were very fast bikes for that time.

As we became more affluent and more mature, we made a very serious decision; we decided to buy a Harley-Davidson. Ten years ago we bought a Sportster Custom 1200, which is a very nice bike. Later we bought a Fat Boy, which my husband still rides, and I purchased a Dyna Low Rider. Eventually I traded my Low Rider in for a Road King with which I am very pleased because it rides very well and is also fast . . . for a Harley.

The transition to Harleys also saw my husband and me become active in the club scene. Today, I am active in the Ladies of Harley, Benelux, and we organize five to seven rides a year. The main event is the Ladies of Harley weekend in Germany, organized by Mary Moelder. Between one hundred and fifty to two hundred ladies come together for this event.

My husband and I live in Spain during the colder months in Europe. In the warmer season, we choose to live in Luxembourg. In Spain, there is a very robust biker scene. We are both members of HOG's Luxembourg chapter, as well as HOG's Costa Blanca chapter in Spain. We share the same passion for Harleys that outlaw motorcycle clubs do, but it depends on the club. Some clearly do not want to talk while others are quite sociable when we meet at rallies or while we are on the road.

My heroes? Well, in sports it's definitely Ayrton Senna. It's a shame that he is not in this world anymore. He had the passion, the courage, the talent, and the guts to be a three-time World Champion in F1 racing. Other than a sporting hero, I would have to say people — some who I know — who suffer from a serious illness or injury and then achieve their dream, enjoying it even more as a result of their determination.

Some really magical rides for me were at the end of the 1970s, when I rode with a group of friends — me being the only girl — to see the motorcycle Grands Prix all over Europe. It was great to be at the places I've previously mentioned and see our heroes on the big bikes. The rides to and from the tracks, and the races themselves, are a real memorable time for me. Riding my Harley in Barcelona at Harley-Davidson's 100th anniversary in 2003 was really special. I would also have to say that the Ladies of Harley rides — sometimes we are about one hundred and eighty strong, all on big Harleys — is a feeling you can't describe!

I do all the repairs on my bike myself, not in the early years, but later, after I had a career in car racing. At the moment, I do a lot of 1960s to 1970s Harley-Davidson restorations; that is where my passion lies these days. My husband cooks so we are really a great team. We've been together for more than twenty-five years.

Some of my favourite sayings are 'Good girls go to heaven — Harley girls go everywhere;' 'You only live once;' and Harley-Davidson's motto 'Live to Ride — Ride to Live.'

Elwira from Poland

I was born into a working-class family. My father was a welder and my mother was a working woman; both were alcoholics. My memories of my childhood are playing football, hanging from trees, playing cowboys and Indians, and playing Zorro with my friends around our houses. Looking for another life, I joined the swimming club in my town at the age of nine. In a very short time I joined the Polish national swimming team. A few of my national swimming records still stand, as they have not been broken by anyone in Poland.

I am in my early forties at the time of writing this story. I have one beautiful daughter who is in the United Kingdom studying for her degree in forensic psychology and criminal justice administration. I am divorced now and happily living life as a single person. I work in the area of life and business coaching. It is based upon identifying strengths in people and then guiding them to help them achieve their potential to do what they hope to achieve in life. I help them to redefine their goals to be even greater than those they set for themselves, and help them to discover the 'diamonds' they are. It is important to understand what I do for employment in order to understand why it is that I ride motorcycles.

My first exposure to motorcycles was a ride I took, when very young, with my uncle who was a soldier and who owned his own bike. From that first ride with my uncle, my dream or greatest desire was to ride a motorcycle. I had to tackle this hidden desire in me in order to be able to be true to what I tell others about achieving their dreams, hopes, and desires. I am no hypocrite so I bought a Kawasaki EN500 motorcycle; one year later I upgraded to a Harley Sportster 883. Two years later, I purchased my current ride, which is a 2002 Harley-Davidson Softail FXST. I have customized my motorcycles to suit my personality: they never look like typical Milwaukee issue. For me, a motorcycle is part and parcel of being a life coach. It is tangible evidence that I followed my inner calling and achieved my goals.

When I think about my riding lifestyle and how I came to riding, I must first say that I have had a desire to ride since the earliest memories of my life. I believe in reincarnation; we souls live and die many times on this earth and continue to do so until we achieve what we are meant to achieve through time. In my case, I believe that my desire to ride is related to the fact that I have identified very strongly with American Indians from my earliest years. I am sure this has to do with a past lifetime, where I was incarnated as an American Indian. To me, as a cosmopolitan European city woman, the horses the Indians rode so gallantly and with wild abandon are exemplified by the motorcycle. When I ride, my spirit feels at one with my kindred American Indian spirits, which I feel are part of my current life on this earth. The freedom, the wind in my hair, the sense of independence all relate to my core being, or rather my previous core identity as an American Indian. For city people like me, the plains and open spaces are gone now; what's left are only roads for the steel and chrome horses we call motorcycles.

I have always been a woman who is more comfortable in the presence of men than other women. Please do not get me wrong: I am neither a rabid feminist nor a lesbian. I am very tolerant and hold no one else's lifestyle in contempt. I simply feel more comfortable hanging around with men. I am a person who respects all people. I do not necessarily love all of them or like all of them, but I do respect them and the lives they choose to live. But I find that most women fill the air with too many meaningless words and are, on the whole, too noisy. They complicate their lives too much for my liking and I have little time for them. It is very strange, I know, but I actually started to act and present myself as more feminine just before I purchased my first motorcycle. I had worn my hair cut short and had spurned 'girly' things all my life, when suddenly I felt the desire to present myself as much more of a woman. Obviously this was in contradiction to buying a masculine machine like a motorcycle.

As a rider, I meet many other riders including members of 1% outlaw motorcycle clubs. The only books available here in Poland are by Sonny Barger and his books do not come near capturing the outlaw scene here. The vision portrayed by his books of alienated World War II veterans forming these clubs is alien to us. Following World War II Poland was a communist nation. As such, anything capitalist — and even more so, American — was seen as subversive to the ideology of the communist state. Riding a Harley-Davidson was seen as a completely rebellious act until the fall of the Iron Curtain. It has barely been twenty years since riding an American motorcycle has become nothing unusual.

It is certainly true that Poland is very close to having two chapters of the Hells Angels Motorcycle Club amongst our riding community. The Outlaws Motorcycle Club is already established here. I assure you that I can see the Sonny Barger obsession with money, domination of turf, and power amongst our home-grown clubs who are now about to become Hells Angels. The Outlaws wear large gold chains around their necks and keep pretty much to themselves. But the clubs here have many different faces and these differences seem to be tolerated.

As for me joining women rider groups here — forget it! The Amazon Motorcycle Club in Poland has absolutely no attraction for me. Two women together is quite enough. Three or more women in a group create confusion, they gossip, and bring out the ugliness of jealousy amongst them. Women and men need each other. It is like yin and yang. That is why I love being the seductress. I ride with only a white tank top, jeans stretched over my bottom, and boots on during the warm months. I just love the look of lust on the men's faces. I particularly like it when a man has a close call in traffic or a small crash as he is looking at me rather than driving his car. But I do believe men are stronger than we are, they have a lot of talents and have more technical knowledge. We women need them, just like these strong men need the tenderness of a woman. For me, all-male or all-female groups are not natural.

I was a member of HOG's Warsaw chapter for one year. HOG gave me the kind of special brotherhood I needed, when

I wanted to join a group of hard-riding, well-experienced bikers. They are good fellows and good riders. I can count on them for a good, hard, safe ride. But on the other hand, I do not like to ride with groups at all. I consider myself to be a lone 'she-wolf' rider. Here is where I experience the fullness of my rides. I ride because I love it, not to prove something. I have been invited to ride with many groups and have politely declined their offers.

There are three rides which I can say were my best rides, if not the most memorable. All were intensely psychological as well as physical. The first was coming from a meeting located 310 miles (500 kilometers) away from my home. I was, of course, riding alone. Thirty miles (50 kilometers) from my departure point the rain came down in buckets. The heaviness of the rain caused the wiring of my bike to become dysfunctional. Slowly but surely electrical components on my bike began to fail. I soon lost my turn signals; a few more miles on I lost my stop lights; and then I lost my horn. I still managed to ride the two hundred and eighty miles (450 kilometers) home, but it was a very trying experience. Then coming home, I was so sick I thought I was going to die. I was washed out. There was water in my boots, in my ears, in my lungs . . . well, everywhere.

The second memorable ride was during a ride to Prague. I was new to motorcycling and was traveling with much more experienced riders. As I think about it, it was quite unusual for them to invite a rookie to travel with them. This leads me to believe they recognized my capabilities better than I did. We came into a tight turn at about 75 miles per hour (120 kilometers per hour), much too fast for my capabilities, and I could feel my body tensing as I came nearer and nearer the curbing. Suddenly, my mind relaxed and my body simply took over. I went up on the curve slightly, followed my instinct, and didn't lose control. I lived inside the moment, not thinking, just acting. When I had cleared the curve, I felt like a wild animal had been released from my over-controlling brain. I am sure that many people will understand: experience your biggest fear and your conscious mind leaves you, letting your soul and body guide you. I can only say that it was exactly like the best orgasm I have ever had. Every cell of my body poured confidence into me and tension out of me. I screamed for a long time under my helmet. It was such a great feeling to experience an event where you learn you can trust your instincts and leave your fears behind.

The third memorable ride was a day excursion over 682 miles (1,100 kilometers). Again, I rode alone. Amazingly, I shook and trembled for two days from the adrenaline of the long ride; every cell of my body seemed to release its tension slowly over the next few days — it was great! It might be that this sort of long ride is like some kind of drug. Or could it have simply been due to doing too many miles for a one-day ride? I can't say, but it happened; my confidence is high in riding my motorcycle. However, every ride is new to me. The full concentration, I find, clears my mind. I treat every trip as a new lesson.

If I had to give one person as my hero, it would be Leonardo da Vinci. The power of his mind and his never-ending potential to follow his ideas through to completion is what makes him heroic to me. As for a role model or golden rule that I try to follow in my present lifetime, I would have to say that what I try to follow is the path that leads to true self-understanding. The experiences which I have described above about my life as a lone she-wolf mean I am almost always on the inside of the action. Being in the midst of the action does not mean being in a crowd, no, being in the middle of the crowd means just that you are in the middle of the crowd and the action occurs elsewhere. The understanding of myself as a true lone she-wolf brings from within me a gratefulness that makes me try to experience this sensation as often as possible. My riding experiences affirm this.

I am truly grateful to have a body that shakes from the thrill of the ride. I am blessed to have such good experiences. I am truly grateful I can live my life and love the life I live even though it hurts sometimes. Having experienced this state of being, personally, I am grateful to the universe which gives to me and other people around me love and happiness.

Goddess from England

I lived for seven years with a member of a 1% outlaw motorcycle club, which provided me with a fascinating insider's view of the scene. I prefer not to delve into my background or discuss my personal life either inside or outside the club scene. But I would like to share these insights about the women I came to know and who, like me, found themselves attracted to the bad boy lifestyle offered by hardcore outlaw bikers.

I would characterize these women as belonging to one of four camps: ladies, strippers, blow-ins, and toys for boys. Others, including some who have studied the biker world, use similar terms, but this assessment is my own. If asked where I fit in, I would say that I belonged to the 'ladies' group. I held myself as such and was treated as such.

The ladies   These women tend to dress and act like 'straights' and basically lead dual lives. They hold mainstream jobs and/ or are devoted mothers. They tend to be well educated, very well mannered, and present themselves as strong and independent women. At the same time, they live as a partner of an outlaw motorcycle club member. Few if any of the ladies use drugs, drink alcohol or party hard with the club. The way they present themselves means they are not harassed in any way by the men of the club, and are deeply respected and well regarded. Of course, there are differences amongst the ladies' attitudes and interests, but overall they tend to be very different from the other camps.

The strippers   The style of the strippers stands in stark contrast to the ladies. They present themselves as scantily dressed, revealing a lot of flesh and generally hold menial jobs which last for only short periods of time, due to a number of factors. The strippers are tawdry and cheap in appearance, and have no apparent interests in life other than the club and their outlaw motorcycle club man. The strippers tend to be more transient than the ladies and can be expected to be around the scene for relatively briefer times, with a few notable exceptions. I would estimate that they are typically around for three to four years, then either move on, go to drug rehabilitation, or simply drift off with another man. Many of the strippers are co-dependent, meaning they are completely dependent on their men to make even the smallest decisions about their lives.

Many of the strippers are, indeed, strippers by vocation. These women turn the money earned from their work as strippers over to their men. The strippers are the direct opposite of the independent woman who characterizes the ladies. The strippers find it very difficult to reach a common ground with the ladies, pretty well negating most chances to successfully socialize with them. By club protocol the ladies are obliged to be respectful of the strippers, but most of the ladies have difficulty showing respect to someone who obviously does not respect themselves.

The blow-ins   These women tend to be like the strippers and form short-term relationships with club men. The primary difference between the strippers and the blow-ins is the time of the relationship with the club and its men. Blow-ins are very exceptional if they make six months. Most depart for various reasons within a month. Most blow-ins are in relationships with club men who are happily married. Almost all blow-ins are much more like the strippers in style and behavior. For the blow-ins, the club is a source of drugs and they are quite dysfunctional with low levels of self-esteem.

Toys for the boys   The fourth camp is a curious group, indeed. It is comprised of women who come to the clubhouse in search of a walk on the wild side. They are often in the scene just one night for any-way-you-want-it sex, drugs, and a chance to associate with the bad boys. These women are 'toys for the boys' and their straight lifestyle is solidly middle class. They may hold down good jobs, and many are married with young children and husbands. After a night of frolicking at the clubhouse they simply return to their homes and, apparently, keep their night-out activities secret from all.

The following are more general points I came to observe:

- Women are attracted to the club for the bad boy image. Club life makes them feel secure. It also gives them a sense of belonging. Even if you are a good girl you're able to live the dangerous life through them.
- Outlaw motorcycle club life is all inclusive; it takes up a majority of your time and lifestyle. The phone is always ringing, someone is always coming by, and someone constantly needs something. It can be a very expensive lifestyle always trying to help your fellow club members out.
- When someone leaves the club, it is a huge lifestyle adjustment for the former members and their wives, girlfriends or ole ladies. The men are bored upon leaving the club and it strains their relationship, because their

entire lifestyle revolved around the club; much like parents whose last child leaves the house.

- Club members are extremely paranoid that someone (law enforcement) is always watching them.
- Most women in the club scene are very subservient. Those who are more dominant can fit in as long as they can also remain quiet when needed. Those who are loud and too pushy are banned from events and leave the lifestyle.
- Most of the long-term members have the same type of women; many are strippers and turn all their money over to their man. Their entire life revolves around taking care of their man.
- Many of the club members and their women are self-destructive. They aren't ever able to get ahead due to the mentality that they don't deserve to have good things. An example would be getting a good job, and then doing something at work to get fired such as not showing up on a certain day or maybe starting back taking drugs. They feel they aren't worthy of such a good lifestyle; maybe because of their childhood.
- Many club members are jealous of what others have. There are those members who take advantage of the hospitality the club provides and are nothing but dead weight for the club.

There is an attractive base for criminal activity in the club given the vast network of contacts that are immediately formed upon joining the club and the extra security the club provides. Most women are not privy to the criminal side unless they help by selling small amounts of drugs. Most of the men recognize the fact that an angry female who leaves the club may go to the cops with information. So the women are never involved in serious criminal activities or told about them.

There is a saying 'What happens in London stays in London' and that holds true to the club also. This is part of the attraction for women and men associated with the clubs, as you can become this other person while being with the club, and then come back to your real life and job during the week. Although club members remain who they are throughout their daily life, the women are allowed to almost live dual roles.

Society today wants women to do it all — raise the kids and family while working fulltime — whereas in the club scene women are able to take the more traditional role and are required only to look pretty and make sure their man and his children are taken care of. They don't have to be like the strong female roles portrayed by television.

I believe there is less criminal activity today amongst most club members, because it is too hard to get away with petty crimes. There are too many tools law enforcement has at its disposal, and the club members today have too much to lose. Jail time is getting longer, the government is able to seize all of their assets, family members can lose jobs, and kids can be taken out of the home; the list is endless.

Section III
Easy Writers

Authors' note

This section is comprised of women who wished to write their own accounts, and to facilitate this, we simply served as editors.

6

Born to Ride: Living on the Edge in a Kilt

Chuff (Scotland)

I have experienced life as an outlaw biker club woman since the age of sixteen. On rare occasions while growing up, I had seen outlaw bikers pass through the small town where I lived flying their club colors and I thought wow, how cool is that! But I never thought I would end up in the biker lifestyle. I came across the local outlaw biker community quite unintentionally, when my brothers wanted to score a bit of weed. That's when I met Bill, who at the time was president of the Barbarians Motorcycle Club. I was a naïve, headstrong young girl when I took up with Bill. My parents, who had high hopes for me as I was a championship highland dancer, needless to say weren't too thrilled with my choice of boyfriend. But I was so strong-minded and having so much fun I wouldn't take any advice from them as to whom I should go out with and which direction I should take my life in.

With the Barbarians, it was drugs aplenty and everything seemed so exciting. I wasn't sure about Bill, but I quickly became consumed by the outlaw biker lifestyle. Bill asked me to come on a run the Barbarians were planning to England to the Kent Custom Bike Show, which was promoted by the Hells Angels. I took him up on the offer. He told me not to worry about a thing; he would take care of me. Being around him I noticed life was one big party. I had never seen so many drugs, so much money — piles of it lying around. It was a buzz — it was exciting! I mentioned to Bill that I needed some new clothes to go to Kent. He told me there was a wad of cash lying around and to help myself to the money and to treat myself. Wow! How good was this! And with Bill being the president of the Barbarians, I felt extra special.

On the run to Kent, I was among the other club women, who looked upon me with disgust, I suppose. But Bill made sure that none of them bothered me. I was so busy with him that I hadn't really taken in the hostility from the other women. It was exciting for a young sixteen-year-old. Here I was riding with those outlaw clubs that I'd seen as a child passing through my little town — now I was part of the scene. We partied all the way to Kent. One night we camped up near Ashford, with a campfire burning and sleeping under a tree. At the show I was in awe. Here were all these people with whom to party. It was my first encounter with the Hells Angels. It was a drug-fuelled weekend. Bill bought me lots of new things including more clothes, and got me my first tattoo from a Hells Angels lady tattooist. It was all very surreal to me but I had a ball.

Back home the parties continued. I moved out of my parents' home to live with one of my brothers. Of course, he got wind that I was hanging around with bikers and I confessed all to him. He gave me a wee pep talk and told me to watch what I was doing. But it was already too late: I was committed to Bill and the biker lifestyle. My brother, who knew the outlaw biker scene as he was into building custom bikes, reluctantly accepted the fact that his little sister was a biker woman.

One night most of the club arrived in our small town and I brought them home to the flat I was staying at with my brother. I was looking out the window at all the bikes lined up down the street and thinking, how good is this? That'll give the neighbors something to talk about! It was around this time that I found out Bill was married. But he said he and his wife had split up so I never thought that much about it. One fateful night the club gathered at a local bar to listen to some bands and my brother and I had been invited along. I was having a great time but at one point I was left sitting in the entrance hall while Bill was off doing his thing. I was surrounded by the other club women who I knew didn't like me. There was obviously some issue they had with me. I was approached by two of them who very subtly asked me into the washroom for a 'word.' I wasn't that stupid to believe I was going in there for a chat and told them if they had something to say to me then just say it.

Things just escalated rapidly from that point on. I had women screaming at me from all angles. As the screaming escalated and then got more heated I jumped from my seat. One of them grabbed the back of my jacket at the neck and wrenched it down, pulling it halfway down my sleeves leaving me helpless. I couldn't raise my arms to defend myself. At this point I saw one of the women take a runner for me and just when I thought here goes, I'm done for, my brother came running through the fracas and I just heard him shout, 'If you can't use your arms use your teeth,' and that's exactly what I did. The next thing I knew the men were amongst us and pulling us apart. I was left spitting out bits of denim and flesh. By this time Bill was back and I was ushered away.

Bill took me back to his place, where I spent the night with him. The next day he went out on business. I remember getting out of bed and looking out the window and seeing his wife and her friend staring up at me. I opened the window and she screamed some things at me. I knew this confrontation was coming and there would be no avoiding it. I got dressed and headed downstairs and outside but by the time I did she was gone. I ended up moving in with Bill shortly after that and the lifestyle of parties continued. I kept my distance from the club women and they kept their distance from me.

On my eighteenth birthday, I found out I was pregnant. I made the decision, without telling Bill, that I was keeping it, even if it meant me leaving and bringing the child up alone. It was a difficult time to say the least. It was the first time he raised his hands to me as he wasn't pleased when he eventually found out. Matters were even more complicated, as at this time there was a major drug bust and Bill was up to his neck in it. They had caught him and a few other club members with a large amount of drugs, mainly cannabis. It was major news in our area. The local high court near us was opened for the first time in seven years to hold the trial. At the time I was six months pregnant. Eventually, Bill was found guilty and jailed for two years.

At this point I moved into my own flat with help from my parents, but I never gave up on Bill. He would write to me promising everything would be okay, and I would visit him in jail. During this time I gave birth to our daughter Candy. She was nine months old when he got out on parole and it was back to the 'lifestyle.' There were always women hanging on, sucked into the scene as I was. Some were mamas who would sleep with numerous club members, used and abused on a regular basis. Others turned up at the parties for free drinks, free drugs, and a walk on the wild side.

It was far from easy being a mother and a club woman. One club woman I did become close to was Jane. To this day, she remains one of my best friends. She joined the club under hard circumstances, too. Digger, her partner, had a long-term relationship before splitting up with his wife and ending up in jail with Bill on drug charges. Jane started writing to Digger while he was in jail and their relationship took up on his release. Jane, too, was never really accepted by the other club women so we hit it off big time.

I spent fourteen years living the outlaw life with Bill. It was hard, but something kept us together, even though I knew he had been with countless others. I even caught him red handed at times. But once you're in the scene it's not easy to walk away. I did try at times, but unsuccessfully. I have witnessed the treatment of the other club women by their spouses. I have seen them come and go. I have experienced and witnessed the abuse, the violence, the drugs, and the crime. Eventually, I was able to open my eyes and move on. After I finally got out I still liked to go to the shows, the parties, and other club events, but on my own terms and as a free agent. I have been to parties like the Bulldog Bash, the Hells Angels biggest United Kingdom show, where I have been a guest of the president of the Hells Angels' Ashfield chapter, 'Rat.'

I have been asked out by Hells Angels and other 1%ers, but I have declined because I prefer not to get involved. I know from experience it's not what I'm looking for. I still see and meet other women who go for the status of being with a club member like a trophy, some being sucked in and the same things happening to them as I experienced, and have seen others experience. I have even cautioned women about what they're entering into. But at the end of the day it's their choice, and it may work for some and not others.

Outlaw biker clubs have an order for the things they value most: first comes their loyalty to their patch (colors), their brothers, then their bikes, then *maybe* their women. If you are really lucky you may make it before their bikes, but this is purely from my experience. I choose to put myself first now. I still have the utmost respect for the clubs and their members. It is a lifestyle and you do need to understand it before you can appreciate what it's all about. I get on great with a lot of club members and they are great blokes to be with, but you've got to be sure you can handle your position in the club. Personally, I like it just the way it is now and I just have loads of good friends. And let's be honest, who says this kind of thing only happens amongst biker clubs? It happens in all walks of life. I feel right now that I'm enjoying the lifestyle on my terms.

The best ride of all time, the one that changed my life, was in 2003 after years of riding pillion or illegally. My brother told me if I passed my bike test he would put me on a Harley. So I went out and got my license. My brother was in the process of building a hardtail Sportster chopper from bits and pieces he had lying about — I fell in love with it! The funny thing was that this was not the bike he had in mind for me and he tried his hardest to talk me out of it, as he had a buyer lined up for it. But I couldn't see past this bike and after nearly falling out with him, big time, he agreed to let me have it.

I had only owned this bike a matter of weeks and had done very few miles on it when he asked me to join him and several friends for a ride to Barcelona on the occasion of the 100th Anniversary Open Road Tour. I jumped at the chance. My brother and his best friend had built two of the most radical custom bikes that the United Kingdom and Europe had seen at that point. We took the ferry from Newcastle, England, to Ijmuiden, Holland. You must understand that I hated riding my bike onto the boat. Even to this day I still get nervous on the slippery surface of a boat. But the minute we got on, the party started! At least eight bottles of champagne were bought, drunk, and splashed about. I knew the adventure had begun.

We got off the next day in Holland, where a couple of friends decided to make a pit stop at one of Holland's famous weed shops for supplies. The rest of us headed towards France and agreed we would catch up with them later. We had all we could carry on the bikes. We would ride, stopping every 50 to 70 miles (80 to 110 kilometers)or so for fuel, coffee, and the like. Then around early evening we would find a campsite, get set up for the night, grab a good meal, a few drinks, and settle in.

The first scary part of the ride was when we encountered the Paris Ring Road. While it's great to see the Eiffel Tower in the distance, the road itself is crazy. There was traffic coming from all directions and they did not seem to care about right of way or converging into lanes and the like. It was as if the driving rules were just thrown away for this road. Staying together in a pack was nigh on impossible, but somehow I survived it.

After we left Paris, direction Foix, my brother developed nasty gearbox trouble so we headed for a service station. We were on a bad stretch of road with many potholes, and I hit one hard. I was on top of it before I saw it — no warning whatsoever. I hit it so hard that I came right off the seat, only my hands remained on the bike. I thought I was going over the bars, but I held on, took some rattle, and then composed myself. I took a long break at the service station to recover while my brother fixed his gearbox with the very basic tools we were able to carry. By the time we arrived in the Foix my butt was seriously black and blue. Ah, the joy of a hardtail chopper, eh? But in all honesty I never felt a thing because I was buzzing. The ride through France, the countryside, and the beautiful weather . . . I was living a dream.

Next, we headed off for the principality of Andorra in the Pyrenees Mountains. This part of the ride was filled with breathtaking scenery I never imagined I would see. The climb up was quite daunting, and the extremely windy roads were quite busy, too. But I could see snow on the mountain tops. We stopped on the way up to take in the views and some pictures . . . it was awesome! Our next stop was in Andorra, and then we were in for the descent from the mount heading for Spain and Barcelona.

I wasn't prepared for what happened next. We were heading over the mountains, enjoying the ride, when all of a sudden I lost power . . . I was freewheeling. Panicking, I waved to show the others I was having trouble. I saw a small lay-by at the side of the road and thought I'd head for that. I slowed down to pull into it and hit the brakes. Unfortunately it was gravel — the whole bike slid sideways and I ended up nearly on my side, just managing to hold the bike up after stopping. When I looked to the left of me I was inches away from a sheer drop of about 40 to 50 feet (12 to 15 meters) into white water rapids and there were no barriers. When the others stopped near me, I could see the look of horror on their faces.

That was definitely my near-death experience and thankfully the only one of the trip. The problem with my bike turned out to be the coil, leaving us with the dilemma of what to do next. There was no choice; the bike would have to be towed to the nearest campsite while someone went to a local dealership for a new coil. My brother tried to get one of the others to sit on my bike while it was towed off the mountains, but nobody volunteered for the job. I said I would do it — obviously a task that the most seasoned rider would balk at. It cannot be imagined how scary it was being towed down a mountain by another bike. I was well warned beforehand to keep an eye on the tow rope, not to let it slacken off or risk it wrapping round the front wheel and whipping me off. Thankfully, all went according to plan and we made it down to a campsite without incident. My brother took off and came back with a new coil, and I was back in business.

We finally reached our destination, a campsite on the outskirts of Barcelona, which was rapidly filling up with bikers from all over Europe. Needless to say we were mobbed by all kinds of people who came to admire our bikes. But this was nothing compared to what we were about to experience. The day of the show I dressed in my bikini, my kilt, and my bike boots. Soon we arrived at Olympics Stadium, which was hosting the 100th anniversary show. The streets were lined with thousands of bikes. We cruised around to where the actual bike show was and when we got around to the gates we stopped at the side of the road. Before I knew what was happening we were mobbed; the road closed in on us and we couldn't move. There were photographers everywhere. I had people running up to me and shoving business cards in my hands and in the waistband of my kilt . . . it went crazy. Everything came to a standstill. So we moved towards the gates and the organizers waved us in. They could see the mayhem. Once inside the gates, we took a few minutes to reflect on what had happened. It was unbelievable!

At first the organizers refused to let us enter our rides for the competition. It was a HOG run and you needed to be a member, which some of us weren't, so we used the names of friends of ours who were. There were also problems registering our bikes because my brother Charlie's and his friend Logie's machines were so radical. But the organizers' better judgement came through — it would have been crazy to send us away, especially back out into that crowd. When the judges came around, I immediately recognized the older man as Willie G Davidson (of the Harley-Davidson factory) and his son. My brother's bike took best in show; Logie's was runner-up. Willie G told them, 'Get those bikes to the States, boys.' He was blown away by them. This was the moment I decided the Sporty was on borrowed time — as much as I loved it, I wanted something special and one day I would have it.

We were all on an absolute high from winning the show. The next night the Rolling Stones were playing at the stadium and we all had tickets. Standing in that arena when the

Stones started playing was great. When it dawned on me what had actually happened, I was overwhelmed by it all. Here I was listening to the Stones live, with a big grass joint in my hand, thinking about what I had achieved, riding down from Scotland on my own Harley chop with a great bunch of mates. My mind drifted back to everything that happened along the way, the response from everyone, the win; it was totally overwhelming. It was better than any high I've ever had — better than any drug. The penny dropped then, and I knew this is what I wanted out of life. If I had died that night I would have died a happy woman.

After this it was time to head for our next destination, which was Sestos in the north of Spain to the Fantasy Bike Show, where we went on to take even more prizes. This time, Logie took 'best in the show' and Charlie was the runner-up. We were on an unbelievable high and we had a great party that weekend, too. But it was crunch time afterwards. A few of us had to start heading home, due to commitments at work and with families. I was already a week late, so I had to go but Charlie and Logie had won plenty in prize money so they were heading down to Faro in Portugal for another show. It was definitely the best road trip ever. It was truly a life changer, that's for sure — full of priceless memories, a few of which I have just shared.

My heroes are my dad and my brother Charlie; both are bikers. From the time I was a kid I was brought up amongst bikers, mainly enduro and off-roaders, as my dad was the British Clubman Champion and he would often take us to events. Then, as my brother got older, he got into road bikes and started to build customs. I owe it all to them. As for a famous saying that I identify with, I would have to say 'I came into this world crying. I will leave it laughing.'

7

I'm Not a Ballerina: Life in the Fast Lane

Toni Sharpless (Canada)

I was born in 1960 in Toronto, Canada. My mother, Elaine, was a registered nurse and my father, Bill, an engineer and avid motorcycle rider/racer. I have two younger brothers, Blair and Todd. All my family rides motorcycles except for my mom who, on her first attempt, ended up crashing our mini-bike and landing face-down on an ant hill. My brothers and I ran over to the crash site with great concern for our mini-bike while Mom had to take her own inventory and blow the ants off her face.

When I was six years old, my parents presented us with that mini-bike under the Christmas tree. I think my mom agreed to give us that bike so we would learn to share. We rode the bike in parkland near our house in Toronto. Back then you could still ride in places like that, but not today. Our dad quit engineering to open a motorcycle shop in Toronto called Sonic Motorcycles. It was then that my brothers and I got our very own bikes. We have a lot of fond memories of riding together after school.

I was nine years old when I first tried competition riding. It was an ice racing event and I soon learned that what I really liked best was speed on a motorcycle. That was the beginning of my addiction to the challenges of motorcycle racing. My brothers and I would go on to successful racing careers in different facets of the sport. Todd excelled in oval dirt track racing, Blair in off-road endurance races, and I in closed circuit road racing.

I was sort of a tomboy in that I was athletic and competitive, but that doesn't mean I didn't play house or with dolls. In fact, once I was playing 'Barbies' with some neighborhood girls outside when a boy kept throwing dirt bombs at us. He wouldn't stop even after being asked to, so I went over to convince him he should stop and ended up giving him a thump on his back. He went home crying only to return with his big brother who wanted to get this guy 'Tony' who beat up his little brother. When I stood up and said I was Toni, big brother then turned to little brother and hit him and said, 'Get home!'

I did not like school at all. I like to learn by doing, not listening, and found it quite boring in school. Racing motorcycles really caught my attention, though, and I dreamed of one day being able to race and make a living from it. I slowly worked my way up the motorcycle racing scene in the dirt. At sixteen my parents let me buy my first street bike. My dad said I could only get one if I could put it on the center stand. At age twenty-two, I bought my first road race bike. Along the way, my mom guided me towards being well-rounded in my activities and encouraged me to attend professional modelling courses and ballet. That quickly dissolved when I showed no dancing qualities and arrived at modeling school with helmet hair and crumpled clothes.

After all my mom's efforts failed, I turned from amateur to a professional road racer at the age of twenty-four. I believe it was simply a continuation of my desire and need for an exciting challenge. My mom became my biggest race fan. I had a poor way of thanking her. One Mother's Day she and my stepdad drove six hours to watch me race and I ended up in a seven bike pile-up on the first lap of the race. Fortunately,

I was one of the few who got up and walked away from the crash site, but my bike was a wrecked ball of metal. I walked back to the pits, where my mom, who had left the stands, was waiting for me. It was then and there that she asked me, 'Are you sure you don't want to take up checkers or chess?' But I wouldn't call myself your typical adrenaline junkie, as I don't engage in risky behavior for an adrenaline rush as much as for the thrill of overcoming a challenge.

During my teen years, I met a guy who was my first love, but he wanted me to quit riding and racing and the relationship soon ended. If it was the bike or the man, the bike easily won. I was thirty-three when I met the man who would become my husband. It wasn't until ten years later that I married Jamie; it was on a Monday evening. I chose that day so that my lucky numbers would be associated with our marriage. The date was 03/03/03. This helps a lot in remembering our anniversary each year!

I raced over ten years on many national and international race tracks on various brands of bikes and won many awards before I married. I achieved my dream of racing two of those years with racing income only. The other years I made a great living selling motorcycle parts and accessories. I continued my racing career until age thirty-two, when I faced a more immediate challenge: cancer of the thyroid. I recovered from the cancer, and the cure of the cancer, and began dirt-bike racing at the age of thirty-five as a form of rehabilitation. I always found off-road racing a great way to stay in shape, because it is so physically demanding and fun.

Because professional riding is addictive, as racers age, we have great difficulties in understanding what we will do with the rest of our lives. That's why some of us work in the motorcycle industry or stay on the race track too long, only to get horrifically injured. It has taken time, but with the help of my husband I have finally found a great pleasure in trail riding a dirt bike. An example of this was during a Michigan six-day dirt-bike event. The entrant is given maps of the course and left alone to ride at his/her own pace.

I was riding with my incredibly talented dirt-bike riding husband and at one point in the race we deviated from the set course. The course went by an American Indian casino, so Jamie said, 'Let's stop to do some gambling.' As long as we were back to the start line before dark and we didn't make the search party go out, we were within the rules of the event. Walking into the casino we thought that two grungy dirt-bike riders would be received less than enthusiastically. How wrong we were! When we sat down to stick a few quarters in a slot machine, a man came walking over to us and we thought, uh-oh, fun is over. But the man asked us if we wanted free drinks, instead of asking us to leave. We thought we had died and gone to dirt-bike heaven. We had a ball gambling and then got back onto the trail. It was just so relaxed and fun. I learned that there was life after road racing.

Due to my successful career as a professional racer, I have access to borrowing Yamaha street bikes for Jamie and me. My husband loves to take trips on road bikes. I tag along, but I can't say that I like riding on public roads a lot. The risks associated with road riding are less controllable than on the race track. Also, you can imagine how I feel crawling around roads rather than experiencing the exhilaration of wide-open throttle on a race track.

In 1992, my brother Blair and I started a dirt-bike school as a business venture. It went really well, but after four years and thousands of customers we decided to sell the business and move on. It is still in operation today. Now Jamie and I enjoy riding our Yamaha dirt bikes on the trails with friends, playing hockey together, and riding snowmobiles. We just bought a summer cottage so now we have added kayaking and fishing to our activities.

Over the years, I've been involved with quite a few motorcycle clubs, especially those involved with racing, but I haven't had much to do with outlaw motorcycle clubs. The one exception was at Daytona Bike Week in 1979, when I and two friends were hired by Harley-Davidson to be Harley's Angels; this was a takeoff of *Charlie's Angels*. Each year before the commencement parade, the outlaw clubs got together to decide who would lead the parade. We went with some employees from Harley-Davidson to the large camp area near Daytona the day before the parade. What I saw was amazing! There was an all-day 'boob contest' on the stage. The club members would take their ole ladies onto the stage handcuffed to their belts. The ladies' tops would then be lifted to bare their breasts.

The roar, or lack of roar, from the crowd determined the winner. I couldn't understand why the women would want to be treated in that manner. We were told by the campground owner that overnight there were stabbings and picnic table burnings and he recommended we leave before dark. This was not the kind of biker world I was familiar with, coming from racing. It was not the kind of biker world I wanted to be associated with. One of the outlaws, nicknamed 'Handle Bar,' took a special liking to me and gave me an American Indian arrow head he had found. He gave it to me as a good luck charm. That was as close as I got to them. We were eventually given permission by the clubs to lead the parade, which was an honor in their eyes.

My favorite sayings are 'The glass of water is half full,' and 'Try hard and never give up.' My heroes are my mom, because she was always there for me and encouraged me to be my own person; and single moms, because it takes so much courage to raise kids on your own. In the racing world, my hero has always been Jay Springsteen. He possessed such a natural talent on a bike, and he was always a gentleman on and off the track.

8

Reborn to Ride: Timeless, Ageless, and Fearsome

Barbara Joans (United States)

Something is out there and we who are part of it revel in its importance. We are women riders who know and respect each other. We ride many scoots and work in many jobs. We take many roles and we make our own rules. We ride different bikes but most of them are Harleys. We are not a great troupe of outlaw women. We are not the female Mafia. No one would wear a 'Property of' tattoo and we are most certainly not a motorcycle club. But here we are. We are bikers with breasts.

What a privilege. I have been extraordinarily lucky. I am included in this rollcall of riders and I know that no one speaks for us all. We each have our own voices and our own style. And we acknowledge one another across the block and across the land. Here's how I know we exist: every time I get information about a woman who rides, who is doing something in the world connected to riding, I put her name down in my Rolodex. My Rolodex of women who jam the wind has a staggering number of entries. I was a columnist for *Thunder Press* for fourteen years, an American Harley magazine, and I got letters, emails, and phone calls from women all over the world. I met easy riders, passionate passengers, timid trikers, hard-assed bikers, scared stiff passengers, Amazonian trikers, and rat-bike bums.

I will get a phone call requesting that I give a talk at this event or that event or that book signing. I meet women riders who are connected with the motorcycle world in their daily lives. They are bike builders and customizers, photographers, and lawyers, especially lawyers who deal with bikers in trouble. They are editors; Internet website producers; saloonkeepers, magazine and newspaper writers; book authors; bed and breakfast hosts; restaurant owners; and advanced rider course instructors. And there are motorcycle map producers, motorcycle racers, and traffic schoolteachers.

I am very lucky. I hear the most outrageous tales — the most wonderful, absolutely hysterical stories from all these women. The tales are so outlandish that if I did not know the women, I would not have believed it possible. But oh . . . they are true! I have seen many of them in action and, if anything, my retelling of the accounts are modest tales compared to the reality. Later, we share. The list is long. In each of the activities, the woman's main focus — her very life's blood — centers around motorcycles. It is not just that she rides — she spends her life and her living in relationship with bikes. Sooner or later, we get in touch.

As I keep saying, nothing in my earlier life could have predicted my romance with the motorcycle: a strong and unwavering bike lust. Most of my life has been spent poor — sometimes welfare poor, other times merely impoverished. Bikes could not have been further from my mind. In fact, if I thought of bikes at all, they were seen as smelly, loud, offensive, and expensive. I lived in East Coast city density. Not even cars were seen as riding options. I had urban concerns and political passions. I raised my children as Greenwich Village street urchins. They were the kids of hippie, radical, commune-living, counterculture, drug-crazed, beatnik, feminist, freaked-out, anthropological dropouts. The kids turned out great.

Throughout my radical, wandering revolutionary days, I studied anthropology. From the welfare lines, I wrote field notes. From the antiwar movement jails, I wrote field notes. From the feminist minefields, I wrote field notes. In the early seventies I got a letter from the City University of New York: it read 'return immediately or be dropped from the Ph.D. program.' That note found me stoned in the middle of an idyllic commune in the middle of Oregon. But I returned. Only a few things had been absolutely consistent in my life up till then. Anthropology is one. Motherhood is another. Unapologetic, unregenerate heterosexuality is a third. I have always been mated. That pretty much sums me up. Then I found bikes.

I started passengering really late in life. My kids were half grown and I had married for the second time. My husband had been riding bikes almost all his life. But ever since he returned from Vietnam it became a serious passion. Through a long, messy, busy, and moving life, his love of bikes remained. He loved Harleys but throughout our lean years could never afford more than a Honda.

Then we moved to California. Everything changed. We were both employed at the same time. We could buy some stuff. He wanted a Harley. For him it was the realization of a lifelong dream. For me, it was a totally new experience. Who knew it would become my obsession? Who knew I would fall in love with bikes? I was fifty-five when I first got on the back of a bike. It amazed me that I managed to passenger. True, Ken had provided a passenger seat that was as big as a barn and as sturdy as an oak. But still I was scared shitless. I was terrified. The movies make it look so easy. You just throw a leg over and away you go. Riding is as American as apple pie, baseball, and Norman Rockwell. The problem is that I am a New York Jew, reared in the streets of Manhattan and the side streets of Brooklyn. Being sedentary, sickly, utterly non-mechanical, and a lover of the great indoors, I was more suited to appreciate museums than motorcycles.

Nothing in my urban, indoor, East Coast experience prepared me for the godawfulness and the glory of riding a bike. When you ride, you are right out there in the middle of nature. You are jamming the wind. I would have preferred to jam the bread. On a bike when it rains, you get very wet. When the sun shines in a cloudless sky, you can swelter. Protection from the elements is so minimal that you make friends with the elements or you don't ride. Nothing in my entire past city life of college teaching, child rearing, short story writing, piano playing, and urban radical activism prepared me for the wonder of riding the wind.

Again, I got lucky. Ken had patience. I had my absolute, stubborn fanaticism. I refused to let my innate, unrelenting cowardice rule my life. I would learn to passenger. I was a slow learner. The first trip took me around the corner. After screaming in Ken's ear to slow down — we were going all of ten miles an hour (16 kilometers per hour) — he decided that one block of riding was enough of a start for us both. Each day we expanded the ride until, a month later, I could ride for half an hour, manage speeds up to 40 miles an hour (65 kilometers per hour), and scream less in his ears. Finally, after joining a local Harley Owners' Group, I was ready to rumble. So what if we rode in the back of the group, came in last every time, and I made enough noise to rouse the neighborhoods? We rode. I was astounded. I was proud of myself. I felt like the queen of the universe!

Then one day my old friend Phyllis called. 'What do you mean you are passengering?' she grumbled. 'Why are you not riding? I want to ride on the back of your bike. I want to be the girl on the back,' she said. What a concept! Could

I ride? The idea had never occurred to me. I saw riding as a young woman's province. Men rode. Girls rode. Women passengered. But I began to observe lots of riding women. So, I mused, why not? At fifty-six, with a lot of help from my friends, I took the beginner's riding course. I bought my first bike, a small, wonderful 250cc Honda Rebel and took to the roads. Actually, I took to the back roads, side streets and alleyways.

The day I passed my motorcycle riding test was one of the proudest days of my life. I remember grinning all the way home. It was right up there with earning a PhD, birthing two children, and marrying for love. I rode with great timidity. While my friends roared down the highways, I putt-putted my slow way home. But I rode. And slowly, the love of riding began to change my life. It was becoming not just an important activity, it started shaping my life. It was time for my Harley.

I bought a Sportster. The bike was bigger, heavier, and far more powerful than my Honda Rebel. A Harley 883 is no slouch of a bike. It is so formidable that it messes with the mind. All of a sudden, I could leap tall buildings in a single bound. When my bike growled, bucked, and kicked me off, I picked it up. Alone and trembling, I managed to haul my five hundred pound (230 kilogram) machine to its wheels. I rode it home and to this very day I do not know how I did it. I did not think about it — I just did it.

After two years of riding my Sporty, it came time to move up to the big twin. My FXD, all six hundred pounds (270 kilogram) of shiny 1340cc Low Rider, is all the bike I will ever need. It is black, of course, the only true color for a Harley. It is sleek, fast, lusty, powerful, and beautiful. It is all the things I would be in the flesh, if I could. It roars . . . it sets off every car alarm within three blocks. It purrs and prances and preens. It sets me free.

And thus began my life as a biker. No, I did not participate in the Iron Butt endurance runs. No, I did not ride with grace, nor speed, nor panache. But I rode. And while only a few friends were willing to ride as slowly as I needed to, there was always someone who would take pity on my husband and ride with us. While he must have gotten tired of always having to ride alongside of me with my slow, plodding ways, he never complained. We did go on HOG runs and while I always came in minutes, sometimes hours, after everyone else, Ken always rode beside me and it worked. My gratitude for his patience and endurance took the form of encouraging him to ride alone with his buddies every chance he got.

Then came the stories. As an anthropologist, I could not resist writing about Harley life. I took care to rarely write about outlaw motorcycle clubs. My writing focused upon the people I rode with and most specifically upon women. Everyone knew what I was doing, gave their heads-up approval, and told me more stories than I had space or wit to absorb. Some events helped. My book, *Bike Lust: Harleys, Women and American Society*, was published to the great approval of my riding community. Writing a monthly column for *Thunder Press* cemented my reputation. Invitations to appear on radio and TV shows, and at readings came in. Women began to use my column to air their views, gripes, pleasures, and problems with male bikers. We had fun. Men as well as women contributed their opinions in the pages of my newspaper column.

I've got a million biker stories, but I want to end with the one that shows that even close women riding friends can have seriously divergent views. My friend Jayne and I had our first fight. I would say we are riding buddies, but she never has the patience to ride as slowly as I need to, so our friendship rarely takes place on the road. I was visiting at her home the other day and she was showing off her latest acquisition. She opened her closet and there hung an absolutely beautiful, full length Canadian lynx fur coat. It was golden and white and full furred and gorgeous.

Apparently a group of biker clients got her the coat in lieu of legal fees. They are very successful bikers and it seemed like a more than fair exchange. I, however, am a member of an animal rights group. I do feel guilty around other animal rights folks because I am still a carnivore and wear leather. Nevertheless, I think that they do good work. But here was my very good friend Jayne parading around in a magnificent fur coat. So I asked her the typically asked question: 'Do you know how many animals had to die to make that coat?' At that point, she turned around to me and in her most humorous manner, looked me square in the face and answered, 'Do you know how many men I had to fuck to get this coat?'

Stalemate . . .

Jayne and I share a number of similar views even though animal rights is not one of them. We are both in love with bikes. I, however, am older and know more of the problems connected with age and riding. As we age we lose some of our faculties. We maintain some of the important ones, but none of them will push us back into youthful agility. Sensuality and sexual pleasures remain, but sometimes have to be coaxed into full life. My bike lets me ride the wind. No, my bike entices me to take in the pleasures of the ride. My bike reminds me that life at any age can be exciting and adventuresome. The spirit does not age. When I ride I am timeless, ageless, and fearsome.

9

Romance, Passion and a Dream Called Hellga

Amy White (United States)

Rather than ramble on about my childhood, which was fairly typical for a girl growing up in Arkansas, I will just cut to the chase and start with the first huge milestone year in my life, which was 1994 — I became a mother to a precious baby boy, Benjamin, whose red hair and big blue eyes still are like looking in a mirror of my childhood. From nearly his first breath he forged a bond with my father, his namesake of sorts; they are still an inseparable pair of 'Bens.' Benjamin still lives there to watch out for my parents every day. He's a great kid.

I also became the wife of a wild-tempered, hell-raising, beer-drinking little redneck named Steve White, who was twelve years and one day older than me at twenty. He had a cute little butt and gorgeous curly hair, and I stood nearly a half a foot taller than him. In a whirlwind relationship of two months that consisted of beautiful shiny new Peterbilt trucks, with long noses and huge sleepers and chicken lights; the huge chrome wheels gleaming in the moonlight as they made their way tearing up speed limits and forging log books from coast to coast. His off hours he sped around in a sexy little Datsun 280 ZX. I didn't have a chance. I became his wife on Labor Day weekend, barefoot beneath my wedding dress so I wouldn't tower over him in the pictures, and trying desperately to hide my first tattoo from my mother. Neither one worked.

One of my favorite stories about Steve is actually our honeymoon. We were on our way back to Monticello the day after we got married, and had had quite a bit to drink. I later learned that this was a common occurrence for Steve . . . having quite a bit to drink, that is. A girl that I had recently become some resemblance of friends with called us to see if she could catch a ride into town, and so we picked her up. She was drunker than a boiled owl, too, and the three of us piled into the fast little two-seater and headed for Monticello. During the ride down the black highway, something possessed her to flash her boobs at my husband of about twenty-six hours. So I hit her right in the face. Hard! Then Steve says something and I, sitting straddled on the console, punched him in the face, too. He flips that car over and over in this deep ass ditch; it rolled three times and landed on four flat tires.

When I got my bearings, Steve was spittin', cussin', and shiftin' gears. He made it a quarter of a mile down that ditch before the cops showed up. This is a very reminiscent view of my marriage to Steve. I quickly learned that alcohol didn't impress me all that much, but that Steve lived for it much as a fish lives for water. That proved, eventually, to be the demise of a rip roaring, gut wrenching, fist-fighting, good ol' redneck marriage. We probably were doomed from the start, because I would always come second to the vaporous vixens who lived in flasks and bottles. But damn, it was pretty fun while it lasted!

In all honesty, I have to admit to myself that I really don't remember much about the exact moments when I first met Bo. In self-defence, though, I hasten to offer, when you are married to a good ol' redneck, you meet so very many marginally different persons whom he refers to as friends, but in actuality are merely acquaintances or drinking buddies, or some such trivial being that it is humanly impossible to remember them all. In fact, the never-ending parade of strange and differing personalities who stopped by to visit or spend a moment or two in conversation in assorted parking lots and restaurants begins to become a bit of a blur. The only ones who truly emblazon themselves into your memory at first meeting are the ones who spill beer on your carpet, are argumentative and disagree with you, or end up in a drunken brawl in the front yard. How strange are the workings of our minds. We can only clearly recall the faces of people we pray we will never have to lay eyes on again.

I do vaguely remember being introduced to Steve's friend Bo in the local Wal-Mart parking lot, but at the time he was of no particular consequence, as he was not belligerent or obnoxious. The brief meeting emblazoned on my mind one piece of powerful information, though, and that is why I remember this meeting. He mentioned the new Harley-Davidson he was on his way to pick up. This led to Steve badgering me for several hours concerning him wanting a motorcycle — again! Steve had at that time nagged me for a motorcycle for the entire five years we had been married. In retrospect, I believe that he also may have mentioned where Bo lived, and a few other bits and pieces of trivia about Bo. However, as time has passed, I can't be absolutely certain as to exactly what was said that night. Somehow I was aware of who Bo was throughout his vague friendship with my husband. He had a tall John Wayne body and Sean Connery good looks, a fifty-four-year-old man with a four foot ponytail. I really had no interest in him or his motorcycle whatsoever at the time, and am fairly certain I tuned out the thought of him after only a few moments.

Some obscure corner of my overcrowded mind reminds me that Bo came by the house to visit on his new Harley. I am fairly certain of it, in fact, and perhaps he came by to visit a few other times as well. But he never made a definite impression on me until he came by the shop that Saturday to get the hinges fixed on his pickup truck's door. That day I remember bits and pieces of our conversation and my feelings with an astounding clarity. I do remember that I wasn't going to charge him for fixing the door, being a friend of my husband and a relatively simple repair, but he insisted on paying for the parts.

He ducked into my office as I made him out a repair slip. He seemed to loom so tall in the tiny office . . . and when he talked to me he looked me right in the eye . . . very cordial . . . and almost intimately. He had this great sexy deep voice, repeatedly called me 'good lookin'' with a deep soft drawl, and smelled so damned good I had trouble filling out the paperwork. I also remember discussing the pay for the door and when I refused to let him pay for the labor, he offhandedly said, 'Well, ya'll come on over to the house tonight and I will take you riding on my bike then. We can all ride to the Crawdad Festival.' He tipped his straw hat and headed out the door.

I stared for a moment in wide-eyed shock. Steve was in the office at the time and then, of course, after Bo had departed, I began to vehemently refuse to accept Bo's offer. Well, Steve put a much expanded guilt trip on me, all about how I couldn't insult his friend. So finally, reluctantly, I agreed to go. I also remember after everyone left the office, I opened the drawer and took out the check he had written me for the parts and looked at it for several long minutes. I didn't really know why, and to this day I still don't. Some sort of premonition perhaps.

By the time the evening arrived, I was a nervous wreck, terrified of getting on this mammoth monster of a motorcycle with this man who was basically a stranger to me. When we arrived at the house, a white frame house surrounded by seven dogs and sitting up on a hill out on the edge of Seven Devils swamp, I noticed the big blue beast was sitting on the front porch. It was a brand spanking new Road King Classic, dressed with all the extras. I had to admit that it was a beautiful machine; the chrome sparkling like so many rivers of diamonds, and the cobalt blue paint shimmering in proud elegance. Everything in my mind sort of faded in comparison to this awesome piece of machinery. I walked over to it and ran my finger down the cold smooth metal of the gas tank. But I was still scared to death.

Tentatively I watched as Bo tied a bandanna around his head. I insisted that he give me a helmet to wear. We agreed that it would be best to get off the gravel road he lived on before I got on with him. I almost changed my mind as we followed him up to the highway in our pickup truck — the thudding rumble from the giant motorcycle making conversation impossible. I was totally afraid as I threw my leg over the back seat. And, as there was nothing to lean against, I had to hang on to Bo, which felt almost embarrassingly intimate for some reason. I just knew I was going to slide off the back of that shiny blue fender onto the pavement. As the engine roared to life again, this time beneath me, I hung on to Bo for dear life. Thinking back, I don't know how he could even breathe as I clutched him so tightly. And God was he sexy and big in my arms compared to my five-foot-five spitfire of a husband. Jeez, what was I thinking?

As we eased out onto the highway he said, 'Relax, I've been riding these longer than you have been alive.' The bike growled a little bit louder each time he shifted gears, and I relaxed a bit more with each shifting. I distinctly remember the smell of Bo's cologne mingling with the scent of a late spring afternoon. The wind whipping my face felt strange, but nice, and the rumble beneath me seemed to have a strange calming effect on me. When we stopped in McGhee about fifteen minutes later, I took the helmet off and put it in his saddlebag. We stopped at a Kentucky Fried Chicken, next to another huge dressed-out Harley. This one was turquoise and creamy white. As Steve eased up behind us in the pickup, another big tough looking leather clad man with a long grey beard winked at Bo, held out his hand to me and said, 'My name's Horace, but everybody calls me Harley.' That night was ten years ago. This was the meeting of the two men who have probably changed my life more irrevocably than anybody or anything ever has. Not long after that night one became my lover. As of that night they both became my best friends.

•

I have to admit I was quite a nervous wreck the two weeks I spent preparing for this unexpected and exceptionally unusual vacation. Finally loading up on the back of a motorcycle with a man I hardly knew and striking out on an iron horsed sojourn towards Gulfport, Mississippi, which is about 600 miles (960 kilometers) away. The fact that my husband and Horace were going as well seemed insignificant. And I seem to recall hearing the first of many speeches alluding to my safety and intelligence from my mother. Ah, well, that is life, I suppose: your mother never stops reminding you to wear clean underwear, don't run with scissors, and don't ride motorcycles.

I was a rookie in the deepest sense of the word. I had neither a clue as to what sort of weekend it would turn out to be, nor did I perceive the sheer velocity of the impact it was about to make on my life. I was in total oblivion to the fact that my mind, heart, and soul were about to be ravished . . . a certain part of me taken and forsaken with the heady feeling of freedom. Some part of me had already succumbed to the road, unveiling a new-found innocence and excitement in a mind that had become jaded long ago in the past. I can honestly admit that I fell deeply in love with that big beautiful Road King from the very second I felt its Milwaukee heartbeat thud between my legs in perfect time, and the first feeling of the wind in my face. I just had no idea of what lay ahead of me.

We loaded all of our things into the trailer behind Horace's bike, and the four of us loaded up on the two motorcycles. Steve crawled up behind Horace and popped a top on a beer at 7 am. I took what was to become my customary place behind Bo. The day was amazing, wonderful, awful, and unforgettable. We passed through summer rain storms, ungodly heat, and miles of open highway on our way to the Gulfport All Harley Memorial Day Drags. Since my first trip to Gulfport in 1999, I made this pilgrimage every year afterwards in sweet remembrance. The laughter, camaraderie, and sheer enjoyment of that day are unforgettable.

I was crying silent tears of pain by the time we reached our motel in Slidell from both my horrid female problems — I would have a hysterectomy later that year — and inexperience on the motorcycle. Bo's comforting hand on my left thigh as he flew down the interstate was a wonderful comfort when I wondered if I would make it just one more mile. Only looking back now do I realize how, from that very first trip, I became calmed by the rumbling symphony beneath me, lulled by the constant pull of wind against my entire body, thrilled with the pulsating heat beating my skin, the way my body naturally molded to Bo's back, and his scent lingering on me even as I closed the door to my motel room.

The weekend was something I never even dreamed existed. We entered a gate into another world of campers, naked girls, and Confederate flags waving a greeting. The dust blew up to linger on the gleaming chrome of thousands upon thousands of motorcycles. I felt myself shiver in excitement as I got my virgin taste of what to me now is my way of life — a melting pot of leather and beer, naked bodies, and vendors upon vendors, the ground quivering beneath my feet to the combined song of thousands of Milwaukee heartbeats. Loud music thudded, scores of men in Bandido vests hovered everywhere, and the scream of the drag bikes tore through the distance.

Steve being Steve promptly dragged Horace away in search of beer and naked girls to photograph. Bo and I spent the entire day sitting on the tailgate of a truck. I have never laughed so hard, saw so much, or had so much fun even in my wildest dreams. Steve and Horace would drift by to visit with us, but we were content to sit and watch the crowd. Probably the highlight of the day was when Steve hid behind a row of porta-potties nearby, lying in wait for girls to go in. He would wait a few moments for them to drop their drawers, giggling like a schoolboy peeking up the teacher's dress, then shake the holy hell out of the potty and roll with laughter when the girls screamed or ran out trying to get dressed. It all ended abruptly when he shook the wrong toilet and a big ol' corn fed woman that looked like a white Muhammad Ali with tits, tats, and three teeth came barreling out and chased him all over the place. By that evening, Steve was drunker than a boiled owl, and settled himself happily in the motel room with a twelve pack of beer and a humongous bag of boiled crawdads. Horace, Bo, and I decided to go across the road and eat a steak. The waitress who took care of us flirted with Horace and referred to me as Bo's wife throughout the meal. He never corrected her.

Of course, the ride home was horrendous on my body, sore and sunburned as it already was. I napped behind Bo most of the way home. He held me on the bike behind him with his left arm around my thigh every time he slowed to a stop. I was wide awake watching the familiar scenery as we came out of Lake Village and headed for the last stretch towards home. I was crying again now that our final destination was at hand, but for a reason that I couldn't even fathom myself. Bo mistook it that I was hurting again, and patted my leg. I was mortified that I was crying and didn't know why. I think it was because my first biker rally was over.

From that weekend on, Steve and I got together with Bo and Horace every weekend. Steve and I bought a neat little Honda 400 Custom that was a few years old but with practically no miles on it. Our lives began to revolve around roaming the two-laned roads of the Arkansas Delta every chance we got. The night air weighed heavily with the scent of endless fields of cotton or tomatoes . . . the wind cooling just enough in the valleys to warrant a jacket, the deep rumble of the motorcycles cutting through the stillness. And without really realizing it, I fell head over heels, predictably, with Bo and his Road King, and how his way of life made me feel so beautiful, so wonderful . . . so alive!

By the end of fall, Steve and I had bought a 1987 Harley Sportster 883. My physical problems required me to have a hysterectomy in late October; I had one son, and I was just twenty-five years old. The first face I saw when I woke up in the hospital was that of Bo. Boy, had I fallen hard, and Lord I didn't know what to do about it. I strongly suspected he felt the same way, and Steve's drinking had gotten nearly to the point that I couldn't take it anymore.

Ten days after my hysterectomy, David Allan Coe was playing in Princeton, Arkansas, about two hours from where we lived. I was not going to miss seeing him, no matter what. We all loaded up and headed to the concert. I still had staples in my belly from the surgery, propped up with a pillow on the back of the Road King. The concert was absolutely amazing!

When the concert was over, it was so cold outside we had to wipe frost off the windshields of the bikes. We made it to Warren and stopped to warm up in a parking lot. Bo kept picking on me to a point where I got aggravated and declared I was riding the rest of the way home behind Steve.

I piled up on the Sportster and ducked my head down with my hands behind Steve to try to keep warm with my breath. We pulled out on the highway and took the formation that we all rode together for nearly seven years: Horace in the front, Steve and I in the middle, and Bo taking up the rear. For some reason still unbeknown to all of us to this day, Bo downshifted that big old Road King and came blowing by us snorting his pipes at us. A moment later I heard the alarming sound of screeching brakes and then metal scraping pavement. Steve hit the brakes hard to bring us to a stop. I was hanging on tight, my head pressed against Steve's shoulder. I couldn't bring myself to raise my head and look to see who went down. I whispered, 'Which one was it?' Steve pulled off his helmet and told me it was Bo.

I felt my insides short-circuit and I thought I was going to throw up. I finally forced myself to look up and there was a doe deer as big as me lying dead on the other side of the road; the last sparks off the upside down Road King disappearing over the edge of the ditch. Horace's brake lights illuminated Bo's body, which was stretched across the highway, his head nearly touching our front wheel. I rolled off our bike onto my hands and knees, tears already streaming down my face, and crawled towards Bo while Steve started trying to flag down cars. The first three cars passed us and sped away. I picked Bo's head up in my lap and started trying to get him to talk to me. His eyes opened and he stammered, 'Is Amy okay?' A car finally pulled to a stop as my tears splashed on his forehead and I coughed out that I was fine. I kept begging him to talk to me; he finally opened his eyes again and looked up at me and said, 'Is my scooter okay?' I glanced toward the edge of the highway where his wrecked bike lay covered in deer shit. I said, 'We can fix it, darlin'. We can fix it.'

The rest was a bit of a blur . . . I was so worried and I felt like we were in a vacuum. A policeman, who failed to find any alcohol on our breath no matter how hard he sniffed, threatened to write Bo a ticket for failure to maintain control of the vehicle. I couldn't believe my ears. I strapped myself in the front seat of the ambulance to ride with Bo to the hospital while Horace and Steve took care of the bike. At the hospital, I perched myself on a crappy little stool as close as I could get to the door they had carried Bo through, clutching his billfold in my cold, shaking hands. I was so frightened that he was hurt bad. All of a sudden I heard a tiny clanging sound, like someone beating on a metal bed pan. Then suddenly I heard Bo's voice booming on the other side of the door: 'I said I'm ridin' home, dammit!' Boy that was a good sound to hear. When all was said and done, he survived the encounter with the deer showing only a scrape on his forehead, both knees, and both elbows. I told him afterwards that his angel must have been riding with us. He replied, 'No, yours was.'

My sanity was questioned again the day an ugly pile of angle-iron, wood, and cannibalized Volkswagen and Kawasaki parts was dragged into my yard. I thought it was absolutely beautiful. My husband and all his bros thought I was nuts — all except for William, the tall, quiet man who had given me this 'trike.' He had built her himself, even ridden it a few times, but the lack of weight on the front end, and the difficulty of combining just the right parts, as well as the temptation of his comfortable Goldwing were just enough to earn her a seat in the secluded bug graveyard beyond his house. He had originally pictured a strangely cute truck used on *The Beverly Hillbillies* television show, hence the wooden moldings around her entire body. I immediately pictured Herman Munster riding such a machine.

I have to admit that my husband was amazing — he didn't laugh with everyone else. He listened to my endless diatribes of ideas, sometimes nodding and murmuring in agreement, or perhaps shaking his head and trying to hide the look of bewilderment in his eyes. Of course, he'd weathered the storm before. He had endured the countless attacks of my paint gun and imagination I applied to his Sportster and various trailers, tanks, and fenders. He was used to it, but I don't think he understood the fire of passion and compassion that flared within me for this forlorn creature with vines knotted through forks, stained with paint and tree sap. I had fallen in love, possessed wholly by this ugly pile of bed rails and rust.

I immediately began my research, poring through websites and magazines for inspiration. I couldn't find it. There was nothing that caught my eye — nothing that looked like me. William probably answered a million questions about VW parts, torsion bars, and motorcycles in general. Most of the time he'd laugh and shake his head, but answered the best he could.

One Sunday, Steve and I rode into town for a late breakfast and happened upon a distant friend who was rebuilding a Yamaha. Amidst our discussion, he mentioned having this rare Italian frame with a cool front end for a trike. We stopped by his house that afternoon to check it out and he came out of the house smiling, holding a beat-up old shoebox. 'There's something I've gotta show ya'll,' he said as he took the lid off the box. Inside there was a tiny model of a wooden c-cab trike, with tiny lanterns, and iron cross mirrors and tail-lights, and a long, sleek, twisted chrome front end with huge rockers. He tried to give me the model, swearing it had been in his closet for years, but I couldn't take it. I didn't need it. I could already see my scooter taking shape. That afternoon, we brought her to my dad's shop, and prayed he didn't faint from laughter the next morning. I knew if anyone could help me build what I could see, Daddy could.

For all the people who wonder why in the world I chose body work, the answer is simple: because my dad did. I grew up as his shadow, his constant companion as soon as I could walk. I've been told he bragged of how I could tell a Ford, Chevy, or Dodge truck apart before I was three. I have been trained as a nurse and dental assistant, but the scent of paint and the cool softness of freshly sanded primer lured me back to the shop, and soon coaxed my husband in as well. Daddy always let me believe I could do anything I set my mind to. My mom was always there with encouragement, too. But I know she would have preferred batons or pom-poms to airplanes, Chevy trucks, and mopeds. I respect my mom, because I know I drove her crazy — still do, for that matter. I mean, really . . . motorcycles?

Well, Dad did laugh like hell when he saw my latest project. Then he mentioned a metal heart-shaped shelf he knew that someone was throwing out, and how it might be nice to have some pieces of curved metal bars. It wasn't long before my project was parked right in the middle of the shop, and he was sitting there staring and frowning, occasionally asking me to measure this or that. He never actually told me what to do; he just offered suggestions or ideas. Sometimes I would tell him what I wanted something to look like, and he would tell me what I needed to achieve it. I must've put 2000 miles (3200 kilometres) on our truck as I ran around to three different metal shops, a boat plant, and countless stores and lumber companies digging for steel rivets instead of aluminium, sheet metal that would be lightweight but sturdy against the vibration . . . so many little things. Steve went home every night for a month with welder burnt eyes. It was about this time I named the trike 'Hellga.'

I still was having problems with that rusted-up Kawasaki front end; the only salvation came in the form of a funky set of twisted chrome ape hangers. I began digging for a piece of Harley; after a half a dozen inquiries to people who either didn't have one or wanted an ungodly price, I finally found something I could afford. I can still see RD smiling at my plight, then telling me he had three I could choose from for one hundred dollars. We left the shop that evening at around 6 pm, and it was already dusk. The air was cold and damp. An hour later, RD turned on the porch light of his shop to see us in. The first front end was probably from a raked Panhead — decent, but not what I was looking for. I asked him if he had one with rockers. 'If you don't mind diggin' for it,' he replied, 'I've got just what you want.'

RD grabbed a flashlight and headed out the back door. Over the fence, ignoring the sleet and the mud, we dug around and a huge piece of metal became visible through the pine straw and vines. I stared at the long, rusty, twisted bars and curving rockers. All of the bolts looked like tiny steeples, and the triple tree was still attached to a scarred, mutilated piece of frame. I looked up at RD and told him it was the ugliest thing I'd ever seen. Then I started pulling the weeds away and motioned for Steve to help me pick it up.

Three months, a lot of pinto beans and sleepless nights later, she was pieced together and starting to look like the trike of my dreams. The meadow green twisted bars reached like winding fingers through the gold rockers, and the deck plate floor boards reflected the chrome skull on the shifter. I'd lost 35 pounds (16 kilograms) and had permanent saddlebags under my eyes, but I was mesmerized by what she was going to be. Shiny Maltese Cross mirrors and tail-lights waited expectantly in boxes. The Camaro wheels, fat tires, and mud flaps gleamed brighter than the gold letters that read 'AMY.' She just needed to be painted.

When I heard about the Easyriders Bike Show in Memphis, I became obsessed with being there. Hellga was still primered forty-eight hours before the show, and I still had three or four insurance jobs that needed my attention in the shop. I almost gave up. But when I looked out the front door that cold Thursday night and saw all of our bros and sisters standing there in ragged clothes with pizza and beer, tears welled up in my eyes as I realized we were gonna make it. After four more hours of body work, around midnight, I began painting the rest of the meadow green metallic and gloss black. At 3.30 am, I set down my paint gun, and looked up at my mom standing in the door of the paint booth in her nightgown and house shoes shaking her head, but grudgingly admitting it was absolutely beautiful. We were gonna make it. I think I fell in bed for an hour or two; morning came early and I dragged myself to my feet for I had cars to paint.

From four that afternoon till about 3 am on Saturday morning, we wired up the lights, added the brass lanterns, four-foot-long fringe on the grips, stereo, and interior pieces, which I cut out and upholstered by hand. We pushed her out of the shop and up on the icy trailer. I stood there, cold, tired, and dirty, and stared at the life size version of RD's model. We had four and a half hours to pack and make the 200 mile (320 kilometer) trip to Memphis. Well, we made it, and I looked down and laughed at the green paint staining my nose and hands.

The state of exhaustion I was in was taking its toll. I could not remember my name for a fleeting moment as I signed my trike in. Once we were registered, we rolled Hellga's sleek long frame into the appointed exhibition spot, which, to my glee, was a prime spot on the corner of a long aisle dressed in some of the world's most beautiful choppers. The huge, drafty, exhibit building was for a moment transformed into

1970s B movie museum, complete with red-braided ropes and strategically placed beautiful lights and mirrors.

I glanced at the clock, and saw I had actually made it . . . fifteen minutes late, but I was there. The aches in my body throbbed in incessant rhyme and my lungs ratcheted with the need to grasp oxygen through the layers of metallic green, and twelve layers of 'clear coat' I had subjected them to not fifteen hours before. My legs shook with the effort to hold up my frame, and the bottoms of my feet beat a cadence in my nasty, cheap, work boots. I felt a tap on my shoulder, and turned to find a man that must have had to reach up to touch me that far up my body. He wore a neatly trimmed goatee and a slick bald head, and his eyes gleamed in quick wit as he inspected the clipboard in his hand. He wore a t-shirt with the word STAFF embroidered over the pocket and was consumed by an air of self-importance.

'What did you say you made this out of again?' he asked in a fast, clipped accent I struggled to follow. I sighed, and again went through the prolific details of the 1969 Bug I had mutilated and the 1945 Harley chopper I had dragged out of the weeds to get that long gorgeous twisted front end. Recapping the back-breaking hours of labor made my body hurt all the more. 'And you really built this all by yourself?' he asked again.

I knew the hair that stuck out in a ratted ponytail from my green tinged baseball cap was clear coated slick. I knew that two thin lines of dark green still smudged my upper lip beneath my dark green nostrils. The jeans I wore were filthy and still had tiny pieces of gold pinstripe stuck to them, as did my ragged thermal shirt. I looked at my hands covered in paint and dried blood. The tiniest little bit of sanity I still possessed must have deserted me in my exhaustion. I drew a deep, painful, paint-scented breath, then straightened to my full six feet and turned to look down at this man full in the face, thinking for a fleeting instant that I must be fatigued to the point of needing hospitalization to not even notice how cute this little stocky guy was . . . and a bald head and goatee at that. God, I needed sleep or a doctor. But I was incensed that he had questioned the fact that I breathed life into this amazing machine, nearly killing myself in the process.

I affected my best southern drawl and bitchy look, and said, 'Look, darlin', do you like tote speakers or dump trash cans or what? Cuz I am a little fuckin' busy here.' He looked up at me with dark eyes that gleamed with devilish humor and then offered me a wicked smile I'll never forget. He held out his nice clean hand to shake my filthy one, and said, 'Good to meet you, Amy. I'm Kim Peterson, editor of *In the Wind*, and assistant editor to *Easyriders* magazine.'

•

For nearly a decade now, my life has consisted of rumbling chrome dragons that breathe hot exhaust, which is a sweeter scent than any flower, for it also carries the scent of freedom, wind, laughter, tears, and memories. Thousands of these amazing memories flood my brain as I try to choose the words that best describe my life as a biker. Perhaps the best way to describe it is through a conversation I recently had with the man I now live with. When he was first contemplating learning to ride with me, he said, 'I guess you will always be a biker's girl.' I answered, 'No, honey, I will always be a biker.'

Throughout the bittersweet years, I have been through four Harleys, a few men, a billion Camels, a million miles, a river of tears, a good bit of whiskey, and a lifetime of highways. Four and a half of these years I spent weeping pathetic tears, for my body finally rebelled against all that paint I breathed, and I became stricken with all manner of autoimmune disorders such as lupus. Through lots of steroids and other type of treatments, I haunted the years that I wasn't able to ride, mournfully admiring the fact that I made it to Sturgis and back to Arkansas as my last real ride. Recently, new developments in treatments, including chemo-type pills, have helped me a lot, and I now am able to ride with Bob on our 2008 Electra Glide for short distances. In an effort not to overstay my welcome shown with the privilege to grace these pages, I must leave you with this excerpt of my return to the leather clad world that I call home, and promise to share more of my stories with ya'll another time.

10

Brotherhood . . . What Brotherhood?

Jane Benson (United States)

I was born in 1955. I am happily married, a doting grand-mother, and live the life I do because I choose to. I was very fortunate growing up with a mother who gave her all in making sure my younger brother and I had a good education and plenty of adventure in our lives. Land and realty being the business our family was involved in, it allowed my mother to take us to explore the different cultures and areas within the United States and Mexico — a much better education than being stationary in one state forever, experience was a 'wonder.'

The early years of my upbringing had nothing to do with me being involved with or looking for the bad boy per se. After being married several times — first to my high school lover, because I wanted to defy my mother's expectations; second to a man from another culture; and third an extremely rich but very boring man — I decided it was time to grow up. As I got older, and my children grew, I learned what I wanted out of life. After being single again, and trying to act as such, I went to a party at a friend's and I saw him, the man I knew I wanted to meet. Because I couldn't keep my eyes off of him a girl screamed out to me, 'He's mine! Quit checking him out!' So I thought it would be best to leave, as I didn't want to cause a scene.

One year later, the same man went to see the girlfriend who had held the party and asked her about me. He wanted to know if I was still single, which I was. Next thing I knew, he was at my doorstep on a very cold night riding his bike; he knocked on my door and asked if I remembered him. 'Um, yeah, I remember you alright,' I stammered. 'Come on in and take a load off.' Well, he came into my home and into my life and never left. We now have five children and nine grandchildren — between the two of us, that is — and have been married eight years. We have been through hell with the 'club' thing and our love and relationship not only survived, it is still very strong. The night he came over he handed me his resume as we sat in front of the fireplace, and that totally amazed me. This was not a job resume, but a personal resume and his expectations of what he wanted out of life and expected from his partner for life. I'm sure glad I never kicked him out that night!

I learned he was on parole for a lengthy period of time for a previous crime . . . drinking being his downfall, but he assured me he had that under control, because he wanted to make something good out of the rest of his life. He soon exposed me to the biker lifestyle, as he was a member of the Wino's Crew Motorcycle Club. This was a great experience for me. I found the members very interesting and exciting to be around: the club was very aggressive and adventurous. In the Wino's Crew, no 'Property of' patches were worn by the women. This was because the founder and president of the club said he did not want such a 'target' riding on the back of one of his brother's bikes.

My immersion into the biker world led me to obtaining my first tattoo, at age forty-five. My man had many talents, one being an accomplished tattoo artist. The tattoo he gave me, which is located on my upper arm near my shoulder, is of a Playboy Bunny with a fiery sunset background. I soon got my second tattoo on my other arm and have been adding to my body art collection ever since.

In the 1980s, the authorities ran the Bandidos Motorcycle Club out of Fort Worth, Texas. This was due to the violent rivalry between the Ghost Riders Motorcycle Club and the Bandidos, which attracted a lot of media attention and subsequent pressure on the authorities to do something about the situation. The cops told the then current Bandidos and Ghost Riders to never come back. The Ghost Riders left and the Bandidos disbanded, sort of; they had every intention of starting up a new chapter again in Fort Worth, before the Hells Angels got a chance to take over what they considered their territory. In the very early 2000s the Bandidos created what is called a 'probationary chapter,' re-establishing the Fort Worth chapter. This new chapter was comprised of five probationary members from the Wino's Crew and five probationary members of a rival club called the Rebel Riders Motorcycle Club, which was based outside the city in farmland country. There was no love lost between the two clubs. In essence, the Rebel Riders were an insignificant club in Fort Worth. The Wino's Crew and Booze Fighters were 'it' in the metropolis.

This presented the first problem trying to create a brother-hood of Bandidos from a group of bikers who didn't get along in the first place. Asking the two groups, who had a history of animosity between them, to call each other brother was like expecting to stick a square peg into a round hole. It didn't take a rocket scientist to figure out where all this was going to lead. The probationary time to become a fully fledged member of the Bandidos was the usual 'hard yards,' which translates into one year. At the end of the probate period, there were only two left from the five original Wino's Crew and three of the original Rebel Riders; my man was one of those left standing.

During this time, I was concerned for my biker man, as he was still on parole and held down a daytime job as a welder. He had been clean from using drugs and alcohol since I had known him and I didn't want to see him return to his old ways. One particular incident that made me uneasy was when he was called upon to join a few brothers on a long road trip. I was worried about him possibly getting into meth in order to make the many miles and hours required for the trip. Thankfully he didn't fall off the wagon and he arrived back home after three days. It was during these years of trial that my biker man said to me, 'I can only be as strong as you are!' Those words would come back to haunt me in the not-too-distant future.

Having completed his probationary period — my man was now vice president of his local chapter — and me having somewhat settled into life as a Bandidos' ole lady, we decided to get married. The marriage ceremony was held in the fall of 2001. It was a fabulous Bandidos wedding, held in downtown Fort Worth on the rooftop of our favorite hangout. Everything was done up in red and gold, which are the colors of the Bandidos. We were surrounded by friends and family and we were on top of the world . . . so we thought.

I was working in auto financing for Mercedes Benz, but still had plenty of time to travel with my husband to many places. We visited other chapters within the Bandidos Nation and met new and exciting people. We were truly enjoying our new extended family and the adventures that came our way. My husband was an 'old school' type who believed in the meaning of true brotherhood. But, alas, our chapter back home was fuming and growing jealous of everything we did, from being free to come and go as we pleased, having the money to do so (because we both worked), to mixing extensively with other members of the Bandidos Nation.

The local chapter looked upon my husband's activities with other chapters and other clubs with extreme envy and the plotting began. According to his constantly quarrelsome chapter brothers he was acting 'without approval.' Soon my husband, and me along with him, began suffering the consequences of internal club politics. His office position was stripped from him as a disciplinary action, just for being the man he was. My husband had become well known throughout the greater Bandidos Nation, and none of the members in the other chapters agreed with how he was being treated. Still, because one chapter can't interfere in another chapter's business, there was nothing they could do about it. In an attempt to make the situation better, my husband wrote a poem trying to get members back to the basics of what 'brotherhood' was truly all about. He penned the following lines . . .

What is True Brotherhood?

The Beginning . . . In the beginning, someone was there for each of us. We were taught . . . and learned . . . how to love, understand, and help each other. No matter how long it takes we still do it. Some take longer than others and some are more experienced than others. The human nature is to look out for only 'you.' Well, my Brothers, we are our Brothers' keepers. If we don't do it, who will? There was a beginning for each and every one of us, no exceptions. In time we all grew as one, to become Brothers, a true loving, understanding, and helping 'Brotherhood.' We can never forget our own true beginnings because each and every one of us has their own story. A true 'Brother' will always look, listen, love, help, and understand one another. True 'Brotherhood' takes more than one or two to hold tight. It takes each and every one of us at ALL times.

Love . . . A true and strong heart for each other, through thick and thin, is Love. To have the ability to forgive and forget mistakes made in life and move on to the important things is Love. To have non-faltering feelings and thoughts for each other's feelings and thoughts is Love and to stand strong together.

Understanding . . . The ability to understand, really understand a person's thoughts or feelings. To be able to understand that we are all human and humans make mistakes. Have ability to be able to help, listen, look at, smile, and understand that we are different. Sometimes others need more understanding and to close our eyes and minds to a Brother that we don't understand . . . is being blind.

Helping . . . To be able to help, you must love and understand. Listening to one another's viewpoints, feelings, and differences is helping. Helping a Brother, mentally or physically, to grow with, to love, to listen, and understand is true 'Brotherhood.' Teaching and laughing with one another is helping. A true Brother will understand, love, and help. Everyone is different and to help a Brother become a true and strong Brother is 'Brotherhood.'

With Love to All My Brothers,
Love . . . Loyalty . . . Respect.

The animosity and jealousy my husband was subjected to filtered, needless to say, down to me. I trusted my husband and our relationship was built on love and mutual respect. Most other ole ladies seemed to just do what they were told, not having an opinion or being able to express their true feelings. That doesn't mean that I didn't meet a lot of good ladies in the club; women I considered my friends and sisters, and still do. These were the ones I had something in common with, like good jobs, good husbands, and a good home life. One such friend and mentor once told me to 'just flutter like a butterfly, smile and say nothing, and as quickly as you can, make that final escape back to reality and away from it all. That will keep you out of trouble.'

By 2003, my husband tried to avoid as much contact as possible with his chapter and we traveled to other chapters for companionship. In June 2004, my husband, who was still on parole, received a call from his parole officer. This kind woman warned my husband that he had been 'snitched out' and that he had about two hours to rid our home of any Bandidos paraphernalia or evidence of other associations with outlaw motorcycle clubs. According to the parole officer the Gang Task Force was going to raid our home and my husband would be sent back to prison for a parole violation if they found proof he was a member of the Bandidos.

My husband was faced with two choices: get rid of everything and leave the club, or go back to prison for life. He was at the time working as a foreman for a major construction company; I still worked for Mercedes Benz . . . and we had our family to take into consideration. Our whole world had been turned upside down. My husband had stayed on the straight and narrow with no record of anything illegal since he had served his time in prison; now, it seemed his only indiscretion was his biker lifestyle and love of motorcycles. We knew what we had to do and made a mad dash to pack up all our Bandidos clothing, paraphernalia including pictures and jewelry, and stashed them in boxes which we then hid in another location.

One thing proved to be a bit of a problem. For my husband's wedding gift, I had a picture of the Bandidos 'Fat Mexican' etched into our glass breakfast nook table top, which was very difficult to hide and/or transport, so I covered it in black lightning bolt contact paper. For a long time no one who visited us knew the difference. They thought it was just a regular tabletop we had bought, not knowing what was underneath it, including some of our club friends who still visited us incognito. When we finally decided to give the table to a brother we considered worthy of owning it, he couldn't believe his eyes when we removed the contact paper in front of him to reveal the etching. He was amazed and proud to own it.

We were to discover later that someone from the brotherhood had taken it upon himself to inform the State of Texas Parole Board that my husband was involved in a motorcycle gang, which could be construed as a breach of parole. Technically, my husband's parole conditions included a clause that he couldn't associate with any Aryan Brotherhood organizations. It didn't state, however, that he could not be involved with motorcycle clubs. To circumvent this little glitch, his parole officer was told by the powers that be to scratch out Aryan Brotherhood on the parole conditions document. Not having any choice the hapless parole officer did what she was told and handwrote 'Bandidos Motorcycle Gang' onto the document. In a show of some kind of defiance, she only initialed the change instead of signing her full name as she was required to.

Once we learned we had been betrayed we decided to hit the road for a while, no longer knowing what to expect from the local chapter or who we could trust. We stayed on the road visiting friends in other areas of Texas and out of state, trying to make sense of it all. At the end of that period, we returned to Fort Worth, but it no longer seemed like home. That same day I asked my husband if he wanted to leave town for good, and start a new life somewhere else. His reply was an unequivocal yes.

We retrieved the boxes containing the Bandidos paraphernalia and sent them to the club's state president in Austin; this signified that my husband was now officially out of the club. Next, we packed up our belongings and moved across the country. We were still emotionally drained from the experience, but feeling very relieved to be away from it all. I accepted a job opportunity in our new state, which came knocking just at the right time in our lives, not unlike that night my man had come knocking on my door. In the following year, we heard from many other Bandidos who also suffered from internal club politics; one member was actually shot and killed by one of his own brothers. Some were forced out of the club and deemed 'out in bad standings,' others were asked to leave and deemed 'out in good standings.'

Once in our new home my husband lapsed into depression in response to the loss of club life, which had been so important to him. He crawled back into a bottle and that's when I saw a side of him I had not seen before . . . and he was a nasty drunk at that. He acted violently and we went through some truly dark times. He was busted in early 2006 for Driving While Ability Impaired. He was waiting at a stoplight and simply fell over, intoxicated on pills and booze. That was the straw that broke the camel's back and he knew he had to get it back together or lose everything. In a way it was a blessing in disguise.

This was the time that his words from a few years earlier about him being only as strong as me really took on their full meaning. I knew I had to be the backbone for both of us and with my encouragement, love, and support he started to crawl back out of the bottle and began to clean up his act. In March of that year, I told him that I wanted to buy a motorcycle. 'That way, we can ride side by side. I can be your brother, your lover, and your best friend,' I said. But being the old school guy he was, he just laughed, believing that women belonged on the back of the bike behind their man. But me being who I am, I just laughed, too, and went out to buy a used 2005 Harley-Davidson Sportster 1200. I wasn't just a biker's woman anymore, I was now a woman biker.

Well, it all worked out just fine. My husband came to terms with his demons and he is no longer depressed and dark. We are still deeply in love, enjoying the freedom of the Rocky Mountain roads together, with me riding next to him and not behind him. And that is a good thing. Sharing those scenic Rocky Mountain roads, on the same path with the man I love, has taught us that we can be happy without the club scene . . . we have lived and we have learned. As for brotherhood . . . well, it starts at home. In some cases you find it outside your home, in some cases it bites you on the ass.

My take on our former local chapter and the club scene in general can only be described as one of amazing contradictions, one where derogatory name calling, bitching, snitching, and infighting more often than not can raise its ugly head. It's sad in a way, because when the club scene was good for us it was really good . . . it's too bad it was ruined by a bunch of small-minded people who, unfortunately, are found in all walks of life, not just in motorcycle clubs.

My favorite ride or most awesome ride was a trip from Oklahoma, where we were visiting friends. The then president of Bandidos Canada was there, too. We all traveled to Angel Fire, New Mexico . . . the ride was magical. I know 'magical' is such a cliché but there is no better way to describe it. I believe I became a stronger person as a result of that trip, which somehow managed to touch a chord deep within me, providing an understanding about the importance of my own identity as a biker's woman and a sister to my many sisters.

Oh, yeah, to find my hero . . . I have to look no further than home, he is my husband.

11

Used, Abused, and Confused

Katie Cole (United States)

I'm attempting to type this with my hand in a cast, thanks to the truck that rear-ended me while I was riding my motorcycle yesterday. After all of the miles through all of the years it was bound to happen some day.

I grew up in an affluent New England family, spending my summers at the country club, the yacht club, or summer camp. If you've ever been to an AA speaker meeting, you've heard my story: I never felt like I belonged. Sometime during one of those upper crust summers, I saw my first Harley-Davidson and knew that was my destiny. Even with extreme hindsight, it's hard to say whether it was the bad boy lifestyle that Harleys represented back then, or if my attraction was purely to two wheels and wicked-cool graphics on a gas tank. I do know that my father was very critical of me, which was something my brothers picked up on. I was constantly berated and was often upset, which then caused me to be criticized for being so sensitive. I longed to be tough.

I dated bikers in my teens, some club affiliated, some plain old dirt bags. When my parents insisted I go to college, I chose Daytona Beach; not for the school, of course, but for the biker culture. I frequented the Boot Hill Saloon and hooked up with a biker here and a biker there. What I really wanted was my own motorcycle. One night I met this guy at a bar and my future as a biker chick jumped into high gear. I won't be busting any stereotypes here.

I'm going to give the condensed version of my first marriage. I made a deal to trade my almost new Camaro for a chopped Sportster and a Shovelhead. I moved to Atlanta and then to northern Georgia with my boyfriend Jimmy to open a bike shop. I fooled myself into thinking that we owned the bike shop and he was a drug dealer on the side, but it was really the other way around. The bike shop was a front. Despite that reality, we did try to create a successful business, but keep in mind we were living in some of the deepest backwoods, redneck, hillbilly country in the south. Not a lot of bikers. Also, this was back at the start of the eighties, when Harley riders were not well-liked or accepted people. The locals constantly tried to find ways to get rid of us.

Life was a combination of visiting with the few people that did come to the shop, parties, small trips, and swap meets. It was drilled into my head that if anyone was ever busted, you didn't say a word. We drank and did a lot of drugs. Like I said, I'm not going to blow away any stereotypes here. Jimmy was not affiliated with a club, but he did some business with the local outlaw motorcycle club from time to time . . . very limited. I have no idea what the deals were, just that we'd visit a clubhouse or have some interaction at swap meets. Being a woman, I didn't have any real information there; for all I knew it could have been all about bike parts.

Jimmy was a talker. He seemed very light-hearted and joked a lot and knew just about everyone. He could talk anybody into anything. He was the king of robbing Peter to pay Paul. He'd manage to get someone to front him some drugs with the promise that he'd pay them back in some specified amount of time. He'd sell them, use that money to buy something else, sell that, use that money to buy something else, ad nauseum.

It was a never-ending cycle that always ended up with a short somewhere, and Jimmy having to smooth things over.

Throughout the relationship I'd have a bike, but it would always get sold. They never really were my bikes. They were bikes that Jimmy would buy or we'd build and then soon after completion it was gone. I never did see the Shovelhead I was promised, and the Sportster was sold early on. The Camaro had been turned over to a drug dealer who wanted his money . . . money that Jimmy had already spent.

One Thanksgiving when I was twenty years old, we had some friends over and were about to sit down for dinner. Federal agents arrived and arrested Jimmy. They had me go down to the shop and open it up so they could confiscate his motorcycle, which wasn't in the yard at the house. A local cop verified that the only bikes there belonged to locals and not Jimmy. I went back to the house, and with the help of a couple of friends, tore apart Jimmy's Panhead, which was sitting on the back porch, and had one of the friends take it in his van to Jimmy's brother's house in Atlanta.

Jimmy got out of jail shortly afterwards; we knew we couldn't continue to pretend we had a business in the mountains and moved to Athens, Georgia. We also knew that someone needed a legitimate job, and I started stripping. That worked out well: a modest, uptight, white girl from a rich Connecticut family not only dancing, but taking her clothes off in front of a bunch of strangers. Alcohol helped, and I soon settled into the groove. While there was a lot more business at the new shop we had opened in Athens, which I was financing, I was much less involved in the day-to-day operations. I often didn't know whose bikes were there and had no idea about the deals Jimmy was making.

I found out what he was really doing, while he was going to court for the charges he faced from his arrest on Thanksgiving. We went through a legal proceeding, with Jimmy maintaining his innocence. Then we went into an office to talk to one of the federal law enforcement agents. No sooner had we sat down, than Jimmy started giving names. I was horrified and sick to my stomach and walked out. It must not have been at that point, but shortly after, he was given his sentence and went to federal prison; I guess the snitching didn't help.

I had planned on sticking around and keeping the shop. A friend of ours was staying there and could do the mechanic work while I continued to make up the difference with my stripper pay. I soon found out what kind of deals Jimmy was making while I was working. Several not-so-friendly people showed up wanting their money. I certainly didn't have it. Sure, if I could have paid them off with a night's worth of tips, I'd have done it. Not so simple. One couple, who'd been growing some damn good pot in North Carolina and got busted by the Feds, had given him all that they'd salvaged and wanted $15,000 from me. That was one of those deals where he'd traded the pot for something else, then sold that to a guy on a front. It turned out that the buyer was a federal agent who'd been taping all their dealings. Clearly there was no money coming from that source.

Salvation came at the strip club. One night a group of bikers from a small local club came by with a man I knew as a 1%er. His name was Buck. He had just buried his wife in South Carolina and had a very young son back in Atlanta staying with his in-laws. Perhaps we both saw an opportunity. Buck stuck around. We rode the bike, stuffing the saddle bags with tequila and tacos by day, and I went to the strip club at night. It worked out well for me, because nobody was going to bother me with Buck around. His reputation was not for his good nature. Eventually, Buck went back to Atlanta while I continued to run the shop during the day and dance at night. I got into trouble at the strip club when a cop was harassing me and I threw an ashtray at his head like a frisbee.

He ducked . . . I got fired! My stay in Athens was history; I shut down the shop, and moved to Atlanta with Buck.

Buck had lived in Chattanooga, but when his son was born with a heart defect, he and his wife moved to Atlanta to be close to her parents and the children's hospital. He soon had to leave the club and get a real job with health insurance to provide for his son's healthcare. Buck and his wife had bought a house in the suburbs; this would become my new home. It wasn't easy moving right into a house whose female occupant had so recently died. All her clothes were still in the closet; her pictures lined the walls. The day after I moved in, I was told that everything that had been mine was now his. If I ever wanted to leave, it was without all of my antique furniture that had been in my family for years; not a good sign.

One evening I left for work in the pickup truck and stopped to get gas. This was long before the days of pay at the pump, and I went inside to pay. When I came out, the bag with most of my stripper costumes had been stolen. I went straight home, very upset. I came in the door and slammed it, starting to tell Buck what had happened. The next thing I knew I was down on the ground, and he started kicking me. Apparently I was not to bang his stuff around. Okay, point taken. About a week into the living arrangement, I was wondering just how badly I'd screwed up. Unfortunately, I couldn't possibly get out of there without the furniture so I was stuck. The damned furniture kept me hostage for a long time. I tried to make the best of it. Buck hadn't worked since his wife died. I was again providing the support by dancing, once all the bruises healed up. My original dream of owning a Harley couldn't have been further away.

Buck received a nice chunk of cash from an insurance policy on his wife, and proceeded to start blowing it. We always had plenty of alcohol and pot, but the money was disappearing like water down a drain. We had talked about buying some property in the country, and ended up purchasing almost 30 acres (12 hectares) on the top of a mountain about an hour's drive north of Atlanta. Although the deed mentioned a right-of-way for utilities, the power company decided it wasn't good enough and refused to provide us with electricity.

Somewhere in this time period, Buck's mother died. She had been a snake-handling, speaking-in-tongues Pentecostal who didn't believe in modern medicine. She had diabetes and was blind. Her condition eventually killed her and Buck lost it — seriously lost it! Some thought it was because he'd so recently lost his wife. I think there was a lot of crazy shit that happened when he was growing up and it all came back to him. He was extremely paranoid and believed there were demons everywhere and in everyone. This man was dangerous when he was sane; insane he was very scary! Complete with a loaded twelve-gauge shotgun in the rifle rack in the rear window of our pickup truck, we took off on a jaunt through Georgia, North Carolina, Tennessee, and back to Georgia.

These were the craziest and most terrifying couple of days in my life. Well, by that time anyway. He was hunting demons and trying to find all the people who were the source of evil in his world. Late one night in Cherokee, North Carolina, Buck slammed on the brakes on a back road. He got out of the truck and returned with a toy tomahawk. He told me this was to be our protection against the demons for the rest of the trip. Later that day, or the next evening, while driving down this back road that starts in North Carolina, does about a mile in Tennessee, and then ends up in Georgia, I got frustrated and hacked at the door with the tomahawk. The head broke off in the process and went flying out the window. Suddenly I was the 'enemy,' for I had destroyed our only defence. Yeah, it was that crazy. At some point the ride ended, and to my surprise, nobody had been killed.

Before too long, the money was depleted, and we were living on top of a mountain in a 10-foot (3-meter) by 20-foot (6-meter) shed without electricity or running water. Buck was still having the delusions. I can't remember how we were eating or buying gas, but at least we were able to haul water up the side of the mountain from a small spring. On my birthday, Buck decided I needed to have a baby and went about successfully fulfilling that desire. So there I was, pregnant, living with a dangerous lunatic, nobody working, and no electricity or water. We also had the added benefit of two killer pitbulls, courtesy of one of Buck's brothers who didn't live in a place where he could keep them.

I had been in touch with my parents somewhat, and they wanted to help without actually giving me money. I don't blame them. I'd made enough really crappy decisions by then. They did help me with finances to attend junior college, which was within walking distance of our mountain 'retreat.' Buck said he'd work to pay for the doctor's bills that we knew would come with the birth of our child. I walked my pregnant self to school every day while Buck occasionally worked for a friend of ours building concrete walls. It was a dirty and hard job and Buck couldn't be bothered to work more than one or two days a week.

At one point, Buck decided to sell this chrome transmission of mine to make a payment to the obstetrician. Off he went to Rome to make the sale and came back with a pound of weed. We were harboring one of his brothers, who was trying not to be found; I was never told that he was on the run. I don't remember what they told me as to why he was there, but he was there hanging out at the compound and sharing what little food we had.

After that, Buck decided to go to Atlanta and work in his field. He was actually a very smart guy, and was well respected in the land surveying community as long as he could hide the fact that he thought everyone was trying to kill him. The psychosis was still there, but had become less obvious on a day-to-day basis. Although he was working while he was down there, he was also living at the home of two women who were not very trustworthy. There was a lot of partying of all kinds going on, and I often got to hear about this girl Froggie, who liked to ride with my husband when he was down there.

While the father of my baby was down in Atlanta having the time of his life, I was still walking back and forth to school and buying groceries with WIC (Women, Infants and Children) nutrition coupons and eating government cheese. One evening I came home from school to find one of the pitbulls loose. I managed to get in the house, but when I had to leave to pee (remember, no running water), I took the shotgun and killed the dog. It's really very upsetting to be pregnant, living in the woods while your man is out screwing other women, and then being forced to shoot a dog. Another one of the highlights of my pregnancy was when I got stung by a scorpion in bed. To this day, when I see happily pregnant women, it upsets me.

There were many other 'fun' incidents throughout the pregnancy. Buck came back to live at home and attempted to work setting up forms for concrete walls again. We had no transportation other than the Panhead, and that's how I was expected to be transported to Atlanta when it was time to have the baby. I wasn't sure how we were going to get home. I can't imagine they'd have let a baby out of the hospital on a motorcycle in December. Two weeks before my son was born, we managed to get a van. I'm glad, because there was no way I would have made it to town on the back of that rigid frame Panhead while in labor.

My son was healthy and incredibly good looking. His father wanted nothing to do with him. He loved him and bragged about him, but he never did anything for the child. When I say he didn't change a diaper, I don't mean that he didn't change them in the middle of the night or after work — he *never* changed a diaper. He never fed the baby or gave him a bath. Back when Buck had been hanging out with Froggie, she had asked him if he knew the baby was his. He told her 'you never know.' He actually told me this, as though it was funny or something I would appreciate. I didn't mind that he never did a thing for the baby, because as far as I was concerned, when he said that about my baby, he was no longer the father. We did get married exactly nine months after the baby's birth, but I only did that so I could have the same last name as my son.

Time went on ... I graduated with my associate's degree about the same time a couple built a log cabin between us and an existing electricity connection. That gave us the easement we needed to get power ourselves, and I secured the loans, hired the subcontractors, and got a septic tank and a well. After more than three years without utilities, we not only had electricity and running water, but a telephone as well. I was working in Atlanta; I think Buck was working in Cartersville at that time. Later, he ended up at a surveying outfit not far from the gun manufacturer, where I was working.

It was Super Bowl Sunday, and we were very broke, but our friends insisted we come over for their party. We told them we wouldn't be able to contribute beer or anything else, but they continued to insist. We got over there and were treated like dogs. Any time one of us grabbed a beer, we were reminded that we didn't bring any. Food was the same way. I'm not sure if this treatment was planned, but it sucked! We left very angry. It triggered a psychotic episode for Buck that went on for months. I constantly had to convince him not to kill them. He told me they poisoned the well, and that's why the pump had to be replaced. I reminded him it got struck by lightning. He didn't buy it; for him two plus two did not add up to four.

One day after work, a co-worker called me to ask if I was okay. I couldn't understand why, because I was fine. When I got to work the next morning, I was called to the conference room, where there were several cops. It seems that Buck had come in the night before, when he came to pick me up, and told one of the executives that his secretary had drugged me and I'd been raped by six guys. I was horrified! They were worried about me, but I convinced them I wasn't in danger. I called a friend for help, and when Buck showed up that afternoon, with a loaded gun hanging from the rifle rack, we talked him into a trip to the psychiatric hospital down the road. Apparently he'd just left work where he'd beaten and hospitalized a guy he had accused of raping me; I've never seen the guy in my life.

After less than a week in the psych ward, the hospital was concerned that his insurance wasn't going to pay and they sent him home. I was terrified. One night we spent the entire night in the bathroom, with his loaded handgun at my head because he thought I was evil. He believed I had been hypnotized at a young age to 'drop to my knees' when someone said the magic word. Yeah, I know your question: What's the magic word? I finally realized that if I wanted to live through the night I needed to agree with him. I said I'd get counseling and we'd work it out. As soon as I was able, I grabbed my son and left for New York — without the damned furniture. I heard about the loss of our family antiques from my parents for a long time. Maybe they didn't know my life was on the line; maybe the furniture was more important to them than I was.

I never saw Buck again. After I got to New York, I got a job, and set out to successfully raise my son. I determined that I didn't need to be drinking anymore and sobered up. I went back to school fulltime, lived off student loans, earned my bachelor degree, and got an engineering job with a large telecommunications company upon graduation. After a couple of years, I transferred to New Hampshire and bought a log cabin on a lake. In June of 2001, I was expecting a call from the Harley-Davidson dealership telling me that my Softail Standard had arrived. Instead, to my unpleasant surprise, the call was from Buck's niece. My heart started pounding! She proceeded to tell me that Buck had been found dead in a storage unit in Chattanooga. Then I got the call about my Harley. It was the best day of my life.

It was nice that the nightmares stopped; my PTSD (post-traumatic stress disorder) symptoms disappeared overnight. I finally had a motorcycle that nobody could take away from me. I rode and I rode and I rode. The first year I logged over 11,000 miles (17,700 kilometers) riding New Hampshire's scenic and winding roads. The day before my bike's seventh birthday, which was the day I got rear-ended, the odometer hit 73,000 miles (117,500 kilometers). I know now that riding a motorcycle is where I belong.

I've dated a little and I've been engaged twice. I find being in a relationship is difficult after having been involved with someone like Buck. A lot of guys seem soft. I know better than to get involved with a bad boy, but how do you find a guy who's tough enough and who will treat you as an equal partner? As long as I have my motorcycle, that's okay.

Section IV
Conclusion

12

What It Is About Motorcycles and Bad Boy Bikers That Attracts Women?

When we first set out on our journey to define the attraction of women to bad boys and big motorcycles we thought that we would be scrounging for reasons with a few themes and a plenitude of stories from appropriate women. How wrong we were! Due to our familiarity with the rider scene, we knew that the existing works had identified a few reasons (which we call themes), and we were likely to find a few more. In fact, we were to find a very wide diversity of reasons or themes which we never could have dreamed we would find.

Furthermore, we expected to find two relatively autonomous groups which would be quite separate with little room for 'grey' areas. We believed that one group would be attracted to motorcycles and the other attracted to outlaw bikers. What we learned, however, was that we were unable to find a clear division between the two groups. Instead, we found a scale where women riders sit at one end of the spectrum with bikers' women who passenger only at the opposite end. To make matters even more complex, outlaw motorcycle club culture has evolved over time as have women bikers and their host cultures. Despite these complexities, we were able to identify many factors which characterize the attractions.

In Chapter 2 we reviewed the existing documentation and literature to develop and provide the dominant stereotype of women who are attracted to members of outlaw motorcycle clubs as opposed to those women riders who shun these clubs. We identified four reasons which were and still are widely regarded as experiences and childhood/family practices which typified a woman rider or passenger associated with outlaw motorcycle clubs. As stated in that chapter, these so-called predictive factors require evidence that the stereotype propagated by mass media sources and heavily supported by both law enforcement (for budgetary purposes) and politicians (for fodder in politics of fear campaigns) is true. These predictive factors were women being raised in lower-class families, coming from dysfunctional families, possessing character deficits or mental health disorders, and being school dropouts and obtaining low grade education.

In light of our women's stories told in Sections II and III, it is clear that these factors certainly do not characterise the vast majority of our women. The myth is well and truly busted. The stereotype is bullshit. It depends upon one's political views to some extent, but the stereotype is simply not supported by the reality. The reasons for the stereotype seem to be politically motivated as stated above.

Be they outlaw club affiliated or not, many women riders did report the presence of four early childhood experiences: a childhood they describe as adventurous — lots of outdoor activities encouraged by parents and family; being an only child; having a motorcycle rider in the family, including brothers, uncles, aunts, grandfathers, and grandmothers; and being more comfortable in the presence of men or being regarded as a bit of a tomboy.

In Chapter 2, we described what the magic of motorcycles was in relation to women's attraction to them. The attraction seems to be comprised of the following qualities or properties of the motorcycle itself: it is variously a symbol of rebellion, non-conformity, and individualism; a device which provides the woman with a sense of freedom; a means to adventure; a device which elicits a sexy feeling in the woman rider; and, finally, a guaranteed adrenaline high in the woman from the risks encountered by riding.

Most proposed reasons given in the existing literature to explain why biker chicks choose to ride, and why some are attracted to bad boy bikers, were supported by the women's interviews. But we found eleven other themes which are not reported in the literature, some of which were highly salient. So let's now turn our attention to what we find when the themes suggested in the literature are analysed in light of the collected interview information.

Some women ride primarily to express aspects of rebelliousness. In the southeastern United States, especially, women indicate that their number one reason for riding a motorcycle is to express rejection of mainstream repression by a sexist and oppressive male-dominated culture. The Chrome Divas' Tallahassee chapter has many such women present in their ranks as do other ladies' clubs and mixed gender clubs like HOG located in more conservative regions of nations globally.

The theme of riding as rebellion is also expressed by several women who specifically mention that their actions to become accepted into the world of the outlaw motorcycle clubs and/or ride was a statement of rebellion made to their parents. Roxy, for example, states 'I was attracted to bad boys because I guess that is how I wanted to live. A non-conforming lifestyle and it annoyed my parents!'

Another example is Lizzie, who came from an oppressive family environment. She recalled her family as being strict to the point of suffocation. Her graduation from high school at eighteen meant little to her, except she was now able to try to escape from the family environment. Having lived in such a family environment, it was predictable that she would rebel against her family values at the first opportunity. She started to dabble in recreational drugs, especially speed, and hooked up with a bad boy outlaw biker.

When we interviewed Sam, she described herself as a teenager who:

> didn't like high school at all. I was always keen to be out experiencing new thrills. I found school to be boring and a real drag. I describe myself as an independent and rebellious teenager who had an insatiable desire to know how everything works and to experience life at its fullest. My parents were pretty straitlaced and I soon learned the art of living a hidden life of my own while appearing to be a good girl.

Chuff related her story of growing up as:

> at sixteen I took up with the president of an outlaw bike club. I was quite naïve, but it was exciting for a sixteen-year-old. You must understand that I was a difficult teenager. My parents couldn't do anything with me. They had high hopes for me as I was a championship highland dancer, but I was so strong-minded and I was having fun and wouldn't take any advice from them at the time.

Indeed, most of the women interviewed considered themselves to be the black sheep of their families. Val stated that 'I am a black sheep in my family. In some ways I think this is part of why women are attracted to bad boys. Black sheep flock together.'

Yet another variation on this theme is a group of women who ride primarily to demonstrate that the spirit of the old south is alive and well in the United States of America. Dixie may have lost the war, but the Confederacy (known colloquially as Rebels) from the time of the United States Civil War generated a mentality that spawned those who refused to be ruled (such as William 'Billy the Kid' Bonner) as unquestionable folk heroes. For these women their primary reason for riding is to make sure the spirit of Billy the Kid and other Rebels is not forgotten. The Rebel flag is also a visual icon which, if you live anywhere in the western world, you will have seen. Old Dixie may have been beaten, but their descendants seem to proudly remember the valiant efforts of the American South to stand up to a massively stronger and better resourced North.

In Australia, a similar folk hero serves as an icon of resistance to a brutal system. Authority unjustly applied seems to be a major factor in the mentality of those who have suffered from the unjust power's sanctions and actions. While there was (unfortunately, many Australians would say) no actual war to gain independence from Britain, there were insurgency icons (rebels) attempting to achieve and organize themselves to that end. Perhaps the best known of these 'bushrangers' (as Australians call them) was Ned Kelly and his gang. Kelly is the Australian equivalent of William Bonner or Jesse James in the United States. Like the Confederate flag of America, the flag of resistance to the established order in Australia was designed by a few Yankees during the Gold Rush years after Kelly was executed. The contest for rule was simply called the Eureka Stockade and the resistance was crushed in a brief but very intense battle. The flag of the miners who rebelled is a hugely popular icon of resistance to authority unjustly applied. Similarly to their American counterparts, members of Australia's biker culture sport many tattoos of Ned Kelly and the Eureka Flag, reflecting rebellion against both positional and civil authority.

For club women, there is yet another twist in the rebellion aspect. Being a club woman allows her to express rejection of 'straight' society by virtue of her association with the club. Some lead dual lives, keeping their affiliation unknown to the outside world. However, on the runs, her expression of freedom and rebellion is full-on. Still others (some of whom did not give us permission to use their stories) fully adopt the trappings, symbols, and displays of being a full-on biker, like one woman whose club name is 'Ornery' (a nickname which we were to learn was not inappropriately given to her). Rockie is another example of these women. We conclude that there is incontrovertible evidence that this is one clear theme derived from the literature which accurately defines a central reason for women to ride or passenger with bad boy bikers as well as for some women riders who shun any contact with these clubs.

Rejection of mainstream society is a clear bridge or theme which manifests itself in unpredictable ways. Many of the women associates of club members are jealous of outlaw motorcycle club members' ability to be part of a visible counterculture to mainstream society. 'Why should the men have all the fun?' was a comment expressed by Wendy, one of our interviewees. Also, being defined as a bad girl biker babe or hardcore biker chick comes with an instant identity of rejection by middle-class mainstream society in every region where we gathered accounts.

Boredom and notoriety were other reasons why, according to the literature, women were said to be attracted to bad boys. Several women provided some insight into this, one of them commenting:

> Women come to the clubhouse in search of a walk on the wild side. They would often be in the scene for one night for any-way-you-want-it sex, drugs, and a chance to associate with the

bad boys. I call these women 'toys for the boys.' These women's straight lifestyles were solidly middle class and they were holding down good jobs. Many are married with young children and husbands and would simply return to their homes. Apparently they kept their night-out activities secret from all.

Red provided us with a similar story: 'There are those women that just come by for a night of debauchery. They are college girls and middle-class women who come down to try and live the scene, with no knowledge about the scene.'

Lizzie says she liked being a display on the back of Tiny's motorcycle and by his side during club events. Sherry noted: 'I happily got my "Property of" patch. I liked the patch because it defined me. And, like the bike and tattoos, it defined me as something very special to the world. I wore the patch everywhere I could.' Clearly the never dull life of a clubhouse has a certain appeal for both short term women (toys for the boys) and much longer lasting relationships as exemplified by Sherry and Lizzie.

Love of Motorcycles — especially Harley-Davidson

Literature sources also suggested that women are attracted to motorcycles simply due to their love of motorcycles, especially Harley-Davidson models. Of course, this theme permeates through all women riders' stories. Wildfire commented: 'The camaraderie and freedom of the motorcycle is what I love about the machine and the lifestyle.' Linda, a Harley riding grandmother, reinforces this as she says about her bike '. . . it is a chance to have something big and hard and throbbing between your legs.'

Some women choose to associate with outlaw bikers because they worship the Harley-Davidson motorcycle. Much like the men, they are attracted to the freedom which the motorcycle symbolizes. Other women grew up around motorcycles and they truly loved them. Chuff told us that 'My heroes are my dad and my brother Charlie. Both are bikers. From the time I was a kid, I was brought up amongst bikers, mainly enduro and off-road bikers. It's all about the memories and the experiences, getting out and enjoying the world, and what better way to do it than on a motorcycle.'

Motorcycles are exciting and thrilling and they sexually turn some of the women on. In Hooper and Moore's *Women in Outlaw Motorcycle Gangs*, Cathy explained:

Motorcycles have always turned me on. There is nothing like feeling the wind on your titties. Nothing is as exciting as riding a motorcycle. You feel free as the wind . . . If you don't ride a Hog, you don't ride nothing. I wouldn't be seen on a rice burner [Japanese model].

In the same book, Pamela commented:

I can't remember when I first saw one. It seems like I dreamed about them even when I was a kid. It's hard to describe why I like bikes. But I know this for sure. The sound a motorcycle makes is really exciting. It turns me on, no joke. I mean really! I feel great when I'm on one. There is no past, no future, and no trouble. I wish I could ride and never get off.

Motorcycle riding appears to attract many women due to the sense of sisterhood and belonging which riding in any collective of women riders provides. This literature-suggested finding is clearly evident in our women's stories. For women attracted to the outlaw club scene, these factors are particularly important reasons for their attraction to their men. The protocols vary enormously between clubs, eras and nations, but the women get the same thing from the club scene as their men. Men truly love the feelings of brotherhood while their partners truly love the feelings of sisterhood. Both men and women associated with the outlaw club scene highly regard the feeling of belonging to a huge extended family.

Wendy commented: 'I am attracted to the bad boy bikers because of the strength and power of the club, and I feel safe and at home as a biker's woman. I think that is the key to understanding women's attraction to bad boy bikers.'

There appears to be a great diversity of opinion, however, about the value of sisterhood and belonging evident in the case studies. For some of the women, the sisterhood is an attraction and for others it is not. One of the women we interviewed, who lived seven years with a member of an outlaw club, describes the difference between what she characterizes as ladies and strippers:

> Ladies tended to dress and act like 'straights.' They led dual lives. They held mainstream jobs and/or were devoted mothers. They tended to be well educated, were very well mannered and presented themselves as strong and independent women. At the same time, they lived as a partner of an outlaw club man. Few if any of the ladies used drugs, drank alcohol, or partied hard with the club. The way they presented themselves meant they were not harassed in any way by the men of the club and were deeply respected and well regarded. Strippers had no apparent interests in life other than the club and their man who belonged to the brotherhood of the club. Strippers were co-dependent, meaning that they were completely reliant on their men to make even the smallest decisions about their lives.

Some women attach themselves to outlaw bikers because they crave a feeling of belonging. One of the Australian women we spoke with calls herself a 'bikie slut.' Shockingly, she left her husband, children, and grandchildren, and moved interstate to be near the outlaw motorcycle club she liked to hang with. She reported that she could not explain it, but she was 'simply, overwhelmingly, attracted to the outlaw motorcycle club' and had literally given up her life to be with the club. The club gave her a cause and a meaning in life and she felt like she was a part of something.

With respect to sisterhood and camaraderie, one clear theme appropriate to women associated with outlaw clubs is the 'Property of' patches and/or belts, and in this regard clubs vary greatly in their treatment of women. Each club has its own protocols for women wearing the 'Property of' patch. Some women wear the property patch if the club they are associated with allows them to wear it out of the presence of the member they are involved with. They do not wear the patch when their men change clubs whose protocols prohibit the wearing of the patch out of the sight of the club member.

Two motives or reasons are given by women who do display the 'Property of' patch. The first is that the patch allows the women to circulate freely at various biker events and open events where the general public, usually intoxicated men, attempt to 'hit' on them. It provides protection and several outlaw club women refer to this in their accounts. The second is that section of the ole ladies who are hardcore biker chicks who seek the same response from the public as the men. The 'Property of' patch provides these women with the ability to make this statement via fashion. On the other hand, the majority of women associates of outlaw motorcycle clubs simply refuse to wear any patch, as don't they consider themselves to be the property of anyone.

On the whole, women associated with the clubs can be characterized as being more subservient than the average woman of today. Women who cannot deal with the required protocols of clubs, or who are too 'pushy' or 'outspoken,' run into difficulties fitting into the sisterhood and club scene. Holly 'Throttle' French suggested to us that the hardcore biker chick elements of the clubs need 'strong men like club members to keep them in line.' Whilst subservience is the 'handle,' it appears that 'man controls the woman' is a widespread belief held by the women of this subculture or section of the ole ladies. Loretta, a biker's woman, filled in the blanks for us:

Women of the outlaw motorcycle clubs still walk in the shadow of their men. They are women who simply do what their men tell them to do or leave the scene. But biker chicks now have their own clubs to ride with. However, like every other motorcycle club, your presence and patch has to be approved by the dominant club in the region. In this case, it's the Hells Angels.

The availability of banned substances has been suggested as another explanation for women associating with outlaw bikers: that is, drug use and abuse. Some of the women attach themselves to outlaw bikers because they have plunged recklessly into a netherworld of alcohol and drugs. In the clubs, there are plenty of drugs and drug-fuelled parties. Chuff commented: 'With the club, it was drugs aplenty and everything seemed so exciting. I wasn't sure about Bill, but I quickly became consumed by it all. Being around him, I noticed it was one big party with them. I had never seen so many drugs, so much money. Piles of it lying around! It was a buzz. It was exciting!' Many bikers' women indicate, however, that they do not approve of drugs and drug use, yet tolerate the behavior in club settings — often with some difficulty.

While obtaining illegal drugs may be the motive for some women who associate with outlaw motorcycle clubs, there is another chemical which certainly drives women to associate with the bad boys — adrenaline! Riders and passengers speak of the adrenaline rush of the ride. The ride focuses the mind. One comes alive by living on the edge. However, a woman can get adrenaline rushes through any number of ways and it is unlikely that this accounts for the specific attraction to bikers or even bad boys.

Love is a powerful emotion and many bikers win the hearts of their women and these women become objects of love as bad boys make them feel truly alive. The women who actually marry outlaw bikers are fiercely proud to be a partner of an outlaw motorcycle club member. Consequently, they endure the hardships of being a biker's lady, because they truly love their man. Chuff commented: 'I spent fourteen years living the outlaw life with Bill. It was hard, but something kept us together, even though I knew he had been with countless others.'

Some women will even go so far as to put their own lives on the line for that of their biker man. In telling us about her experiences, Val related the following incident:

> During a brawl occurring at a club, my ole man was defending himself against an attack by a brother, and another brother came sneaking up behind him with a knife in his hand. I said, 'Don't, I'll fucking kill you!' He still kept coming so I jumped into a position where he would have to kill me to get to my ole man and repeated my words. After a few seconds of consideration, which seemed an eternity to me at the time, the knife wielding brother turned and left the party.

In our research we discovered several other very strong themes not raised in the existing literature which describe biker chicks and their motivations to ride and/or associate with outlaw motorcycle clubs. The first of these themes is that the woman wants to reform the bad boy. Linda commented:

> The women can sense that the man is a bad boy, because he has issues which she believes she can help him with. The women see a fellow rebel and believe that they can help out the bloke in a way that will help him [deal with his issues]. In return, she will have a strong man to keep her strong will in check. I look back on my other relationships and see that I have intimidated the other men in my life . . . I'm not proud of it, but that is the way it is. My bad boy leaves no question as to who the ultimate authority is in our family. But that comes with a mutual love and respect for each other's separate life and passion. I do indeed love my bad boy because he is who I need to keep me in line.

Raine further described reforming:

So many females crave that bad boy and yet when they snag him it's a bait and switch. They then want to change him and switch from approval of the bad boy image to transforming him to fit into the stereotypical soul destroying middle-class man who they were not attracted to in the first instance, because then they want him to conform, dress conservatively, act responsibly, etc. I've always felt this was the height of bait and switch when dealing with a guy. Why on earth would a woman want to change the very elements that attracted her to a guy? Is it a challenge to see if he will change for her?

Some women attach themselves to the bad boy biker because they feel they can tame the wild creature within. Val provided some insight in relation to this:

Some misguided women want to change the bad boys into good boys and that is a guaranteed disaster for the building blocks or foundation for a relationship. It will not last the tests which all relationships are given. Most bad boys have issues which eat at them, and it is probably these issues which have made them bad boys. So, some women see a bad boy and believe that she can be that person who the bad boy needs to deal with his issues. These women are like me. I provide my man with the backbone and strength to deal with his issues and I am a partner in his facing his demons and becoming more comfortable with his issues. To me the combination of being a black sheep of my family and this belief that I stand by him through thick and thin to help him in the spirit of the Valkyries is the attraction for me.

Many women are attracted to bad boy bikers' looks and their overt manliness. Raine expressed her views on what she called banker types:

I'll take a true biker over a banker any day, and a true biker is not a weekend warrior who only rolls the bike out on dry days when the temperature is seventy-five degrees Fahrenheit (24°C). Banker types rattle me, because there is always something hidden beneath the surface, whereas a biker has his true look presented for all to see and, more often than not, he is a true gentleman at heart.

The bad boy biker image has a powerful sexual appeal that draws all types of women. Even good girls can find the bad boy irresistible. Many of the women physically attracted to the bad boy are educated and professional women. These women stray from the norm. Their emotional needs and deepest desires have led them to form attachments with the outcasts of society. Victory Lynn commented:

> What attracts me to bad boys? Well, they are so damned good looking. I love the long hair, the tattoos, and the whole package. To me, they are real men. They have charisma and power. The power is to be strong and reject the pansy filled straight society. Their whole look says 'I think for myself. I love my lifestyle and will kick ass for it.' They are men in denim and black leather. They are the American dream of individualism and reject the host society while still living the American dream.

Several biker chicks stated that they regard themselves as having low levels of any spiritual connection. For these women, riding provides what they define as their 'only spiritual experience.' The ride is their spiritual connection; it touches them deeply in what can only be described as a form of religious experience. Of particular interest in this category is a section of women — both inside and outside the United States — who rarely ride in groups. One excellent example of this mindset reported in Section II is Elwira Stadnik, a Polish biker chick who lives in Warsaw. She speaks of the spirit of the she-wolf guiding her and describes riding or associating with other women as problematic. Two women together is okay, but as soon as there is a third, bitchiness sets in. 'When you get three women, you get the bitchiness and gossiping that I hate,' she said.

Stadnik believes in reincarnation and that past lives influence the present one. She explained her belief system thus:

> We souls live and die many times on this earth and continue to do so until we achieve what we are meant to achieve through time. In my case, I believe that my desire to ride is related to the fact that I have identified very strongly with American Indians from my earliest years, and I am sure this has to do with my past lifetime where I was incarnated as an American Indian. To me, as a cosmopolitan European city woman, the horses the Indians rode so gallantly and with wild abandon are exemplified by the motorcycle. When I ride, my spirit feels at one with my kindred American Indian spirits who I feel are part of my current life on this earth. The freedom, the wind in the hair, the sense of independence all relate to my core being, or rather my previous core identity as an American Indian. For city people like me, the plains and open spaces are gone now with only roads for the steel and chrome horses we call motorcycles.

Karen, like Stadnik a woman biker, summarizes the situation nicely: 'I describe myself as a person who is not well in touch with my spiritual being. To me, motorcycle riding provides me with the ability to find my spiritual self. I am drawn to the magic of the motorcycle.' No bikers' women, however, spoke of the spirituality of passengering. This appears to be one difference which clearly separates the two groups.

Across cultures and countries, there are women who simply refer to their rides as 'magic.' They describe their riding experiences as mystical experiences. They cannot identify any single ride as a 'best' or 'aha' ride, as each ride is their best. This factor is present in both women bikers and bikers' women regardless of the country in which they live. This suggests that 'the magic' is ubiquitous. Clearly part of the magic is the exposure to the environment, wind in your face, and closeness to nature which riders understand so well. The theme of closeness to the environment is an enormous attraction to biker chicks — especially in Europe — but a very strong factor which is shared by all parts of the biker chick world.

Without exception, biker chicks speak of the adrenaline rush that riding a motorcycle provides. They speak of the 'clarity' and 'high' they experience each time they go cruising on their bike. These women thrill-seek in other ways, too, for example, bungee jumping, snowmobile riding, and scuba diving. For these women, the motorcycle appears to be simply a mechanism to achieve both the high of an adrenaline rush and the clarity of thought provided by the concentration required during the high-risk behavior. This factor is present in all riding women and passengers. It appears to be a common theme of women (and many men) riders rather than a factor separating the two groups.

Whilst not a universal theme, there are biker women who hold strongly felt patriotic attitudes and almost a mystic respect for veterans who have served their country in active combat. These women tend to belong to clubs like the American Patriot Guard. Perhaps the highly valued quality of patriotism in the United States means American women are much more likely to hold these beliefs and join clubs that make a strong statement about their patriotism. This theme is not a differentiating factor between women bikers and bikers' women, but rather a major regional or cultural difference amongst our interviewees.

The American Patriot Guard truly illustrates the concern and care for veterans which is characteristic of US women riders, be they club affiliated or not. The precipitating incident for our gal riders was the tragedy of a burial of a young soldier killed in Afghanistan in 2004. An ultra-right wing, family based fundamental Christian church attended the funeral. Once the filming of the somber occasion had commenced, the church members pulled out their signs and disrupted the funeral. It seems that the goal of the cult/church was to protest the US's position on homosexuality. This outraged the nation and the rider culture of the United States stepped up to the plate. The rider community, including biker chicks in all their forms, commenced a semi-club calling themselves the American Patriot Guard. They took responsibility for attending each burial of a soldier killed in the Middle East war and, holding American flags, surrounding the burial sites so that the family could proceed with the awful task of burying their dead without the protesters being allowed to enter the cordoned-off area.

As well, there are several highly important rallies or runs to Washington DC by bikers to support veterans' rights. Of course, biker chicks of all iterations and diversity join these rallies which so accurately express their patriotism, sense of what the veterans have lost for their country, and support for these veterans.

For some biker chicks, their primary motive for riding a motorcycle is to demonstrate or prove they are as good as men. This theme is quite different to the rebellion motive noted earlier. These women take great pleasure in maintaining a riding lifestyle as a statement of their own special abilities which, in their words, prove they are as good as men. While most of the women suggesting this are non-outlaw club women, a few are.

Some biker chicks very much enjoy flaunting their sexuality, for example, riding in scanty clothing with the tacit goal of showing off their beauty and attributes. Again, quoting Elwira:

> Women and men need each other. It is like yin and yang. That is why I love being the seductress. I ride with only a white tank top, jeans stretched over my bottom, and boots on during the warm months. I just love the look of lust on the men's faces. I particularly like it when a man has a close call in traffic or a small crash as he is looking at me rather than driving his car.

Chuff, our Scottish bikers' woman and definitely a biker in her own right, said, 'The day of the show I dressed in my bikini, my kilt and my bike boots . . . There were photographers everywhere. I had people running up to me and shoving business cards in my hands and in the waistband of my kilt . . . it went crazy.'

Several of the women considered themselves to be tomboys and they followed in their father's footsteps, mostly in the area of mechanics and a love of mechanical things. Amy commented:

> As time passed, I found myself spending more and more time in my father's shadow, following his every footstep in his auto body shop, only straying from his side to climb trees barefoot or ride my bicycle as fast as I could pedal. My daddy became my hero early in life, and still maintains that elite position in my mind to this day. A quiet, intelligent, larger than life being that knew how to fix, build, or create anything. He was everything and more than any father could be. Standing at well over six foot and generally tipping the scales at around 400 [180 kilograms], he posed a formidable figure, but was always a fun and happy person with a heart bigger than all outdoors.

Some women try to seek out a man who resembles their father or has some of his qualities. Raine states: 'Dad seemed to always have three bikes being rebuilt at any given time . . . I learned early on that you never picked up any parts that were on the garage floor for a bike he was rebuilding or the earth would go spinning off its axis . . . Much like my father, I had three rides at almost any given time . . . I too believe the earth will go spinning off its axis if anyone "messes" with my things.'

A few women openly admit to being frightened every time they ride. Linda states: 'I am happy each time I arrive home safely after a ride and I thank God for keeping me alive. So, for me, the motorcycle is my means of facing fear head-on and going for it.' For these women, the motorcycle has that magical quality of demonstrating their ability to conquer fear on a regular basis.

The stereotype of bikers' women, even on the fringes of the biker lifestyle, is that they are women who have little interest in riding themselves, preferring to ride on the seat behind their man. Such women comprise a very small proportion of the bikers' women we talked to. In fact, newer outlaw motorcycle clubs and older clubs keeping up with the times have spawned clubs for members' women, supporters, and associates, such as the Devil Dolls, Women in the Wind, the Creed Ladies, Cycle Sisters, etc. This was completely unheard of from the late 1970s to the 1990s. As the picture came into focus it was also clear that recent years have seen the birth of biker clubs comprised only of women who are the wives or partners or 'significant others' of affiliate clubs such as the Hells Angels. The Boozettes, for example, stem from the BoozeFighters, who are notorious for their antics at the so-called Hollister Riot in 1947. These types of women's clubs have become more prevalent in recent years, as they address the hardcore biker women's desires to be like their men. It amazed us that the women basically shared the same desires for expression of rebellion and non-conformity as the men. The Devil Dolls in particular have quite a high profile in the more general biker culture.

But 'hardcore biker chick' doesn't necessarily mean a lack of grace, femininity, culture, and education. Goth Girl, the current president of the Devil Dolls, is a young, gorgeous, blonde bombshell who has been trained as a classical concert pianist. She enjoys employment at a swanky five-star hotel in San Francisco, playing her piano in front of a waterfall backdrop in the massive lobby of the hotel. And in line with her biker image, she also plays at the bottom of a Thunder Dome. While the riders circle around her, Goth Girl's meticulously played Bach, Beethoven, and Brahms create an odd and eerie mood.

During the earlier years, the harder edge club women were by and large sex industry workers. This seems to have been changing in later years although there is certainly no denying there are those outlaw motorcycle clubs whose women associates still include a significant number of sex industry workers, especially those hardcore biker chicks whose experiences stem from pre-1995. But many women partners and family members hold a wide variety of jobs and professions including public service jobs, childcare duties, lawyers, medical technicians, human resources, graphic designers, and a variety of other middle class and some factory occupations. Many had achieved significant levels of education and training. In some cases, the men were the child minders and the women were the primary source of income. In most cases, the money was family money, where the earnings of both the man and the woman were pooled to pay for family expenses.

The main complaint by the women was the police harassment that they experienced as family members of outlaw motorcycle club members. A second was distress experienced during times of war between rival outlaw motorcycle clubs. In one notable example, the women and children of one club were taken to several 'safe houses.' The location of one of the safe houses was leaked to the opposite club and the women had to leave urgently. As the women left, laser dots from gun sights were shone on them by persons unknown — the women were livid!

Later, as they drove through town to another safe house, the woman who had leaked the information was discovered. The driver pulled the car over and the women gave the informant a severe beating. Bikers' women can be very violent and seem to accept aggression as a viable means to 'payback,' or as a means to punish others for their misdemeanours. A deeper analysis of this acceptance of violence would be a fascinating exercise. Much could be learned about the justification of violence, and the rituals and rules surrounding punishment, etc.

All outlaw motorcycle club members interact, to greater or lesser degrees, with their mothers, aunts, and children, particularly female children. His family provides the central meaning of an outlaw motorcycle club member's life, despite the standard politically correct line at the clubhouse and creed of the club: that its members put the brotherhood as all-important. In the vast majority of cases, the children and partners of the outlaw motorcycle club members are the reason for their existence as men. The job of the men is to protect the women and children. The remarkable story of an intimate meeting with the mother of 'Tiny', an outlaw motorcycle club member, is worthy of inclusion as it provides rich knowledge of this aspect of the subculture. It was written by me, Arthur Veno, and is part of my field notes from my work with outlaw motorcycle clubs in Brisbane, located in the far north of Australia. Tiny wanted me to meet with his mother. (I asked another member of the club why he was called 'Tiny.' 'Because he is a fucking giant!' was his response.)

At thirty-five years of age, Tiny had a long history of convictions for assault and possession of narcotics. I was at a bikie function with him on the night we were to meet his 'mum,' as he called her. The function was to end at 9.30 pm, but it had dragged on until nearly 11 pm. Tiny came over to me in the middle of seven people and said, 'Hey, Arthur, it's time to go.' I asked him if we couldn't put it off for another night. I was tired and still had some business to discuss with the crowd gathered around me. Tiny's eyes narrowed and his heavily tattooed arms flexed as he said directly to me, 'What, you don't want to meet my mum?' We departed immediately for Tiny's apartment, which was located in a notorious brothel. His mum had already gained entry and was waiting for us.

It soon became apparent why Tiny had wanted me to meet his mum. She was a medical technician and her ex-husband, Tiny's father, was a senior public servant. After exchanging pleasantries, I asked Tiny to go down to the pub and get me some Tasmanian beer, because it was obvious that Tiny's mum wanted to speak to me directly about Tiny. When Tiny departed she said, 'Arthur, all I really want to know is what happened to my little guy. He was so sweet and loving and then something happened to him when he went to his first school. He was never the same after that.' She had brought along three large notebooks full of memorabilia and pictures from Tiny's life. It seems that mum had recently asked Tiny to write down what he saw as having 'gone wrong' with him. His sister was a court officer and his brother was an ambulance driver and ex-rugby star.

When Tiny got the request from his mum, he worked on it for months and finally produced a letter, which his mum wanted me to read and comment on. The letter indicated that an incident had occurred in his third grade class in which Tiny believed he had killed another child. He claimed that he then split into two characters: one character was benevolent and the other, whom he called 'The Avenger,' emerged whenever situations became threatening for the dominant persona. The Avenger, as the name suggests, was mean and vicious.

Tiny re-entered the room as I finished reading the letter and started to address the issues with his mum. After only moments of conversation, both were crying profusely. Tiny made amazing admissions, including a 'need' for sex up to thirteen times a day, etc. Later in the evening, mum tearfully admitted she was very proud of him, but she just wished he could rid himself of the pain that caused his aggression and his profuse drug use. Tiny's sister came by at about 1.30 am to pick up her mum. After speaking with his sister at some length, it became clear that they were as two apples from the same tree. One apple, Tiny, happened to fall on the outlaw side of the fence while the other, his sister, on the legal side of the fence, becoming a court registrar in the process.

There were several other meetings with mothers and family members that could be discussed here, but hopefully the point is taken. The families are not necessarily, or even mostly, dysfunctional. Much could be learned by spending time with Tiny's remarkable mother and his sister and listening to their stories.

Finally, daughters are a special case, indeed. In most instances, the daughters of outlaw motorcycle club members enjoy an unusual relationship with their dads, who tend to be more protective than the average dad. A good example of this is when it comes to the daughter dating; most potential suitors are extremely wary of alienating the dad for obvious reasons. Many dads have been known to take the potential suitor out behind the barn for a good talking to, and/or have him do some chores around the house first, like washing the car or cleaning out the garage. One biker father was heard to say to his daughter, 'When your new boyfriend comes over to meet me, tell him to bring his lawnmower with him. He needs to mow the lawn if wants to take you to the movies.'

On her first day of high school, the outlaw motorcycle club member's daughter may be taken to school via Harley-Davidson with several members of the club in tow. She will be dramatically dropped off by Dad and a few of his brothers just so the boys at school get the clear picture: 'Mess with my daughter and your ass is grass.'

Many outlaw motorcycle club members take a very different profile with their children's school. These men send their children to private schools and the father hides as much as possible from his children's peers who he is in the club scene.

This seems to be more characteristic when the club is 'notorious.'

•

Biker chicks have existed alongside biker men from the invention of the first reliable motorcycles. These men and women have always had and will always have a reputation for living on the edge, hard partying, and rebelliousness. The iconic image of Harley-Davidson motorcycles and those who choose to ride these machines is a major export of US popular culture.

This book has defined a truly little known subculture which co-exists with the dominant host society. Whilst different from the men riders, women riders have defined their culture in these pages, which stand as a truly global look at this amazing counterculture.

Glossary

ABATE: A Brotherhood Against Totalitarian Enactments. A motorcycle rights organization whose main aim is to fight discriminatory laws against bikers, such as compulsory helmet laws.

AFFA: Angels Forever, Forever Angels.

AFFL: Angels Forever, Forever Loaded.

AMA: American Motorcycle Association. Founded in 1924, the association focuses on motorcyclists' rights, safety related issues, etc. It also sanctions road and off-road riding activities and oversees professional and amateur racing events.

Ape hanger: High rising handlebars on motorcycles; derived from the fact that bikers dangle their arms over them in ape fashion.

Associate: A friend of an outlaw motorcycle club who may ultimately graduate to being a prospect and/or full-patch member.

Back patch: Full 'colors' tattooed on a club member's back.

BACA: Bikers Against Child Abuse. A single issue club with worldwide Chapters in Australia. BUACA (Bikers United Against Child Abuse) is an alternative club with similar goals.

Bible: Harley-Davidson repair manual; frequently used for private weddings and torn up for divorce proceedings.

Big Twin: A Harley model containing a powerful V-twin engine; includes the Dresser and the Low Rider, but not the Sportster.

Bitch seat, bitches box: A passenger seat on the bike that is traditionally reserved for a woman, who is then sometimes referred to as the bitch on the back. Also known as 'riding bitch.'

Bobber: A stripped-down motorcycle which has a relatively stock front end as opposed to the extended front forks one would find on a chopper.

Brain bucket: Motorcycle helmet.

BPC: British Pathfinders Club.

BTBF: Bikers Together, Bikers Forever.

Burnout: Smoking the rear tire of a motorcycle while the front brake is applied.

Cagers: The name bikers use for car drivers in North America.

Cages: The name bikers use for cars in North America.

CMA: Canadian Motorcycle Association.

Catwalk: To drive with the front wheel off the ground; also known as a 'wheelie.'

Chopper: A chopped bike. To chop a motorcycle is to reduce its bulk and pare it down to bare essentials. The bike is redesigned. All unnecessary equipment is stripped off, including the front brake and fenders. Typically the front forks will be raked (extended and the angle increased), the whole bike will be lowered, and the handlebars are set high.

Citizen: Anyone who is not an outlaw biker.

Class: To show class is to do something totally outrageous and shocking to the public.

Colors: The official uniform of all outlaw motorcycle clubs consisting of a sleeveless denim or leather vest with a club patch sewn on the back.

Crash truck: A van, panel truck, or converted school bus that follows or precedes the motorcycle club run, which typically picks up broken-down bikes.

Crotch rocket: A Japanese or European sports bike with enclosed engine and humped tank; a fast bike, known for its turning and cornering ability.

Custom bike: A custom bike may have some of the features of a chopper and/or a bobber, but essentially it is a motorcycle that the owner has customized to make it uniquely his or hers.

Dog: Unattractive woman in North America. In Australia and the United Kingdom, the term refers to someone who tells the police about club business.

Dresser: A Harley Big Twin in the FL series. Usually comes with floorboards, fairing, saddlebags, and a large passenger seat.

FAM: Federation of American Motorcyclists.

Fly colors: To ride a motorcycle wearing colors.

FTW: Fuck the world. A favourite outlaw motorcycle club saying that is typically found on outlaw club membership cards, tattoos, pins, patches, and colors.

Hangaround: An individual who goes to places where they can associate with an outlaw motorcycle club, like a club bar. Being a hangaround is normally an assessment period for potential membership in the club, for both the club and the hangaround.

Hardtail: A rigid motorcycle frame without any shock-absorbing device.

Heat: Law enforcement personnel and their actions when scrutinizing an individual or organization.

HOG: Harley Owners' Group. An association sponsored by Harley-Davidson. Each dealership sponsors its own association within its region, but members must first sign up with the national HOG, which is run out of Milwaukee.

Anyone with a Harley can join by paying dues. Also a term for a Harley-Davidson motorcycle; the term originated in the 1920s, when victorious Harley-sponsored riders would do a victory lap or pose for publicity photos with their mascot, a small pig.

Jamming in the wind: The experience of riding.

Knucklehead: A Harley-Davidson engine design developed in 1936 and produced through 1947.

LOH: Ladies of Harley. An all-female subsidiary group within HOG.

Mama: Any woman sexually available to all club members; these women are also know as club whores.

MC: Motorcycle club.

Nom: A prospective outlaw club member. The nom undergoes a rigorous six-month to two-year period of education and socialization before becoming a full-patched member.

Nomads: Elite chapters of 1%er clubs such as the Hells Angels, Bandidos, etc. Members are recruited from a larger overall area and are not specifically residents of a particular geographic location. They are structured like any other chapter, but do not have a regular clubhouse and members answer only to themselves.

OFFO: Outlaws Forever, Forever Outlaws.

Ole lady: Biker female companion, wife, or girlfriend.

OMC: Outlaw motorcycle club. Originally the term designated to a motorcycle organization that was not a chartered member of the American Motorcycle Association. Today, the term defines any club that has a three-piece patch. All 1%er clubs are outlaw motorcycle clubs, but not all outlaw motorcycle clubs are 1%er clubs.

One-percenter: The '1%' patch is derived from a statement made by the American Motorcycle Association in 1947 that only one percent of motorcyclists are outlaws, the other 99 percent being law-abiding individuals. The 1% symbol has thus become the mark of the outlaw biker and they typically display it on their vest over their heart, and/or have it tattooed on their person.

Out in bad standings: A term for a club member whose membership has been terminated by his club, usually because he has breached club rules. The term is sometimes used to keep former members, who were ousted for political reasons, from joining other outlaw motorcycle clubs. Anyone who has been deemed 'out in bad standings' is (or is supposed to be) ostracized by the entire outlaw motorcycle club community, even rival clubs.

Pack: To carry something special on the bike. Guns and tools are both packed.

Panhead: A Harley-Davidson engine design developed in 1948 and produced through 1965.

Patchholder: A member of a motorcycle club who wears the distinctive club patch on his jacket or vest.

Posers: Citizens who dress as if they are members of outlaw motorcycle clubs. They seldom own a motorcycle. Posers are generally looked upon with disdain by members of a club.

'Property of' patch: A patch worn by a female associated with an outlaw motorcycle club that denotes which club member she belongs to.

Prospect: A prospective outlaw club member. The prospect undergoes a rigorous six month to two year period of education and socialization before becoming a full-patched member. While he is prospecting, the prospect only wears the bottom rocker — the club emblem and name of the club are not allowed to be worn.

Pull a train: A girl having sexual intercourse with each man in the group, any way he would like it, one after another.

Rat: An informant.

Rice burners, Jap crap: Any motorcycle built in Japan.

Road captains: Those responsible for planning club runs, such as mapping out destination routes and run formations, scheduling fuel stops, and preparing contingency plans for breakdowns. Road captains are also responsible for maintaining safety during group rides so they must be able to coordinate long bike formations and initiate any necessary group actions such as passing a slow moving vehicle.

Run: An official club outing. Usually for one day, weekend, or a week to a certain destination, where partying, camping, or special events occur. Sometimes other chapters and/or other clubs may participate.

Scooter: A motorcycle, also known as a scoot.

Scooter trash: An outlaw motorcycle club member or serious hardcore biker.

Shovelhead: A Harley-Davidson engine design developed in 1966 and produced through 1984.

Skid lid: A motorcycle helmet.

Sled: A motorcycle.

Snitch: An informant.

Softail: A Big Twin Harley-Davidson motorcycle. The rear shocks are mounted horizontally underneath the frame, where they are not visible.

Sportster: A Harley-Davidson that is narrower, leaner, more lightweight, and comparatively smaller than a Big Twin. It has a characteristic small, peanut-shaped gas tank.

Sweeper: The rider last in line whose job is to ensure everyone else in the group arrives at the destination safely.

13: Patch worn by some outlaw motorcycle club members; the letter 'M' is the thirteenth letter in the alphabet. It signifies motorcycles, motorcyclism, or marijuana.

Three piece patch: Consists of a top rocker (a semicircular embroidered patch) with the club name, such as Hells Angels; a center patch which bears the club's official insignia, such as the Hells Angels' death's-head; the bottom rocker (looks like an inverted top rocker), with the geographical location of the club, such as New York.

Two-up: To ride with a passenger.

V-Twin: The distinctive Harley-Davidson engine, with two cylinders arranged in a V-shape. All modern Harleys are V-Twin.

Wannabe: A citizen who dresses as a biker would dress and frequents the places that the motorcyclists frequent, but who is not in the club and usually does not own a bike.

Wings: Women's International Motorcycle Association

Wings: An emblem worn by outlaw motorcycle club members as a pin or patch attached to the colors; it is earned for outrageous sexual behaviour, which must be witnessed.

Wrench: To be able to mechanically care for your motorcycle.

Sources

Links

www.abate.org/   A Brotherhood Against Totalitarian Enactments
www.bacausa.com/   Bikers Against Child Abuse (US)
www.bandidosmc.com/   Bandidos World
www.beckysstuff.com/   co-founder Harley Women's Magazine
www.bikerlady.com/   Biker Lady groups
www.boozefighters.com/   BoozeFighters MC World
www.buaca.org/   Bikers United Against Child Abuse
www.chromedivas.com/index.cmf   Chrome Divas
www.devildollsmc.org   Devil Dolls MC World
www.hells-angels.com/   Hells Angels World
www.hog.com   Harley Owners Group
www.outlawsmcworld.com/   Outlaws MC World
wwwpatriotguard.org/   American Patriot Guard
www.route81australia.com.au/index1.html   Hells Angels Australia
www.wima.org.au/   Women's International Motorcycling Association
www.arthurveno.com   Arthur Veno
www.blockheadcity.com   Edward Winterhalder

Documents

Barger, R. (2000) *Hells Angels: The Life and Times of Ralph 'Sonny' Barger and the Hells Angels Motorcycle Club.* Random House: New York.

Barker, T. (2007) *Biker Gangs and Organized Crime.* LexisNexis: New Jersey.

Cohen, S. (1980) *Folk Devils & Moral Panics: The Creation of the Mods and the Rockers.* Oxford: Basil

Curry, G. D. (1998). 'Female Gang Involvement'. *Journal of Research in Crime and Delinquncy, 35,* 100–118.

Deschenes, E. P., & Esbensen, F. A. (1999). 'Violence and Gangs: Gender differences in perceptions and behavior'. *Journal of Quantitative Criminology, 15*, 63–96.

Dicks, Shirley (2002). *Road Angels: Women Who Ride Motorcycles*. Lincoln, NE: Writers Club Press.

Donnelly, G. (1997) *Girls in the Gang*. Wanganui Press: Auckland. (out of print).

Dulaney, W. (2006) Over the Edge and Into the Abyss: The communication of organizational identity in outlaw motorcycle clubs. Unpublished PhD thesis. Florida State University.

Ferrar, A. (2000). Hear Me Roar: Women, motorcycles and the rapture of the road. North Conway, NH: Whitehorse Press.

French, H. (2003). *The Biker Babe's Bible: How to Keep Your Ole Man Happy*. Mountain Press: Boulder.

Grennan, S., Britz, M. T., Rush, J., & Barker, T. (2000). *Gangs: An international approach*. (Women and the Outlaw Subculture). Upper Saddle River, NJ: Prentice Hall.

Guisto, B. (1997) Mi Vida Loca: An insider's ethnography of outlaw bikers in the Houston area. (unpublished PhD dissertation)

Hollern, S. (1999) *Women and Motorcycling: The early years*. Pink Rose Publications and Marketing.

Hopper, C. (1983). Hell on Wheels: The outlaw motorcycle gangs. *Journal of American Culture, 6*, 58–64.

Hopper, C. B., & Moore, J. (1990). 'Women in Outlaw Motorcycle Gangs'. *Journal of Contemporary Ethnography, 18*, 363–387.

Isenberg, S. (1991) *Women Who Love Men Who Kill*. Simon & Schuster: NY.

Joans, B. (2001). *Bike Lust: Harleys, Women, & American society*. Madison, WI: The University of Wisconsin Press.

Joans, B. (2003). *Women Who Ride: The Bitch on the back is dead*.

Kirby, C. & Renner, T. (1987) *Mafia Assassin: The inside story of a Canadian Biker, hit man and police informer*. Methuen: Toronto.

McDonald-Walker, S. (2000). *Bikers: Culture, politics and power*. Oxford: Berg.

Money, J. (1990) *Love Maps*. Prometheus: Boston.

Montgomery, R. (1976). 'The Outlaw Motorcycle Subculture'. *Canadian Journal of Criminology and Corrections, 18*, 332–342.

Mullins, Sasha. (2003). *Biker Lady: Living and Riding Free*. Citadel.

Mullins, Sarah (2008) *The Chrome Cowgirl Guide to the Motorcycle Life*. Motorbooks (nee MBI/Voyager).

Osgerby, B. (2005). *Biker Truth and Myth: how the original cowboy of the road became the easy rider of the silver screen*. (Chapter 5: sisters in Leather) Guilford, CT: First Lyons Press.

Paladin Press. (1989) An Inside Look at Outlaw Motorcycle Gangs – Women).

Person, E.S. (2007) *Dreams of Love and Fateful Encounters: The power of romantic passion*. Americaan Psychiatric Publishing: Arlington.

Pierson, M. H. (1997) *The Perfect vehicle: What it is about motorcycles*. W. Norton & Company: New York.

Quinn, J. F. (1987). 'Sex Roles and Hedonism Among Members of 'Outlaw' Motorcycle Clubs'. *Deviant Behaviour, 8*, 47–63.

Quinn, J. F. (2001). Angels, Bandidos, Outlaws, and Pagans: The evolution of organized crime among the big four 1% motorcycle clubs. *Deviant Behaviour: An Interdisciplinary Journal, 22*, 379–399.

Quinn, J., & Koch, S. (2003). 'The Nature of Criminality within One-percent Motorcycle Clubs'. *Deviant Behaviour: An Interdisciplinary Journal, 24*, 281–305.

Royal Canadian Mounted Police Gazette. (2002) 'Women in Outlaw Motorcycle Gangs'.

Thompson, H. S. (1967) *Hell's Angels: The strange and terrible saga*. Ballantyne: New York.

United States Marshall's Service. (2003) *Outlaw Motorcycle Gangs Manual*.

Veno, A. (2003, 2006). *The Brotherhoods: Inside the Outlaw Motorcycle Clubs*. Allen & Unwin: Sydney.

Veno, A. (2007) *Mammoth Book of Bikers*. Constable and Robinson, London.

Veno, A., & van den Eynde, J. (2007). 'Moral Panic Neutralization Project: A media based intervention'. *Journal of Community and Applied Social Psychology*.

Watson, J. (1980). 'Outlaw Motorcyclists as an Outgrowth of Lower Class Values'. *Deviant Behaviour, 2*, 31–48.

Winterhalder, E. (2005) *Out in Bad Standings: Inside the Bandidos Motorcycle Club*. Blockhead City Press: Ok.

Winterhalder, E. & De Clercq, W. (2008) *The Assimilation: Rock Machine become Bandidos – Bikers united against the Hells Angels*. ECW: Toronto.

Wolf, D. R. (1991). *The Rebels: A Brotherhood of Outlaw Bikers*. Toronto: University of Toronto Pressd.

Wilde, S. (ed.). (1997). *Barbarians on Wheels*. (Mamas and Miss Death) NJ: Charwell Books Inc.

Zentti, G. (Ed.) (2002). *She's a Bad Motorcycle: Writers on riding*. (Girl on a motorcycle). NY: Thunders Mouths's Press.